Criminol
Beginners
Guide

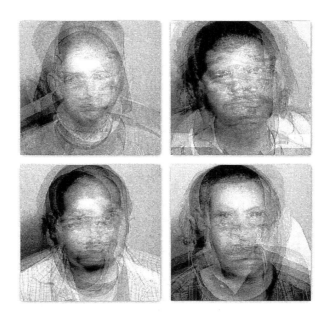

Morrigan L Carey

Angie
know how much
you love a bit of
death!
    Merry Christmas
my darlin

    A xxx *

    21/12/2019

Criminology Beginners Guide

Stubbornness is a virtue

Morrigan L Carey

Chapter 1 - Page 8
Criminological Theory
> * Classical School
> * Positivism
> * Sociological Positivism
> * Types and Definitions of Crime
> * Routine Activity Theory
> * Marxist Criminology
> * Symbolic Interactionism

Chapter 2 - Page 20
Criminological Social Theory
> * Strain Theory, Social Strain Theory
> * Subculture Theory
> * Control Theory/Social Control
Theory
> * Differential Association
> * Labelling Theory
> * Trait Theory
> * Biosocial Theories

Chapter 3 - Page 28
The Brain and Behaviour
> * The Structure of The Brain
> * Sections of The Brain
> * Psychological Approaches to Crime

Chapter 4 - Page 52
Psychopaths and Serial Killers

       * Psychopath/Sociopath
       * Hervey Cleckley (The Mask of Sanity)
       * Robert Hare (Without Conscience, Snakes in Suits and The Psychopathy Checklist)
       * Robert Hare's Psychopathy Checklist
       * Subtypes of Psychopaths
       * Proposed Criteria for Psychopathic Personality Disorder
       * Serial Killers
       * The Organised Serial Killer also known as 'thrill seekers'
       * The Disorganised Serial Killer

Chapter 5 - Page 79
Dangerous Offenders
       * The Dangerous Offender
       * Dr Michael Stone. Scale of Evil
       * Dangerous Sex Offenders
       * The Management of Dangerous Sex Offenders

Chapter 6 - Page 93
Criminal Profiling
       * The Behavioural Science Unit.
       * The Role of Criminal Profiling
       * The Role of Geographic Profiling in Serial Violent Crime Investigation
       * How Geographical Profiling Works
       * Geographical Profiling Process
       * Geographical Profiling Methodology

Chapter 7 - Page 104
Forensic Science
        * Sir Bernard Henry Spilsbury
(16th May 1877 - 17th December 1947)
        * Ballistics
        * Physical Evidence
        * Fingerprints
        * DNA
        * Toxicology
        * Brief history
        * The Science
        * Historical Events

Chapter 8 - Page 146
Crime, Mental Health and Institutions
        * Justifying Detainment.
        * The Mental Health Act 1983
        * Mental Illness and
Imprisonment
        * Broadmoor and Its Residents
        * Oakridge and Experimental
Therapies
        * Insanity Plea Used as Defence
        * Example Cases

Chapter 9 - Page 188
Crime and the Media
        * The Problem of Crime and The
Media
        * The Fear of Crime

* The British Crime Survey
* Moral Panics
* Violence, Video Games and
TV/Film Media

Chapter 10 - Page 197
Punishment, Execution and Social Control
* Justifying Societal Control
* Hanging, Electric Chair and
Lethal Injection
* Types of Punishment
Throughout time

Chapter 11 - Page 223
Policing and Crime Prevention
* History of The Police
* Possible Bias Within The Police
Force
* Primary, Secondary & Tertiary
Prevention
* Theories of Crime: Rational
Choice Theory
* Empirical Research on Rational
Choice Theory

Chapter 12 - Page 249
The Penal System
* The History of Prison
* The Penal System

* The Work of Michael Foucault

Chapter 13 - Page 277
The Criminal Justice System
    * The Law and Society
    * Magistrates' and Crown Court
    * Crown Prosecution Service
    * The Role of The CPS
    * The Decision to Prosecute
    * The Use of Juries

Chapter 14 - Page 310
Violence in Society
    * Dark Figure of Crime
    * Trait Theory
    * Social Learning Theory

Chapter 15 - Page 324
Youth Crime
    * Differential Association
    * Labelling Theory
    * Strain Theory
    * Youth Crime: Summary

Chapter 16 - Page 337
Environmental Criminology
    * Crime and The Social Environment
    * Broken Windows Theory
    * Crime Prevention Through

Environmental Design
> * Defensible Space Theory
> * Opportunity Theory/Routine Activity
Theory

Chapter 17 - Page 356
Victims of Crime
> * Victimology
> * The Development of Victimology as a
Field of Study
> * Types of Victims and Risk
> * Victimology Within The Crime Scene
Investigation
> * Victim and Offender Risk Assessment
> * Victim Proneness/Victim Blaming
> * Victim Recovery Phases
> * Victims as Witnesses

Chapter 1
Criminological Theory

In the mid 18th century social philosophers began to give thought to crime and the concept of law which led to Criminology. Several schools of thought have developed over time. Within early Criminological theory there were three main schools of thought which came about during the period between the mid 18th century and the mid 20th century. These three main schools of thought were, Classical, Positive and the Chicago School. These three schools were the foundation of my other branching theories in criminology.

Classical School

The Sage Dictionary of Criminology McLaughlin, Muncie 2001 Definition:
An approach to the study of crime and criminality which is underpinned by the notion of rational action and free will. In the late eighteenth century and early nineteenth century by reformers who aimed to create a clear and legitimate criminal justice system based on equality. At its core is the idea that punishment should be proportionate to the criminal act and should be viewed as a deterrent. Further assumptions include the notion of individual choice within a consensual society based upon a social contract and common

interest.

The Classical school of criminology is a body of thought about the reform of crime and the best methods of punishment by a group of European philosophers and scholars in the eighteenth century. It took place during the Enlightenment, a movement in Western countries that promoted the use of reason as the basis of legal authority. Italian philosopher Cesare Beccaria is considered to be the founder of the Classical school.

Cesare Beccaria and other members of the Classical school of criminology believed that criminal behavior could be minimized using the basics of human nature. The school was based on the idea that human beings act in their own self-interests. They believed that rational people enter into a social contract in which they realize that having a peaceful society would be in their most beneficial to themselves. The school sought to reduce crime through reform to the criminal punishment system, which they felt tended to be cruel and excessive without reason as well as an ineffective deterrent. Published in 1764 in Cesare Beccaria work on the right to punish and methods to prevent crime. He argued that society should create laws that may infringe upon the personal liberty of the few, but result in the greater happiness of the majority. His approach to crime prevention was that the pain of the punishment should be greater than the potential pleasure resulting from the act.

The Classical school of criminology argued that the most effective deterrent for criminal behaviour would be swift punishment rather than long trials. They felt that criminal actions were irrational behavior and came from people who could not or did not act in their best self-interests or society's. Members of the school contended that punishments needed to be consistently enacted for specific crimes with no special circumstances in order to demonstrate to people that criminal activity will not benefit them because there are definite consequences.

A major part of the criminal punishment reform that the Classical school of criminology fought for was fair and equal treatment of accused offenders. Prior to the schools fight for reform, judges could punish criminals at their own wills regardless of the severity of the crime, which led some to view the criminal punishment system as tyrannical. Cesare Beccaria and other members fought for punishments for specific crimes to be set by legislature and not to allow judges unbridled power. They felt that if judges could only apply legislatively sanctioned punishments, trials would be quick and criminals would receive their punishments faster. The idea behind the Classical school's fight for swift trials and clearly defined punishments was that criminals were more likely to be deterred if they knew what type of punishment they would receive and how quickly. Members of the school believed that preventing crime was actually more important than punishing it, but by having a clear punishment system in place, criminals would use reasoning to deduce that crime would not be in their best self-interests. The classical school of criminology was accepted by European rulers in the late eighteenth century and is considered to have influenced the Western justice system

Therefore, Rational Choice Theory believes that people freely choose how they behave and the main motivation is the avoidance of pain in the pursuit of pleasure. Each individual evaluates their choice of actions in accordance with each options ability to produce advantage, pleasure and happiness. This theory sees people as rational human beings whose behaviour can be controlled or modified by the fear of punishment. Therefore it is believed increasing the punishment will persuade offenders to resist offending. Rational Choice Theory assumes the crime is the personal choice of the offender and it is their individual decision-making process, making individuals responsible for their choice to commit crime so they are to blame for their own criminality. Ration Choice suggests that the offender weighs up the potential benefits and consequences associated with committing the offence and then makes a rational choice based on the evaluation.

Positivism

The Sage Dictionary of Criminology McLaughlin, Muncie 2001 Definition:

A theoretical approach that emerged in the early nineteenth century which argues that social relations and events, including crime, can be studied scientifically using methods derived from the natural sciences. Its aim is to search for, explain and predict future patterns of human behaviour. In Criminology it straddles biological, psychological and sociological disciplines in an attempt to identify key causes of crime - whether genetic, psychological, social or economic - which are thought to lie largely outside of each individual's control

By the early 1929s the development of criminological science - positivism - was to become influential, not only in physiology, but also in medicine, psychiatry, psychology and sociology. Offending came to be thought of as being determined by biological and/or cultural antecedents. It was no longer viewed as simply self determining.

Positivism was criticised for:

> * Denying the role of human consciousness and meaning in social activity.
> * Assuming that there is an underlying consensus in society, of which crime is a key violation.
> * Presenting an overdetermined view of human action.
> * Equating crime with under socialisation or social disorganization rather than accepting the validity of different forms of socialisation and of social organisation.
> * Ignoring the presence and relevance of competing value systems, cultural diversity or structural conflict.

Sociological Positivism

Sociological positivism suggests that societal factors such as poverty, membership of subcultures or low levels of education can predispose people to crime. Adolphe Quetelet made use of data and statistics to gain insight into the relationship between crime and sociological factors. He found that age, gender, poverty, education and alcohol consumption were important factors related to crime. W. Rawson utilised crime statistics to suggest a link between population density and crime rates, with crowded cities creating an environment conductive for crime.

Joseph Fletcher and John Glyde also presented papers to the Statistical Society of London on their studies of crime and its distribution. Henry Mayhew used empirical methods and an ethnographic approach to address social questions and poverty, and presented his studies in '*London Labour and the London Poor*'. Emile Durkheim viewed crime as an inevitable aspect of society, with uneven distribution of wealth and many other differences among people.

Types and Definitions of Crime

Both Positivist and Classical schools take a consensus view of crime, that is, a crime is an act that violates the basic values and beliefs of society. These values and beliefs are manifested as laws that society agrees upon, However, there are two types of law to consider. These are:

* Natural laws which are rooted in core values shared by many cultures, Natural laws protect us against harm to persons, for example, murder, rape and assault. This also applies to property such as theft, larceny and robbery. These form the basis of a common law system.

* Statutes are enacted by legislatures and reflect the current cultural mores, although some laws may be controversial, for example, laws that prohibit the use of cannabis and of

gambling. Certain criminological perspectives such as Marxist criminology, Conflict criminology and Critical criminology claim that most relationships between the citizen and the state are non consensual therefore criminal laws is not necessarily representative of the public's beliefs and wishes and it is exercised in the interests of the ruling or dominant class. Some right wing criminologies say there is a consensual social contract between the state and the public.

Therefore, definitions of crime will vary from place to place, in accordance to the cultural norms and morals, but may be broadly classified as blue collar crime, corporate crime, organised crime, political crime, public order crime, state crime, state corporate crime and white collar crime. However, there have been moves in contemporary criminological theory to move away from liberal pluralism, culturalism and postmodernism by introducing the universal term 'harm' into the criminological debate as a replacement for the legal term.

Routine Activity Theory
The Sage Dictionary of Criminology McLaughlin, Muncie 2001 Definition:
According to Marcus felson mainstream criminology had devoted the majority of its attention

to the criminal, investigating why certain individuals are more criminally inclined than others. As a consequence of this criminology had given very little thought to either the context or nature of criminal acts or the role of the victims as active participants in crime production and prevention. His writings represent one of the most significant attempts to redress this imbalance, and he does so from a rational choice perspective. Crime, for Felson, is first and foremost a physical act and the production of the recurrent, routine activities and structuring of everyday life. This means that the potential for crime is inevitable and constant. A utilitarian motivation to commit crime is taken as given. It also means that criminologists can contribute in a practical manner to criminal justice policy debates by shifting the focus from detection and punishment of the criminal to reduction and prevention of the criminal event.

Routine activity theory was developed by Marcus Felson and Lawrence Cohen. It draws on control theories and explains crime in terms of crime opportunities that occur in everyday life. A crime opportunity requires that elements converge in time and place including:

* A motivated offender
* Suitable target or victim

* Lack of a capable guardian.

A guardian at a place, such as a street, could include security guards, adults or even general pedestrians who would witness the criminal act and intervene or report it to the police. Routine activity theory was explained by John Eck, who added a fourth element of 'place manager' like a property manager who can take protection measures.

Marxist Criminology

The Sage Dictionary of Criminology McLaughlin, Muncie 2001 Definition:

A variety of criminological perspectives that draw on the Marxian tradition in sociological theory in order to explicate the dimensions of crime and its control that revolve around class, power and state. In 1968 a young British sociologist formed the National Deviance Conference (NDC) group. The group was restricted to academics and consisted of 300 members. Ian Taylor, Paul Walton and Jock Young, members of the NDC, rejected previous explanations of crime and deviance. They decided to pursue a new Marxist criminological approach. In The New Criminology they argued against the biological positivism perspective represented by Lombroso, Hans Eysenck and Gordon Trasler. According to the Marxist perspective on crime, deviance is normal, in the sense that people are now consciously involved in ensuring their human diversity. Marxist criminologists argue in support of society in which the facts of human diversity, be it social or personal, would not be criminalised. They further attributed the processes of crime creation not to genetic or psychological facts but rather to the material basis of a given society.

Symbolic Interactionism

The Sage Dictionary of Criminology McLaughlin, Muncie 2001 Definition:

A theoretical approach which focuses on interactions between individuals as symbolic and linguistic exchanges and as a means of creative action. It views the social world as the product of such interactions.

This theory focuses on the relationship between the powerful state, media and conservative ruling elite on the one hand and the less powerful groups on the other. The more powerful groups have the ability to become the 'significant other' in the less powerful groups. The former could, to some extent, impose their meanings on the other and therefore they were able to 'label' minor delinquent youths as criminals. These youth would take on board the label and turn to crime more readily and become actors in what is known as the 'self-fulfilling prophecy' (living up to the name given) of the powerful groups. Later developments came from Howard Becker and Edwin Lemert in the mid 20th century.

Chapter 2
Criminological Social Theory

Strain Theory, Social Strain Theory
The Sage Dictionary of Criminology McLaughlin, Muncie 2001 Definition:

Strain theory argues that people are more likely to engage in crime when they cannot get what they want through legitimate ways. They then become frustrated or angry and they may (1) try to get what they want through illegitimate or criminal ways, (2) Strike out at others in their anger, (3) make themselves feel better through illicit drug use. Strain theory describes the types of strain that contribute to crime, and the factors that influence whether one responds to strain with crime.

Strain theory is also known as Mertonian Anomie after the American sociologist Robert Merton. Merton's theory suggests that mainstream culture, especially in the United States, is saturated with dreams of opportunities, freedom and prosperity, as Merton put it and how we all heard, the American Dream. Most people buy into this dream and it becomes powerful cultural and psychological motivation. Merton also used the term anomie but having a different meaning than it did for Durkheim. Merton saw the term as meaning a dichotomy between what society expected of its citizens and what those citizens could actually achieve. Therefore, if the social structure of opportunities is unequal and prevents the majority from realising the dream, some of them will turn to illegitimate means, crime, in order to realise it. Others will retreat or drop out into deviant subcultures like gang members, homelessness, alcoholics and drug abusers.

Subcultural Theory

The Sage Dictionary of Criminology McLaughlin, Muncie 2001 Definition:

First used by anthropologists, the concept of subculture was applied to the study of delinquency in the mid 1950s. It was used to understand social deviance, and delinquency in particular, by referring to distinctive sets of values that set the delinquent apart from mainstream or dominant culture. It made sense of the apparently senseless by arguing that delinquency was a solution to the structural and cultural problems facing marginalised groups.

Following on from the Chicago school and Strain Theory, and also drawing on Edwin Sutherland's idea of differential association, subcultural theorists focused on small cultural groups fragmenting away from the mainstream to form their own values and meanings about life.

Albert K. Cohen tied anomie theory with Freud's reaction formation idea, suggesting that delinquency among lower class youths is a reaction against the social norms of the middle class. Some youth, especially from poorer areas where opportunities are scarce might adopt social norms specific to those places which may include 'toughness' and disrespect for authority. Criminals acts might result when youths conform to the norms of the deviant subculture.

Richard Cloward and Lloyd Ohlin suggested that delinquency can result from differential opportunity for lower class youths. These youths may be tempted to take up criminal activities, choosing the illegitimate path that provides them with the more lucrative economic benefits than the conventional over the legal options like taking a minimum wage job.

British subcultural theorists focused more heavily on the issue of class where some criminal activities were seen as 'imaginary solutions' to the problem of belonging to a subordinate class. A further study by the Chicago school looked at gangs and the influence of the interaction of gang leaders under the observation of adults.

Control Theories/Social Control Theory
The Sage Dictionary of Criminology McLaughlin,

Muncie 2001 Definition:

A sociological approach to understanding the causes of conformity that focuses on the ability of society and its institutions (parents, peers, schools, spouses and jobs) to restrain human behaviour. From this perspective human nature is assumed to be essentially anti-social - a view that is borrowed directly from Thomas Hobbes's (1985[1651],p 188) description of life in a world without externally imposed control as a 'war of every man against every man'. Thus, the central question is, 'What is it about society that restrains individuals from deviance?' The basic premise is that conformity results when societal ties are strong.

Control theories look for factors that make people become criminals, these theories try to explain why people do not become criminal. Travis Hirschi identified four main characteristics, attachment to others, belief in moral validity of rules, commitment to achievement and involvement in conventional activities. The more a person has these characteristics the less the chances are that that person becomes deviant or a criminal. On the other hand, if those characteristics are not present in the individual it is more likely that they might become deviant or criminal. Hirschi expanded on this theory with the idea that a person with low self control is more likely to become a criminal. Such as, if a person wishes to own something and does not have to money to buy it, lacking in self control they might try to get it by illegal means. Someone with high self control would do without or find a legitimate way of obtaining it. Social bonds can have a great affect on self control. For families of a low socio-economic status, a factor that distinguishes families with delinquent children from those who are not delinquent is the control exerted by the parents. Theorists such as, Matza and Sykes argue that criminals are able to temporarily neutralise internal moral and social behavioral constraints through techniques of neutralisation.

Differential Association

The Sage Dictionary of Criminology McLaughlin, Muncie 2001 Definition:

Initially developed by Edwin H. Sutherland (1883-1950), the concept of differential association is an attempt to account for the acquisition and maintenance of criminal behaviour in terms of contact, or association, with particular environments and social groups.

The attention of criminologist turned to social factors, looking at the role of social organisation and disorganisation in the explanation of crime. The view was taken that young people living in parts of cities that were characterised by social disadvantage and disorganisation were at a greatly increased risk of participating in delinquency. Once a neighbourhood becomes a focus for delinquent culture then the possibility of other young people being drawn into the crime is greatly increased.

As the theory developed sutherland set out a number of postulates:

* Criminal behaviour is learned.
* Learning takes place through association with other people.
* The main setting for learning is within close personal groups.
* Learning includes techniques to carry out certain crimes and attitudes and motives supportive of committing crime.
* Learning experiences, differential associations, will vary in frequency and importance for each individual.
* The process involved in learning criminal behaviour are no different from the learning of any other behaviour.

Labeling Theory

The Sage Dictionary of Criminology McLaughlin, Muncie 2001 Definition:

A sociological approach to understanding crime and deviancy which refers to the social processes through which certain individuals and groups classify and categorize the behaviour of others. On this basis labelled individuals are stereotyped to accordingly. Such reaction tends to reinforce the self conception as deviant and had the unanticipated consequence of promoting the behaviour that it is designed to prevent.

This theory is all about an individual being labelled in a particular way. It was studied in great detail by Howard Becker. It derives originally from sociology but is often used in criminology. If someone is given the label of criminal they may reject it or they may accept it and then go on to commit crime. Even those that initially reject the label can still eventually accept it as the label becomes more well known particular among their peers. This can become even more profound when the labels are about deviancy and it is said that they can lead to deviancy amplification. Klein (1986) conducted a test which showed that labeling theory affected some youth offenders but not others.

Trait Theory

Lonnie Athens developed a theory about how a process of brutalisation by parents or peers that usually occurs in childhood results in violent crimes in adulthood. Richard Rhodes' 'why we kill' describes

Athens' observations about domestic and societal violence in the criminal's background but both reject the genetic inheritance theory.

Biosocial Theories

Biosocial criminology is an interdisciplinary field that aims to explain crime and antisocial behaviour by exploring both biological factors and environmental factors. While contemporary criminology has been dominated by sociological theories, biosocial criminology also recognises the potential contributions of fields such as genetics, neuropsychology and evolutionary psychology.

Chapter 3
The Brain and Behaviour

The Structure of the Brain.

Every kind of animal you can think of has a brain and brains come in many sizes, although the human brain is not the largest it does, by far, give us capabilities far beyond the capabilities of other animals. The human brain has to perform an incredible amount of tasks simultaneously, from regulating blood pressure, body temperature, heart rate and breathing to taking in and processing huge amounts of information from our senses, seeing, hearing, tasting, touching and smells.

The central nervous system is a powerful information processing system connected to the brain, spinal cord and peripheral nerves. The central nervous system in the control centre to everything conscious and unconscious that goes on in a person's life.

The human brain is made up of around 100 billion nerve cells called neurons which gather and transmit electrochemical signals to one another. Kind of like roads with electric bridges. The neurons have the same make up as other cells with the exception of being the electrochemical aspect which allows them to send and receive electrical impulses over long distances. These neurons can come in many sizes depending on their function. As well as different sizes they also come in different shapes which also depends on their function.

We have sections of our brain which are hard wired to do certain things like eat, sleep drink, breath etc which has been termed the reptilian brain and is our instinctual brain, things we do without thinking about it. Information is taken in through all the senses, sight, hearing, touch, smell and taste along with all the other senses created by an experience or an event, the emotional feelings, happiness, sadness, fear, rejection, guilt, joy, love and so on. The initial experience triggers neurons in the brain and a processing path is formed. The various information from all the senses is gathered and processed to ultimately form a reaction or a memory. When we come across the same experience or event for the second time the original neuron path is sparked generating the reaction or memory and feelings and thoughts connected to it. The more the experience or event is come across the more the neuron pathway is reinforced. The same process happens when we learn something new (it can be a positive or a negative experience) for example, learning to play a musical instrument. At first it will be difficult to learn the notes and the order of the notes and to read the music but over time as it is practiced the new neuron path created becomes reinforced and stronger therefore playing the instrument becomes easier as the neurons recognise the incoming information until it becomes quite easy to play a learnt tune without much thinking about it. It is almost like the neuron pathway becomes an automatic pilot. This is a very simplistic view of this process considering that our brains have to process an incredible amount of information constantly throughout the day and we have billions of neuron constantly at work. Each pathway has many branches which can trigger many other thoughts, feeling and memories along the way all intertwined and connected.

A simple example would be if we look at the feeling of rejection. The rejection triggers feelings of lack of confidence, diminished self worth, humiliation, the reluctance to take risks maybe with jobs or relationships. The initial rejection triggers a number of neuron leading to a number of thoughts, feelings and memories which, in turn, can trigger a number of reactions or actions or lack of reaction or action. If someone suffered constant rejection the negative neuron pathways would be reinforced possibly leading to oversensitivity to rejection and diminished self worth to the point where even the thought of rejection can trigger real feelings even though it has not actually happened. It can be very difficult to change reinforced negative pathways.

Sections of The Brain - Lobes of the Brain
Although the minor wrinkles are unique in

each brain both human and animal, several major wrinkles and folds are common to all brains. These folds form a set of four lobes in each hemisphere of the brain. Each lobe tends to specialize in certain functions.

Frontal Lobes

At the front of the brain are the frontal lobes, and the part lying just behind the forehead is called the prefrontal cortex. Often called the executive control center, these lobes deal with planning and thinking. They comprise the rational and executive control center of the brain, monitoring higher-order thinking, directing problem solving, and regulating the excesses of the emotional system. The frontal lobe also contains our self-will the area what some might call our personality. Trauma to the frontal lobe can cause dramatic and sometimes permanent behavior and personality changes. Because most of the working memory is located here, it is the area where focus occurs (Geday & Gjedde, 2009; Smith & Jonides, 1999). The frontal lobe matures slowly. MRI studies of post-adolescents reveal that the frontal lobe continues to mature into early adulthood. Thus, the capability of the frontal lobe to control the excesses of the emotional system is not fully operational during adolescence (Dosenbach et al., 2010; Goldberg, 2001).

This is one important reason why adolescents are more likely than adults to submit to their emotions and resort to high-risk behavior.

Temporal Lobes

Above the ears rest the temporal lobes, which deal with sound, music, face and object recognition, and some parts of long-term memory. They also house the speech centers, although this is usually on the left side only.

Occipital Lobes

At the back are the paired occipital lobes, which are used almost exclusively for visual processing.

Parietal Lobes

Near the top are the parietal lobes, which deal mainly with spatial orientation, calculation, and certain types of recognition like touch and pain.

Motor Cortex and Somatosensory Cortex

Between the parietal and frontal lobes are two bands across the top of the brain from ear to ear. The band closer to the front is the motor cortex. This strip controls body movement and works with the cerebellum to coordinate the learning of motor skills.

Just behind the motor cortex, at the beginning of the parietal lobe, is the somatosensory cortex, which processes touch signals received from various parts of the body.

Brain Stem

The brainstem is the oldest and deepest area of the brain. It is often referred to as the reptilian brain because it resembles the entire brain of a reptile. Of the 12 body nerves that go to the brain, 11 end in the brain stem (the olfactory nerve,for smell,goes directly to the limbic system, an evolutionary artifact). Here is where vital body functions, such as heartbeat, respiration, body temperature, and digestion are monitored and controlled. The brain stem also houses the reticular activating system (RAS), responsible for the brain's alertness.

The Limbic System

Nestled above the brainstem and below the cerebrum lies a collection of structures commonly referred to as the limbic system and sometimes called the old mammalian brain. Many researchers now caution that viewing the limbic system as a separate functional entity is outdated because all of its components interact with many other areas of the brain. Most of the structures in the limbic system are duplicated in each hemisphere of the brain. These structures carry out a number of different functions including the generation of emotions and processing emotional memories. Its placement between the cerebrum and the brain stem permits the interplay of emotion and reason.

Four parts of the limbic system are important to learning and memory. They include the following:

The Thalamus.

All incoming sensory information (except smell) goes first to the thalamus (Greek for "inner chamber"). From here it is directed to other parts of the brain for additional processing. The cerebrum and the cerebellum also send signals to the thalamus, thus involving it in many cognitive activities, including memory.

The Hypothalamus.

Just below the thalamus is the hypothalamus. While the thalamus monitors information coming in from the outside, the hypothalamus monitors the internal systems to maintain the normal state of the body (called homeostasis). By controlling the release of a variety of hormones, it moderates numerous body functions, including sleep, body temperature, food intake, and liquid intake. If body systems slip out of balance, it is difficult for the individual to concentrate on cognitive processing of curriculum material.

The Hippocampus.

Located near the base of the limbic area is the hippocampus (the Greek word for "sea horse," because of its shape). It plays a major role in consolidating learning and in converting information from working memory via electrical signals to the long-term storage regions, a process that may take days to months. It constantly checks information relayed to working memory and compares it to stored experiences. This process is essential for the creation of meaning. Its role was first revealed by patients whose hippocampus was damaged or removed because of disease. These patients could remember everything that happened before the operation, but not afterward. If they were introduced to you today, you would be a stranger to them tomorrow. Because they can remember information for only a few minutes, they can read the same article repeatedly and believe on each occasion that it is the first time they have read it. Brain scans have confirmed the role of the hippocampus in permanent memory storage. Alzheimer's disease progressively destroys neurons in the hippocampus, resulting in memory loss.

Recent studies of brain-damaged patients have

revealed that although the hippocampus plays an important role in the recall of facts, objects, and places, it does not seem to play much of a role in the recall of long-term personal memories (Lieberman, 2005). One surprising revelation in recent years is that the hippocampus has the capability to produce new neurons a process called neurogenesis into adulthood (Balu & Lucki, 2009). Furthermore, there is research evidence that this form of neurogenesis has a significant impact on learning and memory (Deng, Aimone, & Gage, 2010; Neves, Cooke, & Bliss, 2008). Studies also reveal that neurogenesis can be strengthened by diet (Kitamura, Mishina, & Sugiyama, 2006) and exercise (Pereira et al., 2007) and weakened by prolonged sleep loss (Meerlo, Mistlberger, Jacobs, Heller, & McGinty, 2009).

The Amygdala.

Attached to the end of the hippocampus is the amygdala (Greek for "almond"). This structure plays an important role in emotions, especially fear. It regulates the individual's interactions with the environment that can affect survival, such as whether to attack, escape, mate, or eat. Because of its proximity to the hippocampus and its activity on PET scans, researchers believe that the amygdala encodes an emotional message, if one is present, whenever a memory is tagged for long-term storage. It is not known at this time whether the emotional memories themselves are actually stored in the amygdala. One possibility is that the emotional component of a memory is stored in the amygdala while other cognitive components (names, dates, etc.) are stored elsewhere (Squire & Kandel, 1999). The emotional component is recalled whenever the memory is recalled. This explains why people recalling a strong emotional memory will often experience those emotions again. The interactions between the amygdala and the hippocampus ensure that we remember for a long time those events that are important and emotional. Therefore, it is intriguing to realize that the two structures in the brain mainly responsible for long-term remembering are located in the emotional area of the brain.

Cerebrum

A soft, jelly like mass, the cerebrum is the largest area, representing nearly 80 percent of the brain by weight. Its surface is pale gray, wrinkled, and marked by deep furrows called fissures and shallow ones called sulci (singular, sulcus). Raised folds are called gyri (singular, gyrus). One large sulcus runs from front to back and divides the cerebrum into two halves, called the cerebral hemispheres. For some still unexplained reason, the nerves from the left side of the body cross over to the right hemisphere, and those from the right side of the body cross to the left hemisphere. The two hemispheres are connected by a thick cable of more than 200 million nerve fibers called the corpus callosum (Latin for "large body"). The hemispheres use this bridge to communicate with each other and coordinate activities. The hemispheres are covered by a thin but tough laminated cortex (meaning "tree bark"), rich in cells, that is about one tenth of an inch thick and, because of its folds, has a surface area of about two square feet. That is about the size of a large dinner napkin. The cortex is composed of six layers of cells meshed in about 10,000 miles of connecting fibers per cubic inch! Here is where most of the action takes place. Thinking, memory, speech, and muscular movement are controlled by areas in the cerebrum. The cortex is often referred to as the brain's gray matter. The neurons in the thin cortex form columns whose branches extend through the cortical layer into a dense web below known as the white matter. Here, neurons connect with each other to form vast arrays of neural networks that carry out specific functions.

Cerebellum

The cerebellum (Latin for "little brain") is a

two-hemisphere structure located just below the rear part of the cerebrum, right behind the brain stem. Representing about 11 percent of the brain's weight, it is a deeply folded and highly organized structure containing more neurons than all of the rest of the brain put together. The surface area of the entire cerebellum is about the same as that of one of the cerebral hemispheres. This area coordinates movement. Because the cerebellum monitors impulses from nerve endings in the muscles, it is important in the performance and timing of complex motor tasks. It modifies and coordinates commands to swing a golf club, smooth a dancer's footsteps, and allow a hand to bring a cup to the lips without spilling its contents. The cerebellum may also store the memory of automated movements, such as touch-typing and tying a shoelace. Through such automation, performance can be improved as the sequences of movements can be made with greater speed, greater accuracy, and less effort. The cerebellum also is known to be involved in the mental rehearsal of motor tasks, which also can improve performance and make it more skilled. A person whose cerebellum is damaged slows down and simplifies movement, and would have difficulty with finely tuned motion, such as catching a ball or completing a handshake.

Recent studies indicate that the role of the

cerebellum has been underestimated. Researchers now believe that it also acts as a support structure in cognitive processing by coordinating and fine-tuning our thoughts, emotions, senses (especially touch), and memories. Because the cerebellum is connected also to regions of the brain that perform mental and sensory tasks, it can perform these skills automatically, without conscious attention to detail. This allows the conscious part of the brain the freedom to attend to other mental activities, thus enlarging its cognitive scope. Such enlargement of human capabilities is attributable in no small part to the cerebellum and its contribution to the automation of numerous mental activities.

Psychological Approaches to Crime

It has been suggested by many that the key to the development of juvenile offending behaviour is the family. When looking at the subject of families and criminality we are drawn to two main areas of study. Firstly we are posed the question of whether criminal families are more dysfunctional than non-criminal families? And are there similarities between criminals and their biological relatives? There are a number of areas which need to be investigated to give account to these questions, such as biological factors, can criminality be caused by a biological defect?, by chance or by inherited?, can an inherited personality account for criminality or is criminality born out of a learning process developed out of influences from family upbringing and relationships, friends, peers or from their social environment?

Biological factors within a family could play a part in determining the criminality in juveniles. It is quite common for a child to be told how much they are like their parents, but according to Sheldon (1942) these inherited physiques can determine whether a person can be identified as a criminal or not. He stated that a person's body build can be an indication of personality. He identified three body types, the mesomorph, the ectomorph and the endomorph. Mesomorph were said to broad and muscular people with the personality of being, on one habs adventurous, and on the other aggressive. Ectomorphs were thin and bony and were restrained and introverted and endomorphs were large and heavy and tended to be sociable and outgoing. Sheldon based his theory on a study of four hundred offenders and his results showed that mesomorphs largely dominated and differed from a sample of non-offenders which leads to his conclusion. Therefore it would be feasible to say that if a person inherited a broad muscular physique from their family they are more likely to be criminals. This could be argued by considering the possibility that this type of build is something that attracts police attention, which leads to stereotyping offenders. It is also possible that an individual with this type of physique would feel the need to uphold a macho image which is associated with physical appearance of broad and muscular. This can lead to whole families and even generations of families being labelled as criminals just because of their physical appearance.

Another inherited explanation for criminality lies in inherited genetics. This theory states that criminality is inherited directly from parents genetically, meaning criminality is an issue of nature. Like Sheldon, Lombroso (1876) also believed that criminals could be identified by their physical appearance. For example, killers were said to have cold, glassy, bloodshot eyes, curly hair, strong jaw, long ears and thin lips. Lombroso viewed criminals as throwbacks to more primitive times calling these so called throwbacks 'atavistic' once again labelling a person a criminal based only on their genetically inherited physical appearance. Bull and McAlpine (1998) suggested that people often have stereotypes of the facial appearance of criminals and that these stereotypes may even affect judgements of guilt and innocence in court.

Another genetic explanation for criminality can be found in genetically inherited abnormalities. In the 1960's biologists found genetic abnormalities in the calls of humans and discovered an abnormality they called XYY. XYY. This comes from the fact that each person's sex is determined by a pair of chromosomes, females normally have two X chromosomes and males normally have one X and one Y. What the research found was that a small number of the male population had a genetic abnormality and this was XYY. Meaning that some males had double the amount of chromosomes leading to a label of 'the super male syndrome' which was associated with the above average height and below average intelligence. It was claimed to be associated with violent crime. According to this theory nature is the cause of the criminality and not nurture. So the family could play no part in the criminality other than inherited abnormal chromosomes but there is nothing to suggest they are inherited. The main problem with the genetic aspect is that it denies 'free will' and sees crime as a result of forces outside a person's control so no aspect of family life could have any influence on a person's criminality.

One of the basic ideas when investigating the links between criminality and the family is, the closer the biological link, the closer the criminal behaviour should be, criminals come from criminal families (Dugdal, 1910, Estabrook, 1916) which is a long standing popular belief. Osborn and West (1979) found that forty per cent of the sons of fathers with a criminal record went on to have a criminal record themselves, bearing in mind that this means that sixty per cent did not. This does not prove that the tendency is transmitted genetically nor does it consider that socialisation into a criminal lifestyle may have as much to do with the level of criminality in families and the fact that according to Osborn and West thirteen per cent of sons of non-criminal fathers turned to criminality. This cannot simply be explained by inherited genetics. So if criminality in families cannot be explained by genetics, other aspects of the family need to be explored.

Most welfare and public services would state that a substantial amount of crime comes from a small number of families, which would indicate some truth in the statement 'crime runs in families'. This criminality could also stem from years of social deprivation or prejudice. Osborn and West had established the criminal parents are more likely to produce criminal children but being born into a criminal family is not a necessary condition for criminal behaviour (Harrow 2003)

In 1953 David Farrington carried out a longitudinal (a study carried out over a number of years) study of four hundred and eleven working class boys born in the East End of London with a follow up period of thirty years. Farrington discovered that twenty one percent had criminal convictions by the time they were seventeen and another thirteen per cent by the time they were twenty five, so half of the total number of convictions were by just twenty three boys which is just over five per cent. Farrington also identified other factors which he considered relevant to the development of delinquency these included low income, large families, parental criminality and poor child rearing practices. Farrington considered the boys who had a large number of convictions and found that there were warning signs of their possible future criminality at an early age. While at primary school they were considered as troublesome, dishonest, hyperactive, impulsive, unpopular and of a low intelligence. At the age of fourteen they tended to have friends who were delinquent and tended to be aggressive. They were established in delinquent groups by the age of eighteen and were found on average to drink, smoke and gamble more. Farrington also identified them as being more likely to have tattoos, bite their nails, have slow pulse rates and be associated with gangs. This gives possibility to some truth in stereotyping. He continued to study some boys into their thirties where they lived in poor housing, suffered marital breakdowns and found them to be suffering from psychiatric disorders and experiencing problems with their own children. From his study Farrington suggested that if the amount of criminality in society is to be reduced there would need to be improved achievement in school, improved child rearing practices, reduced impulsivity and reduced poverty. Things which most of us would not argue with.

Farrington has indeed identified that the role of the family interaction plays a considerable part in the influence of criminality on juveniles. Extremes of rejection and indifference found in disciplinary styles appear to extend to interactions in delinquent families more generally (Blackburn 2002). A number of factors were found to be important in the early lives of delinquents which included forms of conflict between parents such as arguments, disagreements and marital instability and break ups. Negative attitudes from parents towards their children shows to be more likely in delinquent children, not only this Glueck and Glueck (1956) found that both mothers and fathers of delinquents showed less affection for their children compared with parents of non-delinquents. It also appears that delinquents have negative perceptions of their families and a noted lack of involvement with the parents (Hirschi 1969). There is a distinct lack of overall involvement in almost all aspects of parent child relationships within delinquents, but this seems to have more effect on boys than girls. A longitudinal study by McCord (1986) showed that a lack of affection by the mother when the child is between ages five to thirteen was significantly related to property crimes by the son. Crimes against the person were associated with parental conflict and aggression towards the child (Blackburn 2002). Domestic violence and the physical abuse of a child also plays a part in delinquency and can lead to antisocial behaviour. Although evidence suggests that most abused children are not antisocial and other studies suggest the physical abuse may not be a significant factor in the development of delinquents. McCord's follow up longitudinal study suggested that parental rejection was more significant. According to McCord serious juvenile crimes were committed by fifty per cent of children who had been rejected, but only twenty per cent of those were abused and neglected and only eleven per cent of those who were loved (McCord 1986). Overall it appears that there are many aspects of a child's family life which can affect the amount of delinquency in later life, Not only with the interaction between child and parent but also with child rearing practices.

Hoffman (1984) identified three patterns of child rearing which are, power assertion, which involves physical punishment, criticism, threats and maternal deprivation, love withdrawal, withholding affection as a sign of disapproval and induction which may be considered as the most important as this involves explaining to the child what the consequences if their actions are for others. The pattern which is most associated with families of delinquents is that of power assertion (Bandura and Walters 1959) where parents often ridicule the child and inflict physical punishment which can lead to low self esteem and high aggression. According to Patterson (1982) it is not necessarily the use of physical punishment which is damaging but the use of severe and inconsistent punishment. This happens more often in larger families where there are many young children

Large family size is another influence on juvenile delinquency. Studies show that delinquents were more likely to come from families with four or more children (West 1982) and a similar relationship for self reported delinquency was found by Hirschi (1969). Recidivism from other family members is common but is more common with boys than girls. Large families are difficult to control as the attention of the parents has to be spread among the whole family with each one competing against each other for attention. Some children can be more demanding than others and this tends to leave the quieter ones unnoticed and neglected, which can leave them to look to their siblings as role models (Blackburn 2002).

Some research into siblings has been done, specifically twins. These twin studies have an advantage over family studies because the inheritance is constant therefore any variation in criminal behaviour between twins must be due to factors other than genetics. Two types of twins are identified as identical twins, monozygotic or MZ; share the same genes, and non identical twins, dizygotic or DZ, who have fifty per cent of each parent's genes. The aim of the twin studies is to establish any genetic relations in areas such as intelligence and criminal behaviour. The idea is that if twins share the same environment then major differences between them would support the genetic perspective. The result of these studies showed a higher concordance level for identical twins than for non identical twin in criminal behaviour showing that genetic factors do play a part in the development of criminal behaviour although this effect seems to be more distinct in relation to adult crime rather than juvenile delinquency (Goldsmith and Gottesman 1995). More recent studies have shown a high concordance rates for both identical and non identical twins which is more likely to be the result of a common environment than genetic factors (Lyons 1996).

Another area which has been of interest to researchers is adoptive studies. These studies look at the links between criminality in children, the adoptive parents and the biological parents. If a child's behaviour is closer to that of the biological parent then this would prove there to be a genetic link. In

1974 Crowe found that adoptive children whose mother had a criminal record fifty per cent had a criminal record by the time they were eighteen and the control group only showed five per cent, showing that family environment was influential.

Other theories of child criminality include psychoanalytic theories. Bowlby (1944) suggested that if there is any disruption of the attachment bond between mother and her child in the early years could lead to criminality later in life. Mainly because it causes an inability to develop any meaningful relationships (Bowlby 1944). Maternal deprivation was a concern for a long period of time and focused on the quality of mothering when the mother worked. Bowlby drew on Freud's work to develop his theory. He stated that if a child is raised within a dysfunctional family it may cause long term damage to the superego or conscience, which would result in not being able to control anitsocial impulses and would lack guilt. In contrast to this an overdeveloped superego would produce a desire for punishment, unresolved guilt and develop an 'acting out' type of behaviour. This theory does not take into account that some crime requires rational planning. It has been claimed by Aichorn (1955) that the cause of delinquency is an underdevelopment of the ego and the reality principle. This would lead to a person relying heavily on the pleasure principle and is not fully socially developed and this lack of socialisation leads to delinquency. If a person relies too heavily on the pleasure principle and immediate gratification this will reduce their effective functioning within society (Alexander and Healey 1935). Sublimation can also be used as an explanation for criminality developing within a family. This theory suggests that sublimation happens when instinctual impulses are channelled into other thoughts, emotions and behaviours. This results from a failure to form deep emotional tied with close relations like parents. Basically it suggests that the child's inner frustration causes them to commit a criminal act. Healey and Bronner (1936) compared non delinquents with delinquents and noted that the delinquents came from less stable families and showed greater emotional disturbances. The key points of psychoanalytic approach an unresolved inner conflict, an emotional instability and it occurs in childhood. As with many studies of this type there is a lack of scientific support.

One area which has been widely researched and debated is that of learning approaches. One of the main learning approaches is differential association. This theory attempts to explain the social conditions necessary to produce crime and the process in which a person becomes a criminal (Sutherland and Cressy 1974). Sutherland came up with nine stages within the process of becoming criminal. This theory claimed that criminal behaviour is learned and this learning occurs through association with other people but the main part of the learning occurs within close personal groups. This type of learning includes techniques to carry out particular crimes, specific attitudes towards crime and favourable drives and motives towards crime. These drives and motives are learned from a favourable or unfavourable perception of the law, usually passed on from parents to children. What makes a person criminal is when their definitions favourable to law breaking outweigh their definitions to non violation (Sutherland 1974). This theory also stated that the process of learning criminal behaviour is no different from learning any other behaviour and points out that criminal behaviour is an expression of needs and values but the crime cannot be explained in terms of those needs and values. What they learn is a method to acquiring something. This theory is linked to operant learning.

Overall it is difficult to say what actually causes criminality within families. The best possible conclusion would be to think of a criminal as having their own unique individuality the same as everyone else and what makes a non delinquent is just as individual as what makes a delinquent. Criminality could be a combination of a huge number of factors including circumstances, experiences, influences, environment, interaction, social learning, individual biology and many more.

Chapter 4
Psychopathy and Serial Killers

Psychopath/Sociopath

There has been much confusion over the years with the terms Sociopath and Psychopath. The words can be used interchangeably whereas others make a clear distinction between the two terms. To clarify this the first port of call must be the DSM-IV, Diagnostic and Statistical Manual of Mental Disorders. In the DSM-IV there is the criteria for Antisocial Personality Disorder (ASPD) this criteria is a list of personality traits for Antisocial Personality Disorder included in the list is, lack of remorse, impulsivity, deceitfulness and a failure to conform to the social norms. The full criteria is as follows:

A. There is a pervasive pattern of disregard for and violation of the rights of others occurring since age 15, as indicated by three (or more) of the following:

A1. Failure to conform to social norms with respect to lawful behaviors as indicated by repeatedly performing acts that are grounds for arrest.

A2. Deceitfulness, as indicated by repeated lying, use of aliases, or conning others for personal profit or pleasure.

A3. Impulsivity or failure to plan ahead.

A4. Irritability and aggressiveness, as indicated by repeated physical fights or assaults.

A5. Reckless disregard for safety of self or others.

A6. Consistent irresponsibility, as indicated by repeated failure to sustain consistent work behavior or honor financial obligations.

A7. Lack of remorse, as indicated by being indifferent or rationalizing having hurt, mistreated, or stolen from another.

B. The individual is at least age 18 years of age.

C. There is evidence of Conduct Disorder with onset before age 15.

D. The occurrence of antisocial behavior is not exclusively during the course of Schizophrenia or a manic episode.

By definition, all individuals with Antisocial Personality Disorder had preceding Conduct Disorder as a child. Among those with Childhood Conduct Disorder, however, only about 40 percent of males and 24 percent of females are diagnosed with Adult Antisocial Personality Disorder. The highest reported rate of diagnosis is among the male adult population, averaging between ages 25 and 44. These are also the ages of most convicted serial killers with Antisocial Personality Disorder.

Among those criminals with Antisocial Personality Disorder few ever make it into old age, because of an abnormally high rate of early death from suicide, homicide, accidents, and complications of drug and alcohol abuse.

Patterns emerge in the evaluation of the histories and backgrounds of individuals with Antisocial Personality Disorder. There is a recurring course of childhood deviance in which their problems start at a young age and tend to continue into adulthood.

Because the criteria for diagnosing Antisocial Personality Disorder emphasize overt violations of social rules, it is not surprising that it correlates so well with criminality. Research on American criminals showed that 25 to 30 percent of the imprisoned inmates meet the criteria for Antisocial Personality Disorder. Canadian researcher Robert Hare (1983) reported that 40 to 50 percent of the convicted prisoners in Canada met the criteria for Antisocial Personality Disorder and that in some Canadian prison populations the rate was as high as 75 percent. Psychopathic prisoners on average, have longer sentences and are less successful in staying out of prison than non psychopathic prisoners.

Hervey Cleckley (The Mask of Sanity)

Hervey Cleckley was an American psychiatrist who published a book called The Mask of Sanity in

1941. The reason for this title was because he believed that psychopaths appeared to the outside world as normal and this book was also to clarify the psychopathic personality traits. In his ground-breaking work Hervey Cleckley developed a list of psychopathy symptoms.

* Considerable superficial charm and average or above average intelligence.
* Absence of delusions and other signs of irrational thinking.
* Absence of anxiety or other "neurotic" symptoms. Considerable poise, calmness and verbal facility.
* unreliability, disregard for obligations, no sense of responsibility, in matters of little and great import.
* Untruthfulness and insincerity.
* Anti-social behaviour which is inadequately motivated and poorly planned, seeming to stem from an inexplicable impulsiveness.
* Inadequately motivated antisocial behaviour.
* Poor judgment and failure to learn from experience.
* Pathological egocentricity. total self-centeredness and an incapacity for real love and attachment.
* General poverty of deep and lasting

emotions.

       * Lack of any true insight, inability to see oneself as others do.

       * Ingratitude for any special considerations, kindness and trust.

       * Fantastic and objectionable behaviour, after drinking and sometimes even when not drinking. Vulgarity, rudeness, quick mood shifts, pranks for facile entertainment.

       * No history of genuine suicide attempts.

       * An impersonal, trivial, and poorly integrated sex life.

       * Failure to have a life plan and to live in any ordered way (unless it is for destructive purposes or a sham).

Hervey Cleckley published a second edition of his book in 1950 in an attempt to clarify the psychopathic personality.

Robert Hare (Without Conscience, Snakes in Suits and The Psychopathy Checklist)

Dr Robert Hare is one of the leading experts in psychopathy. He is professor emeritus at University of British Columbia in Canada, and sits on the Research Board of the FBI's Child Abduction and Serial Murder Investigative Resources Center. For many years, Dr. Hare also sat on the advisory panel for the Home Office in England, set up by Her

Majesty's Prison Service to develop treatment programs for psychopathic offenders, and he still frequently consults with the English prison service as well as with other prison services and law enforcement organizations in North America and England. In addition, he belongs to the International Fellowship for Criminal Investigative Analysis, and has received several honors, such as FBI citations, the Silver Medal of the Queen Sophia Center in Spain, the Canadian Psychological Association's award for distinguished applications of psychology, the American Academy of Forensic Psychology's award for "Distinguished Contributions to Psychology and Law," And the American Psychiatric Association's Isaac Ray Award for "Outstanding Contributions to Forensic Psychiatry and Psychiatric Jurisprudence." He has also written the the books Without Conscience, Snakes in Suits as well as the Psychopathy Checklist.

Robert Hare's Psychopathy Checklist

1. **Glib and superficial charm.** the tendency to be smooth, engaging, charming, slick and verbally facile. Psychopathic charm is not in the least shy, self-conscious, or afraid to say anything. A psychopath never gets tongue-tied. He can also be a great listener, to simulate empathy while zeroing in on his targets' dreams and vulnerabilities to be able to manipulate

them better.

2. **Grandiose self-worth.** a grossly inflated view of one's abilities and self-worth, self-assured, opinionated, cocky, a braggart. Psychopaths are arrogant people who believe they are superior human beings.

3. **Need for stimulation or proneness to boredom.** an excessive need for novel, thrilling and exciting stimulation. Taking chances and doing things that are risky. Psychopaths often have a low self-discipline in carrying tasks through to completion because they get bored easily. They fail to work at the same job for any length of time, for example, or to finish tasks that they consider dull or routine.

4. **Pathological lying.** This can be moderate or high, in moderation form, they will be shrewd, crafty, cunning, sly and clever, in extreme form they will be deceptive, deceitful, underhanded, unscrupulous, manipulative and dishonest.

5. **Conning and manipulativeness.** The use of deceit and deception to cheat, con or defraud others for personal gain, distinguished from item 4 in the degree to which exploitation and callous ruthlessness is present, as reflected in a lack of concern for the feelings and suffering of one's victims.

6. **Lack of remorse or guilt.** A lack of feelings or concern for the losses, pain and suffering of victims. A tendency to be unconcerned, dispassionate, coldhearted and unempathic. This item is usually

demonstrated by a disdain for one's victims.

7. **Shallow affect.** emotional poverty or a limited range or depth of feelings, interpersonal coldness in spite of signs of open gregariousness and superficial warmth.

8. **Callousness and lack of empathy.** a lack of feelings towards people in general, cold, contemptuous, inconsiderate and tactless.

9. **Parasitic lifestyle.** An intentional, manipulative, selfish and exploitative financial dependence on others as reflected in a lack of motivation, low self-discipline and the inability to carry through one's responsibilities.

10. **Poor behavioral controls.** expressions of irritability, annoyance, impatience, threats, aggression and verbal abuse, inadequate control of anger and temper, acting hastily.

11. **Promiscuous sexual behaviour.** A variety of brief, superficial relations, numerous affairs and an indiscriminate selection of sexual partners. The maintenance of numerous, multiple relationships at the same time. A history of attempts to sexually coerce others into sexual activity (rape) or taking great pride at discussing sexual exploits and conquests.

12. **Early behaviour problems.** A variety of behaviours prior to age 13, including lying, theft, cheating, vandalism, bullying, sexual activity, fire setting, alcohol use and running away from home.

13. **Lack of realistic, long term goals.** An inability or persistent failure to develop and execute

long term plans and goals, a nomadic existence, aimless, lacking direction in life.

14. **Impulsivity.** The occurrence of behaviours that are unpremeditated and lack reflection or planning, inability to resist temptation, frustrations and momentary urges, a lack of deliberation without considering the consequences, foolhardy, rash, unpredictable, erratic and reckless.

15. **Irresponsibility.** Repeated failure to fulfill or honor obligations and commitments, such as not paying bills, defaulting on loans, performing sloppy work, being absent or late to work, failing to honor contractual agreements.

16. **Failure to accept responsibility for own actions.** A failure to accept responsibility for one's actions reflected in low conscientiousness, an absence of dutifulness, antagonistic, manipulation, denial of responsibility and an effort to manipulate others through this denial.

17. **Many short term relationships.** A lack of commitment to a long term relationship reflected in inconsistent, undependable and unreliable commitments in life, including in marital and family bonds.

18. **Juvenile delinquency.** Behaviour problems between the ages of 13 - 18, mostly behaviours that are crimes or clearly involve aspects of antagonism, exploitation, manipulation or a callous, ruthless tough mindedness.

19. **Revocation of conditional release.** A revocation of probation or other conditional release due to technical violations, such as carelessness, low deliberation or failing to appear.

20. **Criminal versatility.** QA diversity of types of criminal offences, regardless if the person has been arrested or convicted for them, taking great pride at getting away with crimes or wrongdoings.

Subtypes of Psychopaths

According to source there are four different types of psychopath with one of the first distinctions being made by Cleckley in 1941 being the distinction between primary and secondary psychopaths.

1. **Primary psychopaths.** Do not respond in the normal way to any kind of punishment regardless of disapproval by others or being caught by the police. This type of psychopath can han have good hold of their antisocial impulses to suit their purpose at the time and not because of conscience or the fear of disapproval. Cleckley outlined a condition of primary psychopaths he call 'semantic aphasia' suggesting that words do not mean the same to a psychopath as they would to you or i. Psychopaths are incapable of experiencing any genuine true emotion of anything or anyone and they do not follow any form of life plan.

2. **Secondary Psychopaths.** This suggest that

they are not full psychopaths which could be due to genetic variations but they are still as vulnerable to everyday stress the same as the average person is yet they expose themselves to more stress than the average person. They are still big risk takers but they are more likely to be worriers and prone to guilt.

3. **Distempered Psychopaths.** Powerful cravings are the main driving force in this type of psychopath. They can be obsessed with powerful sexual urges for a large part of the time and have a very strong sex drive. They are prone to drug addiction, illicit and/or illegal indulgences, peadiphillia and kleptomanis. Excitement and risk taking provide this type of psychopath with the 'high' or 'rush' they crave. Distempered psychopaths can fly off into a rage very easily and can even resemble an epileptic fit.

4. **Charismatic Psychopaths.** This type of psychopath can use their charm, fast talking, powers of persuasion and lies to con someone out of everything they own. This can be seen in cult leaders who persuade people into giving them their own life. They usually have some kind of talent which they will use to their own advantage when manipulating others. They can lie to the extent of becoming to believe their own lies. They consider themselves irresistible.

In 1980 Robert Hare provided a summary of psychopathic traits which included,

* Inability to develop warm, empathic relationships.
* Unstable lifestyle
* Inability to accept responsibility for anti social behaviour
* Absence of psychiatric problems.
* Weak control over behaviour.

According to Hare the difference between antisocial personality disorder and psychopathy is that antisocial personality disorder refers mainly to a cluster of criminal and antisocial behaviours while psychopathy is a syndrome defined by a cluster of both personality traits and social deviant behaviours. He produced a list of key symptoms of psychopathy which he divided into interpersonal traits and antisocial lifestyle.

Interpersonal
* Glib and superficial
* Egocentric and grandiose
* Lack of remorse or guilt
* Lack of empathy
* Deceitful and manipulative
* Shallow emotions

Antisocial lifestyle
* Impulsive
* Poor behavioral controls
* Need for excitement
* Lack of responsibility
* Early behaviour problems
* Adult antisocial behaviour

It must be noted that the distinctions Hare makes between psychopathy and antisocial behaviour is not universally accepted.

In 2000 Bartlett and Sandland pointed to the fact that Section 1(2) of the Mental Health Act 1983 defined the terms used in the Act and whilst they accepted the definition of other terms in the sub section they strongly contest the validity of the definition of Psychopathic Disorder basing their argument on the fact that the criteria for definition are not distinct from the results of that behaviour. They argue that, 'abnormal aggressive or seriously irresponsible conduct does not merely characterise the disorder/illness, they are indistinguishable from it, at least in current medical understanding. They suggest the medical profession consider the term psychopathy outdated and prefer antisocial or dissocial personality disorder.

In 2008 Putwain and Sammons cited the work

of Mitchell and Blair of 1999 suggesting that the underlying problem with psychopathy is lack of empathy with others stating, 'humans have inherited mechanisms which allow them to terminate aggressive attacks when submissive signals are shown by the victim and this is absent in psychopaths. These studies were based on the work of ethologist Lorenz 1966, Violence Premeditated.

It is interesting to note that an early definition of psychopath was produced in 1968 by American Psychiatric Association which includes the personality traits as,

* Incapacity of loyalty
* Selfishness
* Irresponsibility
* Impulsiveness
* Inability to feel guilt
* Failure to learn from experience

This suggests that psychopathic behaviour results from personality traits.

A DSM-IV field trial was done that aimed at improving criteria for antisocial personality disorder. The criteria are based on the revised Psychopathy Checklist, an interview procedure that also draws on information from any other available source, such as criminal or case records. The proposed disorder was named Psychopathy Personality Disorder. The first five characteristics pertain to a subscale consisting of selfish, callous, and remorseless unstable and antisocial lifestyle, and the other five pertain to chronically unstable and antisocial lifestyle. In the first edition of the DSM-IV which was published in 1952 used the term sociopath to diagnose a person who possessed these personality traits.

Proposed Criteria for Psychopathic Personality Disorder
1. Inflated and arrogant self-appraisal
2. Lacks remorse
3. Lacks empathy
4. Deceitful and manipulative
5. Early behavior problems
6. Adult antisocial behavior
7. Impulsive
8. Poor behavioral controls
9. Irresponsible

Serial Killers

Serial killers are known to be the most feared and dangerous individuals of society. The most common definition of a serial killer is an individual acting alone or with another serial killer or a partner who commits two (some sources state three) or more separate murders over a period of time with what is termed a 'cooling off' period between each murder. Killings in two or more different locations with no cooling off period is a killing spree. This cooling off period can range from hours, days, weeks, months or even years. It is also common that this 'cooling off' period can become shorter as the killer claims more victims, as they grow in confidence, as they go undetected and as they perfect their modus operandi. The first time they kill it releases feelings of power, control and feeds an internal need. This internal need can be a range of things, a hatred of women, a need for power and control, a need for revenge, a sexual need or simply because they enjoy the suffering of others, all needs are requiring some form of satisfaction. There is usually no actual connection between the killer and their victim but the serial killer's victims will usually have something in common such as, young women with blond hair, teenage boys, prostitutes or elderly women or something more general like age, sex, race or occupation.

There has been many studies into the question of what makes a serial killer and there are many types, labels and categories assigned to the serial killer. These include sociological traits, psychological and biological categories (Siegel 1998). As well as factors such as mental retardation, brain disorders etc but today we are more familiar with the psychopath and the narcissist. Because these labels main trait is a lack of conscience it makes it easier to understand why serial killers kill. If an individual has no feelings of guilt or remorse for what they do it would therefore make it easier for them to kill. It is far more common for a serial killer to be male as shown by a study conducted by D. K. Rossmo in 1995 that showed that over 90% of serial murders were carried out by males. He also found that the average age of a serial killer was around the mid 20's further to this he stated that 73% of serial killers were white males and 22% were African American, 3% hispanic and only 1% Asian (Hickey 2002). There are three targets associated with serial killers, these are, the stranger, the acquaintance and the family member. The problem with the serial killer is they came from all walk of life. Some are well educated, but mostly only up to high school level, and some are not, some come from privileged families and some from poverty stricken families. The type of employment does not seem to be relevant either. One factor that most serial killers do have in common is a prior criminal history with offences ranging from property offences, sex crimes, drugs, arson and assault.

Eric Hickey's study of serial killers also looked at the methods used to kill, which to some researchers is the most important factor. He found that 41% used firearms some of the time. 42% of the serial killers included in his study used a combination of methods. These are, 37% strangulation, 34% stabbing, 26% some bludgeoning, 19% used firearms only, 13% only stabbed and the final 2% used other means of killing (Hickey 2002). Although this information give us an idea of the most common methods and a most likely offender it is still very difficult to fully categorise and understand the serial killer. According to the Federal Bureau of Investigation (FBI) there are three distinct types of serial killers. These types are based on the way they carry out their murders. Firstly there is the 'Medical Killer', One of the first serial killers that comes to mind for most here is Harold Shipman. Dr Shipman killed up to around four hundred of his elderly patients by the time he was caught giving him the title of the 'the greatest serial killer the world has ever known'. Even with all the evidence against him and fifteen life sentences. He continued to claim his innocents and committed suicide by hanging on January 13th 2004 in prison Although this type of serial killer is very rare there are those who go into the medical profession for the sole purpose of carrying out murders. This providing them with the perfect cover for their crimes as it is common for people in hospital to die. They are very good at covering their murders and are usually very intelligent. The usual way is to make the death look like natural causes involving their ailment so there is no reason for any suspicion. This type of killer is also known as the 'angel of death' or the 'angel of mercy'. There can be a number of reasons why they choose to kill within this profession. Theses can be:

* Sadistic killers, use their position as a way of exerting power and control over people who are helpless and cannot defend themselves. An example of this is Richard Angelo
* Malignant hero, this is when they deliberately endanger a patient's life to almost the point of death in order to save them and appear to be the hero. It has also been know for the patient to be already dead and a fake attempt at resuscitation is made. For example Beverly Allitt
* The mercy killer, this is when the killer believes that there is no hope for the patient and they are only suffering so it is an act of 'putting them out of their misery'. For example Jane Toppan

The Organised Serial Killer also known as 'thrill seekers'

As the title suggests this type of serial killer is very organised and can be one of the most difficult to identify and to catch. They are usually well above average intelligence, some may even be at what is considered genius level. They can be so organised that it can be almost ritual like. Every detail of the murder will be well planned out from start to finish. They will be well aware of forensic evidence and will take every precaution not to leave a single trace at the crime scene, the body dump site or at their home. The first stage in their planning will be the victim selection and can watch their victim for several day or even weeks beforehand. They will take note of their everyday activities and routines as well as the comings and goings of other family members and friends. They will come to a decision as to whether this potential victim is or is not a good target. They will use their observations of the victim to come up with some ploy to lure them to go with them or to get in their car. For example, they were sent by another family member to pick them up or a family member has been involved in an accident and they must go with them to the hospital. This is the main reason why prostitutes are commonly the targets of serial killers, they willingly get into a car with someone unknown with the intention of going to a secluded location. The victim will then be taken to the kill location or even to the killer's own home, and killed. This type of killer will 'hide the body' or hide the body until they want the body to be found. It is not uncommon for this type of serial killer to want to 'play games' with the police, they see it as some kind of challenge between them and the police. They will often refer to their killings as their 'work'. They will follow the newspapers and tv reports closely and may even keep a scrapbook of newspaper cuttings related to their murders. Because this type of killer is usually psychopathic they get great pleasure out of seeing the authorities trying to solve the crime and believes they are too intelligent for the police to catch. It is also common for this type of serial killer to take something from the victim. This might be a watch or item of jewelry, a piece of clothing, a shoe, an id card or in some cases a body part. They do this in order to have something to remind them of their murders so when holding it or looking at it they can relive the murder over and over in their mind.

The Disorganised Serial Killer

This type of serial killer is more opportunistic and is more down to the victim being in the wrong place at the wrong time. Their killing are very rarely planned with very little, if any, steps taken to cover up their victim or the crime. The 'urge' to kill will build up to a point they cannot contain it any longer and will go out looking for a victim. The body will usually be left where the crime was committed and no, or very little, attempt is made to hide the body. They may drag it into undergrowth or behind bins in an alleyway but the body is usually found very easily. This type of serial killer will move around from town to town or, in the US, state to state to avoid being caught. Opposite to the organised serial killer, the disorganised serial killer will be of low intelligence. They will usually be very antisocial, have very few, if any at all, friends and be estranged from their family. As a way of diminishing their responsibility or disassociating themselves with the crime when they are caught this type will often claim they hear voices in their head and the voices told them to do it or they may claim that they have no memory of the event at all.

All serial killers share a certain amount of typical characteristics, these are:

* The very organised serial killer will usually be of high intelligence as will the type of killer that uses bombs but on average the serial killer is of low intelligence and will have a low IQ.

* They were often brought up by a domineering mother and the father had left the family unit when they were a young age.

* They may have attempted suicide a high number of times throughout their life.
    * They usually come from families that have a high level of alcoholism, criminal behaviour and psychiatric problems.
    * They were often abused by a family member. This may have been any, or a combination of physical, sexual or emotional abuse.
    * They tend to be in menial jobs and struggle to keep a job.
    * From an early age they can be intensely interested in things to do with sex and violence and will be very involved in fantasising.
    * Were usually bullied as a child.
    * May have been involved in petty crime, mainly dishonest offences like fraud.

In 1963, a psychiatrist J. M. MacDonald published a paper in the American journal of Psychiatry titled 'The Threat to Kill'. In this paper he outlined three behavioural characteristics which could be used to predict violent behaviour especially in relation to serial offending. This was termed the 'MacDonald triad' or 'triad of sociopathy' or the 'homicidal triad' These three behavioral characteristics are:

    * A fascination with setting fires.
    * Especially in children that have not

reached sexual maturity there is an involvement in sadistic activity. This sadistic activity may take the form of torturing small animals.

     * Bedwetting beyond the age of 12 years. Statistics claim more than 60% but these figures are questionable.

The motives is a question that is asked a lot when dealing with serial killer. Why do they do what they do? These motives can be a number of things and each type of serial killer is put into a number of categories with four main categories of motive, Visionary, mission oriented, hedonistic and power/control.

Visionary

This type of serial killer believes at times that they are another person, like a split personality or entities such as God or the Devil has made them kill. They suffer with psychotic breaks with reality.

Mission Orientated

This type of serial killer will justify their killing by saying that they are ridding the world of a certain type of person that is considered undesirable to the world such as prostitutes but this can even be people such as homesexuals or people of different religions or race. This type of serial killer is not usually psychotic. They view themselves as 'doing the world a favour' and changing society for the better.

Hedonistic

This type of serial killer, to many, is considered as the most psychopathic because they kill for the thrill of it and and derives much pleasure from the killings. To them people are considered as expendable and can be nothing more than a means to their intended goal. The hedonistic serial killer has been put into three subtypes by forensic psychologists. These are 'lust' 'thrill' and 'comfort'.

* **Lust:** For the 'lust' serial killer sex is the primary motive to their killing and fantasy plays a huge part in this. For the lust killer it does not make a difference if the victim is dead or not. They derive sexual gratification by torturing and mutilating their victims and the gratification depends on the amount of torture and mutilation. The cooling off period for this killer will get shorter the more they kill and over time the amount of stimulation they get from the killing will increase. They usually use personal methods of killing such as the use of a knife or strangulation.

* **Thrill:** This type of killer is looking for an adrenaline rush. The thrill they get from

hunting and killing their victims. Their main aim is to instill terror and pain in the victim. There is usually no sexual aspect to this type of killer, it is only about the kill and when the victim is killed it is not usually a prolonged process but there aim is also to commit the perfect crime and will spend a great amount of time perfecting and refining their methods. Unlike others their cooling off period can last for long periods of time. They will usually follow their victim for some time and they are usually strangers.

* **Comfort (profit):** For comfort killers a comfortable lifestyle and material gain are the main motive to this type of killer. Their victims are usually family members and close acquaintances. Insurance or inheritance is the usual motive. To avoid any suspicions from family members and the authorities they will wait a long time before killing again. It is usually women, but not all, who are comfort killers and the usual method is poisoning by arsenic or ethanol glycol (anti freeze).

Power/Control

The exertion of power over the victim is the main goal for this type of killer. The need for them to do this usually comes from their childhood when they were abused which has left them with feelings of inadequacy and powerlessness when they become adults. They inflict these feelings on to their victims by sexually abusing them. The power and control serial killer may rape their victim but it is not about the sex like with hedonistic killers they use it as another form of exerting power and control.

Chapter 5
Dangerous Offenders

The Dangerous Offender

The first idea and definition of a 'dangerous offender' was introduced into the Criminal Justice Act 2003. But it is very difficult to define what is considered 'dangerous' or 'dangerousness'. It would make sense to use the Criminology concept 'offenders who are seen to pose a significant risk to the general public' and these actions are not the result of any kind of mental illness. The number of people who may be a significant risk to the public due to a mental illness would be confined to mental institutions requiring treatment whereas dangerousness without mental illness would lead to the penal system. There are many questions that arise from the simple statement of 'dangerous offenders'. If we first look at the concept of dangerousness in the criminal offender, we must first assume that the offender has been assessed by professionals as to be, not suffering from any form of mental illness and deemed not to be insane. The next stage would be the proof of guilt of an offence which is considered as dangerous. The problem here is that there appears to be very little guidance on what type of behaviour can be deemed as dangerous. So there are no distinct guidelines to determine the difference between dangerous and non-dangerous offenders. When looking at the little guidelines there are, criminal behaviour that is considered as dangerous would be those that are considered as creating risk of 'grave harm to others'. Under this term it would be reasonable to consider such acts as murder, rape, assaults and many other violent and sexual crimes as 'grave harm to others' but the category of dangerous may also include arson, dangerous driving and many others. The list could become endless and we must also consider that what may be considered as dangerous to some may not be considered as dangerous to others.

For offenders that are considered as dangerous they will at some point come to the end of their sentence and be released back into the community. They then become the responsibility of a group of organisations referred to as the 'responsible authority'. In 2001 Multi Agency Public Protection Arrangements (MAPPA) was set up under the authority provided by the Criminal Justice and Court Service Act 2000. The aim of MAPPA is to bridge the gap between the offender, who has served time in prison for their crime, and has the right to liberty and the protection of the public through supervision. This is provided in the European Convention on Human Rights (ECHR) Article 5, which states the 'Right to

Liberty and Security'. The term 'dangerousness' is attributed to specific crimes under the MAPPA model and limits the supervision to violent and/or sex offenders. Some of these offenders are considered as 'high risk' offenders (offenders who are most likely to reoffend) in these cases they are referred to a more specialised organisation known as MAPPP, Multi Agency Public Protection Panel. Therefore the main aim of these organisations is to find a balance of supervision that protects the public and their rights but at the same time protecting the rights of the offender under article 5 of the European Convention on Human Rights. The problem with this MAPPA model of classification of what constitutes as dangerous is limited to violent and sexual crimes and the 'grave harm' with other types of crimes that also cause 'grave harm' are overlooked, for example, money laundering, embezzlement and fraud. These types of crime can cause 'grave harm' to others which can be more widespread. The term 'dangerous' and 'dangerousness' should not be solely concerned with violent and/or sexual crime but should encompass other crimes which cause 'grave harm' to others. The second problem with this model is its focus on the offender and the crime committed and not the wider social problems that generate these types of crimes. It is a bit like treating the symptoms and not attempting to cure the cause. This system simply punishes and imprisons offenders from the most deprived and poverty stricken areas and skimming over the other types of crimes committed by corrupt institutions committing crimes of fraud, embezzlement and money laundering that can destroy people's lives and continue to have a knock on effect to others. Therefore the term 'dangerous' used in the legal concept ignores social problems, and focuses on only a small number of types of criminal activity.

Dangerous Offenders: Dr Michael Stone

Scale of Evil

Dr Michael Stone is a forensic psychologist at Columbia University, USA. In 2001 he created a scale to categorise 'evil'. The scale takes those believed to be the most evil killers ever documented and categorized them into a scale escalating in severity of evil ranging from 1 to 22. The scale is used to psychological profile a suspect or defendant and is used by many law enforcement agencies all over the world.

The Scale of Evil

1. Those who have killed in self defence, and those who do not show traces of psychopathy.

2. Jealous lovers who committed murder.

Although egocentric or immature, they are not psychopathic.

3. Willing companions of killers. Aberrant personality, impulse ridden with some antisocial traits.

4. Those who have killed in self defence but had been extremely provocative towards the victim for that to happen.

5. Traumatised, desperate persons who killed abusive relatives or other people but who show remorse for their crimes and are not psychopaths.

6. Impetuous, hotheaded murderers, yet without marked psychopathic traits.

7. Highly narcissistic, but not distinctly psychopathic persons, some with a psychotic core, who kill persons next to them, with jealousy as an underlying motive.

8. Non psychopathic persons with smoldering rage and who kill when the rage is ignited.

9. Jealous lovers with marked psychopathic features.

10. Killers of people 'in the way' such as witnesses. Extremely egocentric, but not distinctly psychopathic.

11. Psychopathic killers of people 'in the way', such as close friends or even family members.

12. Power hungry psychopaths who kill when they are 'cornered.

13. Psychopathic murderers with inadequate, rageful personalities, rage being the reason of their killings.

14. Ruthlessly self-centred psychopathic schemers who kill to benefit themselves.

15. Psychopathic cold-blooded spree killers or multiple murderers.

16. Psychopaths committing multiple vicious acts with repeated acts of extreme violence.

17. Sexually perverse serial murderers: Rape is the primary motive and the victim is killed to hide evidence.

18. Psychopathic torture-murderers, where murder is the primary motive and the victim is killed after a torture that was not prolonged.

19. Psychopaths driven to terrorism, subjugation, intimidation, and rape, but who are short of murder.

20. Psychopathic torture-murderers, where torture is the primary motive, but in persons with distinct psychoses (such as schizophrenia).

21. Psychopaths who do not kill their victims, but do subject them to extreme torture.

22. Psychopathic torture-murderers, where torture is the primary motive. In most cases, the crime has sexual motivating factor.

Dangerous Sex Offenders

In today's society sex offenders are considered as high risk offenders but it needs to be understood that some sex offenders are considered as low risk. These are offenders that are considered as very unlikely to re-offend. As most sex offenders cannot be sent to prison indefinitely then there is a call for treatment and rehabilitation programmes. What constitutes as a 'sex offence' has changed over time and place as with the ideas of what is considered as normal sexual behaviour and abnormal sexual behaviour. Laws and views on sexual offences is different all over the world and so is the age of consent. In some countries it is as low as 9 years old going up to 21 in others. There are many different types of sex crimes such as sexual harassment. grooming, incest, rape, child molestation, child pornography etc, and there is no way of determining who is a sexual offender and who is not, they look the same as everyone else. It is also a misconception that sex offences are committed by strangers when in fact most sexual offences are committed by someone who is known to the victim. There has been many theories as to why people commit sexual offences but it is more probable that it is a combination of various theories. Ellis (1989) identifies two main theories as explanation as to why some people become sex offenders. These are Social Learning theory and Evolutionary theory.

Social learning theory suggests that people learn certain types of behaviour by being exposed to those behaviours from an early age and to such an extent that they become considered as normal behaviour. Social learning theory was first introduced by Bandura and Walters in 1963. They conducted a number of experiments to show how social learning was linked to aggression rather than from an inner drive or force and that aggression was learnt through a process of observation. reinforcement and modelling. Behaviours can be learnt through a child observing the behaviours, seeing the rewarding consequences of the behaviour and then imitating the behaviour. So using this theory can explain how when a child is exposed to certain things like, pornography, sexual acts, victimisation etc, they can become to see this as the normal way to behave and act and then models themselves on what they observed. Evolutionary theory which is concerned with genetics and male aggression suggesting that certain behaviours are passed on genetically. The highest risk sex offenders appear to have the following characteristics according to the Review of Sex Offender Treatment Programmes 1998, psychopathic or antisocial personality, low victim empathy, criminal history, emotional loneliness, antisocial lifestyle and low problem solving abilities, but not all sex offenders have all of these characteristics.

The Management of Dangerous Sex Offenders

The aim of these treatment programmes is to, 'challenge offenders distorted thoughts and reasoning in relation to their victims and to help manage their impulses by providing alternative courses of action which they view as being more rewarding' (Worrall and Hoy 2005). Some treatments are on a one to one basis for the high risk offender and on a group basis for the low risk offenders. It is required that all sex offenders have at least eighty hours of treatment. In order to reduce crime rates The British Prison Service introduced the Core Sex Offender Treatment Programme (SOTP) which states ten criteria that SOTP should have to be effective and successful. These are

* Explaining how the programme will bring change.
* Including who the programme is intended for and why.
* Underline the risk factors.
* Treatment methods.
* Teaching different types of skills to avoid re-offending.

* Inform them that there are links
between the management and the programme.
 * Enforce engagement of participants.
 * Explaining the sequence and duration.
 * Monitor if the programme is being
delivered properly
 * Evaluate the efficiency of the
programme.

Over a number of years now the Criminal
Justice System has continued to strengthen legislation
and punishments for sex offenders and have looked
more at the public's safety and more at rehabilitation.
There had been no significant change in the laws
regarding sex offences since the Sexual Offences Act
1956 until the Criminal Justice Act 1991 and then
again later with The Sex Offenders Act 1997. The aim
of The Sex Offenders Act 1997 was to make it easier
to identify and manage offenders once they were
released back into the community. Under this act sex
offenders had to register their names and addresses
with the police which, in turn, would enable the police
to uphold the protection of the public. Further to this,
the Crime and Disorder Act 1998 section 58, extended
the post release supervision of sex offenders to a
maximum of ten years regardless of the length of
prison sentence and introduced the Sex Offender
Order in section 2. This also enabled the Magistrates

Court to place a number of restrictions on the offender, for example, preventing the sex offender from going to certain places (Legislation.co.uk). 2003 saw a further change in the laws so longer sentences could be put in place and life sentences were put into effect (Pakes and Winestone 2007). In addition to this the meaning of rape was redefined and internet grooming was added to the Sexual Criminal Act.

Nearly two thirds of sex offenders go to prison immediately (Home Office 2003c). The other offenders are put under the supervision of the probation service or are bound by supervision orders or fines and for some they are discharged completely. All sex offenders who are charged or convicted are required to sign the sex offenders register. This register is divided into different levels and are public information. Depending on the offence the offender will be on the register for life or for a determined length of time. The Sex Offender Registry enables members of the public to know if a sex offender is living in their area but this may cause problems if the register is not updated regularly.

The main aim of the sex offender register and treatment programmes in to ensure the offender does not re-offend. In order for the offender to take part in any of the treatment programmes they must first admit to the offences they have been charged with.

The offender can be sent back to prison if they do not do this. These offenders are also expected to talk about a number of issues or could also face going back to prison, these are, have remorse for their crimes, discuss their behaviour and talk about and express their feelings.

It is not uncommon for medication to be prescribed to sex offenders to decrease their sexual arousal as it is considered as one of the main factors in sexual offending. This is prescribed by psychiatrists who work with the prison service, probation service and treatment programmes. These programmes involve a number of elements, these are,

* Identifying emotions.
* Changing sexual arousal patterns.
* Anger management.
* Social and interpersonal skills.
* Future planning.
* Victim understanding.
* Problem solving.
* Skills therapy.
* Psychotherapy.
* Psycho-education.
* Pharmacological approaches.

(Centre of Sex Offender Management 2000)

It has been suggested by recent studies that further attention needs to made to other issues regarding the offender these are,

      * Low self esteem.

      * Confidence.

      * Loneliness.

      * Attachment issues.

The main focus of these approaches is,

      * Uses of medication.

      * Getting out secrets.

      * Increasing victim empathy.

      * Learning about the law.

There are many organisations and agencies involved in the treatment of sex offenders and usually starts when they are sentenced to a prison term. These include the following,

      * Drug and alcohol abuse workers.

      * Psychologists.

      * Therapists.

      * Probation officers.

      * Prison officers.

      * Cognitive behaviourists.

      * Teachers.

      * Police officers.

      * Prison chaplains.

It has been noted that Sex Offender Treatment Programmes (SOTP) have had a significant impact on the treatment of what are considered as medium risk offenders and low risk offenders but not so with high risk offenders. This is assumed because some have no intention of changing their behaviour and have a high dropout rate. Research has shown that cognitive behavioural and pharmacological treatments have been the most effective in treating offenders.

Chapter 6
Criminal Profiling

The Behavioural Science Unit.

The Behavioural Science Unit was opened in 1972 with eleven agents and Jack Kirsch as the official chief serving for eight months and then followed by John Pfaff. At this point the Behavioural Science Unit offer local police advice on many different types of crime with their speciality in serial murder coming later. Howard Teten began the process of analysing crime scenes by looking at the behaviour of the offender while in the commision of the offence, he looked for the personality traits and also for any evident mental disorders. The initial eleven staff were hand picked especially for their ability to have the 'knack' for behavioural analysis. Over time many of the staff involved began to specialise in certain types of crimes such as, sadistic sexual crimes, child abuse and satanic ritual abuse. The staff at the Behavioural Science Unit went out to various local jurisdictions to teach the 'art' of profiling but at the same time they were helping to solve many difficult crimes and cold cases. As the reputation of the unit grew they began to get requests for their assistance from police departments from all over the country. This required the training of more agent to keep up with the demand for the service. This saw the emergence of the Criminal Personality Profiling Program and the Crime Analysis Program. The identity of the Behavioral Science Unit grew and by 1977 it comprised of three initial purposes, profiling, crime scene analysis and the analysis of threatening letters. The profilers did not take up the cases they wanted to but only took up cases that they were invited to do so because the investigating authority was struggling to solve the case or they had came to a standstill with the case or there was a clear indication that it involved a federal crime.

Two major figures in the Behavioural Science Unit were Robert K Ressler, one of the early agents and John Douglas who eventually became the unit chief after joining in 1979. Both of which have wrote books on their experiences within the Behavioural Science Unit. 'Whoever Fights Monsters' by R. K. Ressler and 'Mindhunter' by John Douglas. Both highly recommended.

The work of the Behavioural Science Unit was new and exciting in the world of offender detection and the program was gradually introduced to law enforcement agencies all over the country. This was. what many consider to be the most important breakthrough into the understanding of the most brutal and extreme aspects of human behaviour. John Douglas and Robert Ressler conducted prison interviews with what was considered as dangerous criminals in order to find out more about their crimes and their motives. The idea was to create a database of the information gathered on the common traits and behaviours of these offenders. As the program advance the methods were refined and proved to work time and time again.

The Crime Scene Analysis has a number of steps to follow which help to put all the information gathered into a conclusion, these steps are:

* The profiling Inputs. This is the collection of all the evidence.
* Decision Process Models. The evidence is examined and arranged in order to locate patterns.
* Crime Assessment. All the evidence collected is organised and the crime scene is reconstructed.
* Criminal Profile. This is where the first three steps of the process are used by the profilers to create the profile of the offender. In this will be included the motives, physical qualities and the personality of the offender.
* The Investigation. The profile compiled will then be given to the investigators who are work on that particular case. It will also be given to to various organisations who may have the data that could lead to the identification

of the killer.

    * The Apprehension. The arrest of the offender.

  Overall, criminal profiling works and has been show to work in many cases around the world. It has helped to catch many offender quickly and efficiently. It gives the investigating authorities, not only a type to focus on but a good direction to lead the case forward.

The Role of Criminal Profiling

  During the 1950's and the 1960's murder rates were rising in America. Among this murder rate the authorities saw an increase in murders of victims by strangers and J. Edgar Hoover, founder of the FBI, was given a wider jurisdiction. His first attention was to area of serial crime called pattern or repetitive crime areas. Between 1951 and 1993 it was estimated that there were around 300 to 400 serial killers at large.Therefore a new unit was formed to take on the task of catching these killers.

  Criminal profiling is gathering information that shows regular patterns and traits for a general description of an unknown subject (UNSUB). The profilers will make a number of determinations from the information gathered. They will look at the psychological and behavioural characteristics of a murder and the victim. They will be looking at how the murder was committed:

      * If a gun or a knife was used, was it a blow to the head or strangulation etc.
      * The age, sex and physical description of the victim.
      * Has a sexual assault or rape taken place.
      * Is there any mutilation or signs of torture.
      * Was the victim killed where they were found or killed elsewhere and brought to a dump site.
      * Are there signs that the killer spent time with the victim at the sight. For example, is there cigarette butts or other items discarded.
      * Are they forensically aware. Wiped prints or 'cleaned up'.
      * Are there tyre and/or footprints.
      * Determining if the offender is on organised or disorganised offender.

Who the victim is also plays a large part in the criminal profiling. It can give good indications as to what type of person committed the crime and their motivation. They would be looking at:

      * The victim's age, their mental age and their intelligence.
      * Their appearance, are they well

groomed or not.

 * Their family background and where they were brought up.

 * The kind of lifestyle they had.

 * Their demeanor and personality.

 * Their employment history and what type of job they did if any.

 * Where they lived in relation to where the crime was committed and where the body was found.

 * Their sexual history.

 * Their arrest record if they have one what type of crimes were they involved in.

 * Drug and alcohol history.

 * The victim's movements during the days and hours leading up to the event.

 * The risk level of the victim, for example, a prostitute would be considered high risk.

The criminal profilers will also be looking at the offender's 'Modus Operandi' and their 'Signature' if there is one. The Modus Operandi is what the offender has, in their own mind, what they have to do in order to accomplish the crime. The Signature is something that tell the profilers a lot more about the offender they are dealing with because this is something that the offender has to do to fulfill or satisfy themselves emotionally. A signature will be used by an organised killer and can be used as a way of taunting the police or for a sexual or perverse reason. All the above information can be used by criminal profilers or behavioural scientists to build up a personality and psychological behavioural profile of an offender which can help them to narrow down suspects or eliminate suspects and to help predict the behaviour of the offender. The profiling is not only for serial murders it can be also used for serial rape, arson, kidnap, bombing and product tampering.

The Role Of Geographic Profiling In Serial Violent Crime Investigation

Thanks to films like silence of the lambs, many people associate criminal profiling with the methods and techniques developed by the FBI at the Behavioral Science Unit at Quantico. There are a number of other approaches that can be used in the course of a criminal investigation and one of these other approaches is geographic profiling. Geographic profiling is an information management system and investigative methodology that evaluates the locations of connected serial crimes to determine the most probable area of offender residence. It can be applied in cases of serial murder, rape, arson, robbery and bombings.

The name most closely associated with geographical profiling is Kim Rossmo. Rossmo began studying geographical profiling as part of his PhD studies at Simon Fraser University (British Columbia, Canada). He studied under professors Paul and Patricia Brentingham, who had developed a theoretical crime model which examined where crimes were most likely to happen, based on offender residence, workplace and leisure activity.Put simply, the Brentingham model maintains that we all have an 'activity space' related to the areas in which we live, work and play and that this activity space produces a pattern of movement around the area. In relation to criminal activity, therefore, it follows that an offender has to know about a particular geographical area before he or she begins selecting crimes to commit; and where the offender's movement patterns intersect within this geographical area, will to a large extent determine where the crime takes place. Kim Rossmo noted that the Brentingham model was examined mainly in relation to crime prevention and was interested in approaching the topic from the opposite perspective by asking the question, what does the location of a crime say about where the offender might live? Acknowledging the potential investigative use of this research the Vancouver Police Department established the world's first Geographic Profiling Unit in 1995. Since it's launch, Scotland Yard, The FBI, The New York Police Department and The Royal Canadian Mounted Police have all used the services of geographic profiling

How Geographical Profiling Works

Geographic profiling works on the basis that the location of a crime site can provide the police with crucial information. It assesses and predicts the offender's most likely place of residence, place of work, social venues and travel routes etc . Geographic profiling consists of both quantitative (objective) scientific geographic techniques and qualitative (subjective) components e.g. a reconstruction and interpretation of the offender's mental map. The primary geographic technique is a computerised system known as Criminal Geographic Targeting (CGT). This means, spatial data such as, data relating to time, distance and movement to and from the crime scenes is analysed to produce a three-dimensional model known as a jeopardy surface. The jeopardy surface contains height and colour probability codes which when superimposed onto a map of the area in which the serial crimes have been committed give an indication of the likelihood of where the offender lives or works. Although the science underpinning geographic profiling can be difficult to understand, it's easy to see how this approach can offer practical assistance in the course of a criminal investigation. As Rossmo points out:

'By establishing the probability of the offender residing in various areas and displaying those results on a map, police efforts to apprehend criminals can be assisted. This information allows police departments to focus their investigative efforts, geographically prioritise suspects, and concentrate patrol efforts in those zones where the criminal predator is likely to be active'.

Geographical Profiling Process

A geographic profile would be used in a criminal investigation as follows:

* A series of crimes is committed.
* The crimes are investigated via traditional means.
* Linking analysis conducted to ascertain which crimes are connected.
* Psychological profile of the unknown subject conducted.
* Geographical profile constructed.
* New investigative strategies developed and pursued.

Geographical Profiling Methodology

In preparing a geographic profile, a number of procedures will be followed. These include:

* Examination of the case file: Witness statements, autopsy reports & psychological profile (if available).
* Inspection of the crime scene.

* Meetings and discussions with lead investigators.

* Visits to the crime sites when practical.

* Analysis of local crime statistics and demographic data.

* Study of street, zoning and rapid transit maps.

Chapter 7
Forensic Science

Sir Bernard Henry Spilsbury (16th May 1877 - 17th December 1947)

Spilsbury was born to James Spilsbury, a manufacturing chemist, and Marion Elizabeth Joy in Leamington Spa, Warwickshire and was the eldest of four children. He became one of the leading figures in the development of forensic science and worked on many famous cases throughout his career. He was educated at the Magdalen College in Oxford where, in 1899, he took a BA in natural sciences and in 1905 he took an MB BCh and in 1908 an MA in the same subject. At the same time as these studies he also studied at St Mary's Hospital in Paddington, London from the beginning of his studies in 1899. Spilsbury specialised in what was then known as the new science of forensic pathology. He was then appointed as the resident assistant pathologist in October 1905 at St Mary's Hospital. At this time the London County Council insisted that all the general hospitals in the London County Council area must appoint two qualified pathologists to perform autopsies following the sudden death of a person.

The first case Sir Bernard Spilsbury was involved in which brought him to the public's attention was the case of Hawley Harvey Crippen in 1910. Dr Crippen practiced as a homeopath in New York. It was here where he married his second wife Corrine (Cora) Turner in 1894. Dr Crippen and his wife moved to England in 1897 where he worked as a distributor of patent medicines. After he was sacked from this job for taking too much time off work to manage his wives stage career Crippen took the position of manager of Drouet's Institution for the Deaf in 1903. It was here that he met a typist called Ethel Le Neve who would later become his lover. Mr and Mrs Crippen moved around various parts of London before settling into 39 Hilldrop Crescent, Camden Road, Holloway, London in 1905. At this new address the Crippens began to take in lodgers in order to subsidise their low income. Cora had an encounter with one of these lodgers, at this, Crippen began an affair with the typist Ethel Le Neve in 1908. The Crippens held a party at their home on January 31st 1910. It was after this party that Cors disappeared. Crippen's lover, Ethel Le Neve soon moved into Hilldrop Crescent and even began wearing Cora's clothes and jewellery. Dr Crippen said that his wife had decided to move back to America but later stated that she had died and been cremated there. Suspicions grew and the house was searched.

During the ongoing investigation the Crippen

house was searched another three times and it was on the fourth search that the police came across the remains of a body which had been concealed under the brick floor of the basement. This is where Sir Bernard Spilsbury came into the case. It was his work which enabled the finding of traces of scopolamine, a calming drug, in the remains of the body. He was also able to identify the body as that of Cora Crippen from a piece of skin from the abdomen. They never found the head and limbs of Mrs Crippen. Undoubtedly, without the work of Spilsbury the method of murder and the identification of the body may not have taken place.

By now Spilsbury was the leading figure in the development of forensic science and worked on many cases. One of the most interesting cases for Spilsbury was that of George Joseph Smith in 1915, also known as the 'brides in the bath murders'. This case was a significant case in the development of forensic detection and pathology. This case was also one of the first cases where crimes were connected by the similarities between them and showed that crimes were deliberate.

George Joseph Smith was born in London and showed signs of being trouble from the age of nine when he was sent to a reformatory and then in 1896 he talked a woman into stealing from her employers and was sent to prison for a year. Using the name of Oliver George Love he married Caroline Thornhill in 1898. The following year he married another woman, his first bigamous marriage. His wife worked for a number of employees in London where she stole from them for Smith. When she was caught she was sent to prison for a year but when she came out of prison she confessed her husband's involvement and he was sent to prison for two years in 1901. When he came out of prison she moved to Canada and Smith went back to his other wife just to empty her bank account and left.

Florence Wilson was Smith's next wife in June of 1908. Taking money from her savings and selling her property he left on the 3rd July. At the end of that month, in Bristol he married Edith Peglar. While married to her he would spent much time away claiming he was away on business selling antiques but he continued to come back to Peglar with plenty of money.

George Rose Smith was the name he used to marry Sarah Freeman in October of 1909 and, like the others, he cleared out her bank account and left. Alice Burnham and Bessie Munday were his next two wives and victims. Using the name Charles Oliver James in September 1914 he married Alice Reid. Between 1908 and 1914 Smith married seven times bigamously.

Joseph Crossley owned a boarding house in

Blackpool in January of 1915 and sent two newspaper clippings to Detective Inspector Arthur Neil, one of the clippings was regarding the death of Margaret Lloyd who was found in the bathtub by her husband John Lloyd and the landlady at the lodgings in Bismarck Road, London, the article was dated 1914 just before christmas. The other clipping was dated December 13th 1913, this one was about a woman called Alice Smith, in Blackpool, who also died in the bathtub in a boarding house. Her husband George Smith found her in the bath. The clipping were brought to the attention of Detective Inspector Arthur Neil in early January. A Mr Charles Burnham along with Crossley and his wife were concerned and suspicious the the two incidents seemed very similar and expressed the matter to be investigated by the police. When Arthur Neil went to Blackpool to investigate the matter he found it odd that the women could drowned in a small bath which was only three quarters full. The only injury found on the body was a small bruise above the left elbow. He then discovered that an insurance policy had been taken out on the woman only three hours before she died and the beneficiary was her husband and all her savings had been taken out the bank the same day. When Neil confronted Mr Lloyd/Smith at the lawyers office while he was claiming the insurance money he admitted to being John Lloyd and George Smith and after being questioned he was arrested for bigamy and on suspicion of murder and Sir Bernard Spilsbury was called in to determine how the woman had died.

After the exhumation of Margaret Lloyd's body Spilsbury had a number of tasks. Firstly he had to determine that the cause of death was drowning and whether it was by accident or by force. What Spilsbury determined from his examination of the body was that death was almost instant. He then ordered a toxicology report to see if she had been poisoned with negative results. Spilsbury, along with Neil, then ran some experiments with the same bathtub set up in the police station. During this time Neil was sent another report of a similar death in Kent where a Henry Williams had rented a house for him and his wife Bessie Munday who he had married in 1910. The house had no bathtub but Williams had rented one shortly after moving in. William claimed that his wife was having epileptic fits and consulted a doctor. On July 13th 1912 it was reported that Bessie Munday had drowned in her bathtub while having an epileptic fit. Williams claimed the insurance which had been stated in Mundays will only five days before she died.

Spilsbury also conducted an autopsy of Alice Smith and discovered the same results as that of

Margaret Lloyd, at this Spilsbury had the bathtub sent to London and took measurements of the bodies. By this time it was discovered that Henry Williams, John Lloyd and George Smith were all the same person. At the same time Spilsbury discovered what he called 'goose pimples' on the skin of the women's bodies including that of Bessie Munday which he claimed as a sure sign of drowning. Considering all the evidence and much thought Spilsbury determined that considering the size of Bessie Munday and the size of the bathtub and the process of an epileptic fit it was impossible for her to have drowned in the bathtub. Through reasoning he determined that Smith must have grabbed her by the feet and pulled them up towards himself pulling the upper part of the body under the water. The sudden gush of water into the throat and nose would cause a quick loss of consciousness which would explain little signs of drowning and minimal signs of injury to the body. Spilsbury tested out his theory with some female divers and one of these almost died during the experiments proving it was very possible to kill someone this way. Spilsbury's work led to the arrest and the charge of George Joseph Smith for the murders of Alice Smith, Margaret Lloyd and Bessie Williams (Munday) on 23rd March 1915. A demonstration of how Smith had killed his wife was held in court and on 1st July 1915 George Joseph Smith was sentenced to death. If it was not for the work of Spilsbury he may have continued killing without detection.

Another famous case which lead to a conviction due to the work of Spilsbury was that of the Herbert Rowse Armstrong. Armstrong was a retired Territorial army major living in Hey-on-Wye working as a solicitor at 53 years old. Armstrong's wife, Katherine, was believed to be a hypochondriac who constantly nagged and domineered Armstrong. In July of 1920 Katherine was certified insane and was sent to an asylum for several months. Once Katherine returned home she suffered some sort of illness which was agonising for her which was later diagnosed by a doctor as gastritis. After Armstrong returned from a holiday he took to get over his wife's death he found himself in a dispute with another local solicitor named Oswald Martin. In order to settle the matter Armstrong invited Martin to tea where he handed him a scone. Martin became violently ill later that day. It happened that Martin's father-in-law was the town's chemist and told the doctor that was treating Martin that Armstrong had made several purchases of arsenic from him. A sample of Martin's urine was sent for analysis and was proven to contain arsenic. On New Year's Eve of 1921 Armstrong was charged with the attempted murder of Oswald Martin. The now famous pathologist Bernard Spilsbury exhumed Katherine Armstrong's body in order to carry out a post-mortem. He discovered that her body contained 208 mg of arsenic. The body is said to have been in a good state of preservation and this was due to the arsenic having a mummifying effect on the body. Armstrong was hanged on 31st May 1922 and was the only solicitor ever to be hanged in England.

Later in his career Spilsbury with member from Scotland Yard put together what was know as the 'Murder Bag' a kit containing all the things needed to collect forensic evidence at the crime scene. It contained evidence bags, gloves, tweezers, magnifying glass, swabs, compass etc. The contents of the bag have changed over the years with advances in forensics.

Ballistics

Ballistic has been a major development in the forensic sciences and have contributed to a large amount convictions which would have not been possible without the expertise of ballistics. In order to have a good understanding of ballistic we need to understand how a gun works.

Guns that fire cartridges are revolvers and semi automatic pistols which are the type of guns more commonly used in a majority of gun related incidents due to them being easily concealed and easy to carry. Here we will start with how a bullet if fired from a handgun. Firstly there is the casing of a bullet which we are all familiar with. The actual bullet is positioned at the top end of the casing and the lower end holds the explosive powder (gun powder). Right at the bottom end is the primer, the primer is what starts the process of firing. When the trigger of a gun is pulled it forces a hammer pushed by a spring which hits a firing pin, which, in turn, hits the primer which causes the powder to light. The powder gives off gases which expand, rapidly accelerating the bullet through the barrel of the gun. The barrel of the gun has swirling grooves throughout it which causes the bullet to spin giving it more speed. When a bullet is fired there are markings left on it which can be used to identify the gun it was fired from. The main marking left by the gun are the ones caused by the bullet travelling through the barrel and these are called striations although other markings left by the firing process can be used for comparison. The striations are compared by clamping them to a macroscope that is optically connected to another. The bullets are rotated to match the striations. This enables investigators to match bullets from different crime scenes and bullets to guns by test firing.

The size, weight and shape of a bullet is also used when narrowing down the type of gun used in an incident. Some bullets may have only been used in a rare type of gun or were only made during a certain time period. The way the firing pin hits the primer in different makes and models of guns can also be used in linking bullets to guns as each make and model leaves different markings or scratches on the primer. These are known in forensics as 'breech marks'. After a bullet is fired the casing is extracted from the gun by a round groove at the base. The extractor hooks on to this groove and extracts the empty casing from the chamber and is then ejected by the ejector. Both these processes can leave unique markings on the casing which can be used to match a bullet to a certain gun.

1. The first recorded use of ballistics being used as evidence was in 1835 when Scotland Yard's Henry Goddard uses a visible flaw in a bullet traced back to the mold as comparison to convict a murderer.
2. In 1889 Professor Alexandre Lacassagne of forensic medicine attempted to individualise bullets to a barrel which he based on the number of shots hit and the grooves that could be seen.
3. Photomicrographs were taken by Paul Jesrich a forensic chemist in 1898 to compare two bullets.
4. 1913 saw the first article published by Victor

Balthazard individualising bullet markings, later to be known as striations.

5. The pioneer in striation analysis in tool marking comparison was an American criminalist called Luke May in the 1920's.

6. This decade also saw the perfection of the comparison microscope to be used in bullet comparison by Calvin Goddard along with others.

7. Again it the 1920's came the first catalogue manufacturing data of weapons by Charles Waite.

8. It wasn't until 1959 that Gilroy and Harrison first introduced the qualitative colorimetric chemical test which enabled them to detect the presence of antimony, lead and barium on the hands of someone who had fired a gun.

9. At the Aerospace Corporation in 1974 they used a scanning electron microscopy with electron dispersive x-rays technology to detect gunshot residue.

10. Huge advances were made in 1991 with the launch of the Integrated Ballistics Identification System. This was an automated imaging system used to compare markings left on a fired bullet, shell case and cartridge case.

11. The following year in 1992 an automated imaging system to compare the same bullet markings called Drugfire was helped to develop by the FBI.

Physical Evidence

1. One of the first known cases where physical evidence was used in solving a crime was in 1235 where a murder was committed by using a sickle. It was then ordered that everyone who owned a sickle was to lay them out in the sun in the middle of the village, eventually files gathered around the sickle attracted by the blood, inturn identifying it as the murder weapon.

2. In 1248 The Washing Away of Wrongs, His Duan Yu, the Chinese book was the first recorded use of applying medicine to solve a crime where he describes how to distinguish the difference between strangulation (broken neck cartilage) and drowning (water in the lungs).

3. One of the first recorded medical autopsy was performed by Bartolomeo da Varignana in 1302 regarding a suspected murder of a nobleman.

4. The French Duke of Burgundy's missing teeth were used to identify his remains in 1447.

5. In 1590 Zacharias Jansen and his father Hans Jansen were Dutch spectacle makers who discovered, by experimenting with lenses, the first microscope.

6. A Systematic document examination treatise was first published by Francois Damelle in 1609.

7. Adipocere was discovered in 1658 by Sir Thomas Browne. Adipocere was described as a soap like, fatty, waxy substance that formed on human bodies when they had been buried in air free, moist places.

8. One of the first uses of physical matching was first documented in 1786 in England was the case of John Toms who was convicted of murder on the evidence of a torn piece of paper found in his pocket matched a piece of paper found in a pistol.

9. In 1817 T. Bateman notes dark purple blotches on a body and from this determines that they must be due to the pooling of blood in the dermal tissues. He calls this senile ecchymoses.

10. Thomas Bell, in 1829, first describes 'pink teeth' he takes this to be a sign of drowning or hanging.

11. In the 1830s the work of Bertillon is used by Adolphe Quetelet from Belgium to prove that no two human bodies are the same.

12. Petechial haemorrhages, red speckled rash like marks, occurring in asphyxial deaths (choking or drowning etc) was first brought to attention by Ambroise Auguste Tardieu in 1855.

13. In 1863 a paper was written by Taylor and Wilkes showing how a fall in body temperature can be used in determining the lapse of time since death.

14. The first test for the presence of blood was discovered by a German scientist in 1863. This involved to oxidation of hydrogen peroxide by the haemoglobin.

15. The following year, 1864, saw a huge advance in criminal evidence with the documentation of evidence and crime scenes and the use of photographs to identify criminals which was advocated by Odelbrecht.

16. The study of hair and the recognition of its limits was first studied by a German pathologist, Rudolf Virchow in 1879.

17. 1880 saw the introduction of temperature graphs in order to determine the time since death.

18. The first description of the many uses of physical evidence in solving crimes came in 1891 when Criminal Investigation was published by Austrian, Hans Gross.

19. The basis for cheiloscopy, this is where lip traces are used for the purpose of identification, was first put forward by R. Fischer in 1902 when he describes the system of grooves on the lips.

20. The first in depth study of hair was published in 1910 by Professor of medicine Victor Balthazard.

21. The first use of a vacuum to collect trace evidence was in California by Albert Schneider in 1916.

22. In 1923 the absorption-elution tests for the blood typing of stains was developed by Vittorio Siracusa.

23. The first recognition of secretion of group specific antigens (a toxin or a foreign substance that triggers an immune response in the human body) into body fluids other than blood was by a Japanese scientist called Saburo Sirai in 1925.

24. Two years later in 1927 the development of the MNSs and P typing systems www.bloodbook.com was lead by Landsteiner and Levines' first detection of the M, N and P blood factors.

25. In 1928 the first medical legal investigator Meuller suggests the identification of salivary amylase (this is an enzyme that breaks starch down into sugar) as a presumptive test for saliva stains.

26. K.I. Yosida in 1929 was the first to conduct a comprehensive investigation which he established the existence of serological isoantibodies in fluids other than blood.

27. Absorption inhibition AB typing techniques was developed by Franz Josef Holzer in 1931 and this became the basis of the technique commonly used in forensic laboratories today.

28. Walter Specht in 1837 developed the chemiluminescent reagent luminal as a presumptive test for blood.

29. The 1940s was the first use of dental records comparisons with the teeth from bodied.

30. In 1945 Frank Lundquist developed the first acid phosphatase test for seman.

31. The tape lift method of collecting evidence was first developed by Max Frei-Sulzer in 1950.

32. De Saram , in 1955, publishes a paper of temperature measurements taken from executed prisoners which was considered a landmark in when determining a time since death from the cooling of the body.

33. Mocker and Stewart developed the skeletal growth stages in 1957.

34. In 2007 The Forensic Science Service in the UK launched the first online footwear coding and detection management system calling it Footwear Intelligence Technology.

Fingerprints

When a forensic team enter a crime scene one of the most well known forensic applications is fingerprinting. Fingerprints can very easily be destroyed if great care is not taken. How fragile the prints are will depend on whether they are on a porous or nonporous object. When fingerprints are on surfaces that are nonporous like glass, plastic, ceramic or metal touching them, even with glove on, can destroy the fingerprint and so can dusting then vigorously. The prints can also be destroyed by placing them in a plastic bag, so great care needs to be taken. The procedure is for the object to be secured in a box corner to corner so it cannot move and the prints will be secure. This would only be done if it was impossible to perform a 'Cyanoacrylate Fume Test'. Cyanoacrylate is superglue. This is a simple but effective way of obtaining prints. All that is needed is a box, a heat source, such as a cup of hot water or a light bulb, which would speed up the process, to provide water vapor. Something to hold a small pool of superglue, such as some aluminum foil and something to suspend the object, a piece of string would do. Be warned, if you do try this at home make sure it is in a very well ventilated area and all safety measures are taken. If you use a cup of water make sure it is discarded immediately after. <u>Do not drink it</u>. The residue from the fingerprint reacts with the cyanoacrylate fumes and the water vapor which creates a white powder called polycyanoacrylate. The powder sticks to the ridges in the fingerprint resulting in white visible print which is hard. This can then be photographed and recorded. Fingerprint can be taken from porous surfaces like, a body, sheets, cigarettes etc. Fingerprints can also be seen from a single light source, such as a torch, used at the right angle. Light which emits at certain wavelengths such as a laser light can make some prints glow making them visible.

Fingerprints have patterns to them. The ridges are in three basic patterns, loops, whorls and arches and each pattern has sub groups to them such as ulnar loops and radial loops to determine the direction of the loop and depending on their shape there are plain and tented arches. There are also accidental, plain and double loop whorls. The fingerprints are analysed on three levels. The first stage looks at the general flow of the ridge and the pattern it forms but this is not enough to identify a suspect with so the analysis moves on to the second stage. The second stage looks closer at the features of the ridges, these are, where a ridge splits and then rejoins, known as a lake. The bifurcation, one ridge splits into two. The end of a ridge is the termination. A short ridge is an independent. Every variation in each and every ridge is named and recorded until the print it completely analysed. Once a qualified examiner has come to their conclusion the print will be passed on for another examiner to avoid mistakes being made.

There are four categories of fingerprints these are, patent, latent, plastic and inked.

Patent: These are fingerprints which are caused by the transfer of something such as blood and are impressions of the fingerprint. This type of fingerprint can be easily seen and photographed

Latent: These are impressions of fingerprints that are left at a crime scene by accident whether they are visible or not. Any fingerprint that is left at a crime scene that can be made visible by one technique or another regardless of the surface it is on, is known as a latent print. There are various techniques that can be used other than fuming and light sources such as the use of different coloured powders so one powder shows the ridges and the other shows the surface. Another technique is iodine fuming, some prints have fatty deposits and oil in them which the iodine reacts to making the print visible. Lifting tape is one of the more well known ways of securing fingerprints.

Plastic: These are prints that would be left at the scene of the crime in some soft surface or substance like clay or putty or some kind of grease.

Inked: These are controlled prints and are known, recorded prints. The prints that are taken by the police when a suspect is brought in for questioning. The more well known way of doing this is for the suspect to roll each finger and thumb in ink and then onto a card known as a ten-card. The palmprint may also be taken. These days it is more common for a copier to be used, much like a scanner but will pick up all the ridges and grooves on the fingers and the palm.

1. It is known that even in pre 700 BC in ancient Babylon fingerprints were used on clay tablets for business transactions.

In his treatise the spirals, loops and ridges in fingerprints were noted by Marcello Malpighi, a professor of anatomy in 1686.

2. As a way of identifying books he published, Thomas Bewick used engravings of his own fingerprint.

3. In 1823 a thesis discussing 9 fingerprint patterns was published by anatomy professor John Evangelist.

4. Thumbprints on documents were used by Sir William Herschel to verify document signatures and as a substitute for written signatures in 1856.

5. 1877 saw the first suggestion of using palmprints and fingerprints as a way of identifying criminals by Thomas Taylor.

6. In 1880, in a Tokyo burglary, Henry Faulds uses fingerprints to eliminate an innocent suspect and to prove the burglar. He then publishes a paper suggesting that an offender could be identified by the fingerprints left at the scene of a crime.

7. As a way of safeguarding himself from forgeries in 1882 Gilbert Thompson put his thumbprint on wage chits (a short official note, memorandum, or voucher typically recording a sum owed)

8. The same year saw the development of the Fingerprint Classification System by Juan Vucetich. It is later used in Latin America.

9. The Fingerprint Classification System that would

be later used in North America and Europe was developed by Sir Edward Richard Henry in 1896. Then in 1901 he became head of Scotland Yard and enforced the replacement of anthropometry (the scientific study of the measurements and proportions of the human body) with the Fingerprint Identification System.

10. Henry DeForrest pioneers the first systematic use of fingerprints in America by the New York Civil Service Commission also in 1901.

11. For criminal identification in America fingerprints were first used by the New York State's Prison system in 1903.

12. In 1918, as the work on fingerprinting develops Edmond Locard suggests 12 matching points as a positive fingerprint identification.

13. 1977 saw a major development in forensics with the introduction of the beginnings of Automated Fingerprint Identification System (AFIS) by the FBI this was the first computerised scans of fingerprints.

14. The same year saw the development of latent prints using the superglue fuming method by Masato Soba.

DNA - National DNA database

The National DNA Database (NDNAD) was set up in 1995, and it has since become a very potent tool in fighting crime. It can be argued that the database is infringing civil liberties by retaining the DNA profiles that the Police have collected, this issue will be discussed. There are also human rights issues that will be addressed. However, the NDNAD has helped to secure many convictions and prevented miscarriages of justices which will be given consideration in this work.

The NDNAD is a forensic detection tool used by the Police. It stores Deoxyribonucleic Acid (DNA), found in virtually every cell in the body; each person's DNA is unique. It can be found in blood, semen and saliva left at a crime scene. It allows the Police to identify a suspect early in an investigation and gain convictions. There has been calls for a nationwide database but this has met with strong resistance and the current database is also under scrutiny, because it is seen by many as an infringement of civil liberties. However, the benefits of a NDNAD can be clearly shown. In 2005, the NDNAD was responsible for twenty thousand convictions; four hundred and twenty two of which were murders and manslaughters. As laid down in Article 2 of the Human Rights Act 1998, you have an 'absolute right to the life and this must be protected by law'.Using the NDNAD the police are catching murders in some cases before they can strike again . Crime figures for

2005 show there were seven hundred and sixty five murders, and nine hundred and twenty two manslaughters. Conviction rates could have been even higher with a nationwide database. There are no statistics available to show how many crimes the NDNAD has prevented. Yet, as one of the government's primary duties is to protect its citizens from crime, it is fair to assume that NDNAD is acting as a deterrent. NDNAD is protecting civil liberties and freedoms that are expected in a liberal society. The Database is also responsible for solving 'cold cases'; a crime which has remained undetected for a long period of time, in some cases years.

When considering civil liberties, consideration must be given to Sean Hodgson, whose liberty was removed for 27 years for a murder he never committed. In 1982 he was convicted of strangling Teresa De Simone in Southampton. Mr Hodgson would never admit he was guilty, so was never eligible for parole. After DNA tests were performed, on items preserved from the car Teresa was strangled in, it was found not to be that of Sean Hodgson. The NDNAD can stop these horrendous miscarriage of justice. The argument that innocent people on the NDNAD, will not catch criminals, because the innocent have nothing to hide, nothing to fear, is a fallacious argument. This is ideology, assuming that people are born criminals, and there are those, walking around in society today, who will never commit a crime. 'Psychology and Crime' explains that criminal behaviour can occur as a matter of a person's circumstances. Christopher Woods [4] is a prime example; Woods was a well respected man who worked in a charity shop, he had had his home reposed in 1986 and had been living in a council house ever since. He began to fall into arrears with his rent and, when the council threatened to repossess, he went out and robbed two building societies to pay the rent. Christopher Woods was an innocent man until he was fifty three years old. There are beliefs that civil liberties are being breached by NDNAD. There are also concerns about the powers that the Police have to obtain a DNA profile, place it on the database and retain it indefinitely. It has also been suggested that the NDNAD could lead us into a Police state. The arguments against the NDNAD are equally as strong as those in favour.

The Police have powers to add innocent citizens to the NDNAD, that have been arrested and not convicted, they can also add volunteers, that have given their DNA to be eliminated from an enquiry; for instance a rape case. These DNA profiles are put on the database and never removed. If a sample of DNA is found at a crime scene, it is then run through the NDNAD to see if there is a match. Innocent people are having their civil liberties breached by being turned into 'pre-suspects'. The common law principle is innocent till proven guilty. The NDNAD is turning the nation into suspects. Any society that is democratic, must strike a balance between the rights of privacy, a person's right of innocence, and the need to fight crime. New powers given to the police to take DNA samples from people for the most minor of offences such as a dog fouling the pavement or begging in the street, combined with reports in the media that the Police are arresting people, purely to add them to the NDNAD, is tipping that balance towards a Police state.

One third of all Young black males are on the NDNAD. This again is in direct violation of their human rights which says 'you will not be discriminated against because of skin colour'.[5] Any interference with these rights are to be proportionate, clearly this is not the case. Black males are being stigmatised by Police. The Police with an over eagerness, are causing alienation among the ethnic minorities by pre judging them as lawbreakers. This, once again, is underling there civil liberty as in the Race Relations Act 2000. There have been calls by senior members of the government and Police for a nation wide NDNAD, with DNA being taken from newborn babies and being added to the database.

These would remove the problems associated with discrimination, but this would prove not to be cost effective and the benefits to society would be disproportionate to the intrusion of privacy. The Data Protection Act 1998 exists to protect organisations from sharing personal information about citizens. The NDNAD holds the most personal of data, your genetic signature. Section 35 of the Data Protection Act, allows the Police to share this information with anybody. This violates your Human Rights which states that everybody has a right to privacy.

In conclusion, both sides of this argument have been addressed, and both are equally strong. The advantages of the NDNAD can easily be seen, and the case of Steve Hodgson highlights this. However the civil liberties infringements are also apparent and the misrepresentation of ethnic minorities needs addressing by the government. The usefulness of the NDNAD cannot be ignored and a balance needs to be found in the way that the Police use and retain this information and how long they hold the profiles for. A summary offence should only be held for 2 years and an indictable offence 20 years I believe this would strike a fair balance. A Walker, C Kershaw and S Nicholas "Home office statistical bulletin"

Toxicology - A Poison is described as 'a substance

that is capable of causing the illness or death of a living organism when introduced or absorbed'. Poisons are commonly used as a form of pest control but are also commonly used as a method of murder so it is important that toxicologist are able to detect these poisons in the tissues of a body. Although there are many different kinds of poisons the ones most commonly used for murder are arsenic, cyanide, strychnine and ethylene glycol more well known as anti-freeze. There is no test that can be done to reveal what type of poison someone died from so it is a case of evaluating the evidence and testing for the most likely poison used or a process of elimination. There are six levels of toxins with cyanide and strychnine being at the top of the scale at number six.

Arsenic: Arsenic comes in a number of forms with the most common being a white powder called arsenic trioxide which is found in insecticides, weed killers and rat poisons. There is also arsenic trihydride which is a gas created by the reaction of arsenic with acids and is said to have the smell of garlic. Arsenic affects the digestive system and it depends on how much arsenic has been ingested as to how long it would take for a person to die. If a large amount is administered then the symptoms can start after around 30 minutes but can take up to around twenty four hours. This can be determined during the autopsy. If only traces of arsenic is found in the digestive tract and the stomach is inflamed it can be determined that the victim dies quickly. There skin may also have a yellowish look to it due to red blood cells being destroyed by the arsenic. If the arsenic was administered over some time then the arsenic would be found in other organs of the body like the kidneys and the liver. The symptoms of arsenic poisoning are abdominal pain, headaches, vomiting, severe diarrhea, drowsiness, dark urine, dehydration, coma and finally death.

Cyanide: Cyanide is highly toxic and can come in a number of forms these include hydrogen cyanide which is also known as hydro cyanide acid and prussic acid. This is a gas or a liquid. potassium cyanide which is a small crystalised colourless substance that can easily be dissolved in water. And sodium cyanide which is also a white crystalline which is soluble, when it becomes damp it gives off hydrogen cyanide. Cyanide can be ingested, absorbed through the skin and inhaled. Inhaling cyanide causes the most damage. It is said that cyanide has a bitter almond smell but not everyone can smell it. This is due to some unknown genetic reason. The main effect of cyanide is that it interferes with the absorption of oxygen in the body. As the brain and the heart use more oxygen than other parts of the body it is these that are affected first. Ingesting cyanide can take between four to twelve hours to kill a person but only if a large dose is given or taken in suicide, whereas cyanide gas can render someone unconscious immediately and death comes soon after.

Strychnine: Strychnine is also a very lethal toxin. Victims of strychnine poisoning are sometimes found with the look of agonising pain still on their faces after they have died. Strychnine has a fine crystalline powder appearance, it is colourless and is said to have a bitter taste. It can administered in a number of ways, taken orally, inhaled or mixed with another solution and injected directly into a vein. Strychnine comes from a plant found in India, South Asia, Australia and Sri Lanka called 'Strychnos-nux-vomica. It is mainly used in pesticides in particular rat poison. Strychnine interrupts the chemicals that control the nerve signals to the body's muscles causing the muscles to go into very painful spasms. In the latter stages of poisoning the person is unable to breath and finally death. When ingested strychnine symptoms can begin after only around fifteen minutes but can take up to around an hour. This would take slightly longer if the person had just had a large meal. A large dose of strychnine administered by any means could kill a person from between fifteen and thirty minutes. The symptoms of strychnine poisoning are, jaw tightness, muscle pain, stiff limbs, painful muscle spasms, fever, liver and kidney problems, restlessness, agitation, breathing difficulties, respiratory failure and brain death. Strychnine can be detected in the blood and tissues of a body after death but only for a limited time.

Ethylene glycol: Ethylene glycol is more commonly known as antifreeze and has been used as a means of murder and suicide for some time. It is odorless, colourless and is a sweet tasting liquid. Because of its sweet taste it can be easily mixed with other liquids that are regularly consumed. It can also be found in many other substances such as, deicers, engine oil and brake fluid. It is not the ethylene glycol itself that causes the major poisoning but the metabolites contained in it which are oxalic acid and glycolic acid. The symptoms of ethylene glycol poisoning are many with the main being the feeling of intoxication which leads to some people drinking it as a substitute for alcohol. This intoxicated feeling it the first symptom felt which can come about within a few hours depending on how much is taken. When ethylene glycol is used as a means of murder it is usually given in small amounts over a longer period of time therefore the symptoms would get progressively more severe over a prolonged period of time, until eventual death. The symptoms are due to the poison disturbing the chemistry within the body. After the first feeling of intoxication the main symptoms are, nausea, vomiting, blurred vision, tiredness, cramps in the legs, rapid breathing and heart rate, convulsions, coma and ending in death.

Ethylene glycol can be detected in the blood and urine as well as x rays of the lungs which would show fluid in them and swelling of the brain which would be shown in the brain scans. During autopsy a toxicology screening would take place where ethylene glycol would be detected.

Brief history of Toxicology

1. In 1775 a discovery was made by Karl Wilhelm which would later play a huge part of the detection of arsenic. He found that he could change arsenious oxide in to arsenious acid which, when comes into contact with zinc it produces arsine.

2. Considered as the father of toxicology, Mathieu Orfila publishes a toxicology book in 1813.

3. Sir Robert Christison publishes documents on poisons in 1829 which is regarded as the standard work on toxicology for many years.

4. James Marsh an English chemist in 1836 develops the 'marsh test' which is a test for the presence of arsenic in body tissues and he is also the first to use toxicology in a jury trial.

5. A chemistry professor for Brussels, Jean Servais Stas, in 1851, is the first to identify vegetable poisons in body tissues. **6.** By this year arsenic was being commonly used as a means of murder in Britain so the arsenic act was passed in order to have control over the availability of arsenic.

The Science

There are many great scientific breakthroughs that have made the advance of forensics possible but scientific application did not show force until the 1800's and has grown rapidly since then. Having said that, a form of forensics are known to have taken place as far back as pre 700 BC and around 287-212 BC it is thought that Archimedes talked about being able to prove that a crown was not made of gold by immersing it it water and using buoyancy and density as a guide.

1. In 250 BC the first idea of a lie detector was discovered by an ancient Greek physician, Erasistratus when he noticed that people's heart rates increased when they were telling lies.
2. In Germany in 1810 a document known as the Konigin Han Schritt was chemically tested for a particular kind of ink dye and this is the first recorded use of document analysis.

3. The Nicol Prism or the polarising light microscope was invented by William Nicol in 1828.

4. In 1831 Leuchs discovers amylase (an enzyme found in saliva that converts starch and glycogen into simple sugars) activity in human saliva.

5. One of the first attempts recorded when determining the time elapsed since death using body temperature was by Dr John Davy in 1839 when he experimented on dead soldiers using a mercury thermometer.

6. H Baynard was the first to publish reliable procedures detecting microscopic traces of sperm and he also noted the microscopic differences on different fabrics in 1839.

7. Ludwig Teichmann from Poland was responsible for the first microscopic crystal test for haemoglobin using hemin crystals in 1853.

8. The first use of photography for photographing inmates for prison records came about in 1854 when Massox, an English physician developed dry plate photography.

9. In 1862 a Dutch scientist called J. Izaak Van Deen develops a presumptive blood test using guaiac (a brown resin that comes from a guaiacum tree)

10. Based on his invention of anthropometry (the scientific study of the measurements and proportions of the human body) Alphonse Bertillon in 1883 identifies the first repeat offender.

11. The precipitin test for species was developed in 1901 by Paul Uhlenhuth a German immunologist.

12. This year also sees the discovery that blood can be grouped into different categories by Leone Lattes.

13. Professor R A Reiss in 1902 sets up the first academic curricular in forensic sciences.

14. The presumptive test for blood based on benzidine was developed by Rudolf and Oscar Adler in 1904.

15. A test using diatoms (a singled celled alga that has a cell wall of silica) that could be used for distinguishing whether a person was submerged in water before or after death was a conceived idea by Revenstorf in 1904.

16. In 1912 another microscopic crystal test from blood is developed by Massaro Takayama using hemochromogen crystals.

17. The hyperbola spectrograph was the first mass spectrometer (an apparatus used for recording and measuring spectra, especially as a method of analysis) built by J J Thomson in 1913.

18. Two years later in 1915 professor Leone Lattes introduces the first antibody test for ABO blood types.

19. During the 1920's botanical identification use in forensics is pioneered by Georg Popp.

20. The portable polygraph was designed by Leonard

Keeler and John Larson in 1921.

21. Also in 1921 Schuller makes the suggestion that frontal sinuses could be used for identification.

22. The diphenylamine (a synthetic crystalline compound with basic properties, used as an insecticide) test was introduced in 1933 by Teodoro Gonzales to detect gunshot residue.

23. Frits Zernike a Dutch physicist in 1935 invented the first interference contrast microscope.

24. The first paper to be published stating the usefulness of secretor status for forensic applications came from a paper published in 1937 by Holzer.

25. In 1938 M Jayle and M Polonovski are the first to identify haptoglobin (a protein present in blood serum that binds to and removes free hemoglobin from the bloodstream).

26.. Vincent Hnizda was thought to be the first to analyse ignitable fluid in 1940.

27. A S Weiner and Landsteiner in the same year were the first to describe Rh blood groups.

28. The study of voice print identification was first suggested in 1941 by Murray Hill.

29. In 1946 Mourant is the first to discuss the Lewis blood group system.

30. In the same year the Kell blood group system is described by R R Race.

31. Then the Duffy blood group system came along in

1950 by M Cutbush.

32. Only to be followed in 1951 by F H Allen's Kidd blood group system.

33. 1953 saw a huge breakthrough in forensic science by James Watson and Francis Crick with the publication of their landmark paper that identified the structure of DNA.

34. The Breathalyser used for field sobriety tests is invented by R F Borkenstein in 1954.

35. The H-lectin to determine positive O blood type was introduced in 1958 by A S Weiner.

36. In 1959 Hirshfeld was the first to identify the polymorphic nature of group specific component (Gc).

37. In 1960 the application of gas chromatography (the separation of a mixture by passing it in solution or suspension or as a vapor which is used in the case of gas) was used to identify petroleum products in a forensic lab by Lucas he also noted the limitations of being able to identify a brand of gasoline.

38. Also in this decade the Ouchterlony antibody antigen diffusion test was adapted by Maurice Muller for testing to determine species.

39. In 1963 there was D A Hopkinsons identification of the polymorphic nature of erythrocytes acid phosphatase (EAP) and then in 1964 there was R A Fildes and H Harris's identification of the polymorphic nature of red cell adenylate cryclase (AK)

40. The development of the immunoelectrophoretic technique for haptoglobin typing in bloodstains was developed in 1966 by Brian Culliford and Brian Wraxall.

41. Gel based methods to test for isoenzymes in dried blood stains was initiated by Culliford in 1967. He then, in 1971, publishes 'The Examination and Typing of Bloodstains in the Crime Laboratory.

42. In 1976 Zoro and Hadley were the first to use GC (group specific component)-MS for forensic use.

43. A multisystem method for testing the polymorphic nature of different blood cells was developed in 1978 Brian Wraxall and Mark Stolorow. They also developed different methods for typing blood serum proteins.

44. In the same year a test called electrostatic document analysis (ESDA) was developed to obtain document impressions.

45. We now come into the 1980's were huge developments and advances in forensics came into play with the discovery, by American geneticists, in 1980, of a region of DNA that does not hold any genetic information and is extremely variable between each individual person.

46. One of the most groundbreaking advances in

forensics took place in 1984 with Sir Alec Jeffreys when he discovered a way to identify individuals from their DNA. The full name of this method is 'Restriction Fragment Length Polymorphism (RFLP) This is more commonly known as DNA fingerprinting.

47. The following year in 1985 saw the first use of DNA profiling by the British police force.

48. Advances in the DNA profiling were made by Kerry Mullis in 1986 with the discovery of Polymerase Chain Reaction (PCR) This is a method of replicating particular regions of a DNA molecule.

49. In the same year Colin Pitchfork is on trial for the murder of two girls in the Midlands and Jeffreys uses DNA profiling to prove his guilt. This was the first time Dna profiling was used to solve a crime.

50. This year also saw the first use of a PCR (polymerase chain reaction) typing kit which was specifically for use in forensics. The PCR technique was developed by The human genetic group at Cetus Corporation for clinical and forensic purposes.

51. It was in 1987 when we saw the first use of DNA profiling in the American criminal courts.

52. Homogenous enzyme immunoassay (EMIT) was a procedure for analysing the whole blood for drugs that was introduced in a papers published in 1988.

53. In 1992 a paper was published that suggested the

use of short tandem repeats for DNA analysis by Thomas Caskey.

The world's first national DNA database came into use in 1995 in the UK.

54. The following year, 1996, saw the introduction of computerised searches by the FBI of AFIS (Automated Fingerprint Identification System). Also in this year Mitochondria DNA evidence is used in court for the first time in America.

55. Again in 1996 the UK police establish the National Criminal DNA Database.

56. Two years later in 1998 the FBI introduces its own DNA database, NIDIS (National DNA Index System).

Historical Events.

1 1810 saw the first detective force called the Surete of Paris which came about due to Eugene Francois Vidocq who, in return for a suspension of arrest and a prison sentence makes a deal with police to establish the force.

2 Arthur Conan Doyle publishes the first Sherlock Holmes story in 1887.

3 Due to a mistaken handwriting identification of Bertillon in 1894, Alfred Dreyfus is convicted of treason.

4 There is some confusion at a Kansas Prison when a

new inmate is confused with another inmate in 1904. This confusion came about by using anthropometry (the scientific study of the measurements and proportions of the human body).

5 Geological evidence is used for the first time in 1904 by Georg Popp in a criminal case.

6 Theodore Roosevelt, the US president establishes the Federal Bureau of Investigation in 1905.

7 The first police crime lab was established in 1910 by Edmond Locard in Lyon.

8 In the same year Albert Osborne publishes Questioned documents.

9 In Oakland, California in 1915, The Association for Criminal Identification was established. It later became known as the International Association of Identification (IAI).

10 In 1920 the Locard's Exchange Principle is announced by Edmond Locard.

11 1923 saw polygraph test results ruled as inadmissible in court cases. The case Frye v. US brought about this change.

The first US crime lab was established in 1924 in California by August Vollmer.

12 The FBI crime Lab was created in 1932.

Hendon, in 1935 saw the establishment of the first British forensic lab.

13 In 1950 the (AAFS) The American Academy of

Forensic Science is established. And in the same year the School of Criminology and University California Berkley are established in California by August Vollmer. Compassing theory and practice, kirk published, in 1953, 'Crime Investigations' this is the first comprehensive criminal crime investigation papers.

14 In 1975 'The Federal rules of Evidence' became a congressional statute. The Forensic Science Service is established as an executive body in 1991.

Chapter 8
Crime, Mental Health and Institutions

Justifying Detainment

One of the main problems with detainment under the mental Health Act is that an individual can be detained without a conviction or even without any offence being committed. Then the problem of, what is considered as dangerous or deviant behaviour which requires the individual to be detained. This could come under the umbrella of any behaviour that deviates from whatever that particular society considers as the 'norm' or the 'collective conscience'. Therefore, under this definition it could include people are considered to annoy other people but do not actually pose any risk to others or themselves which would be considered by most as unacceptable reasons to detain someone. For this reason there is the existence of the DSM, Diagnostic and Statistical Manual of Mental Disorders which is a list of defined mental disorders used by professionals to diagnose psychological and personality disorders. For example, an individual with a personality disorder would show patterns of certain behaviours and one of the common personality disorders is Borderline Personality Disorder. This type of disorder displays a number of highly unstable characteristics:

* Intense anger outbursts.
* Difficulty controlling anger.
* Low tolerance for frustration.
* Drastic mood swings.
* Self destructive behaviours.
* Suicide attempts.
* Manipulative.
* Self mutilation/self harm.
* Instability in close relationships.
* Disturbances in identity/sense of self.

Although many people may consider this list of characteristics as dangerous or possible risk of harm to others very few people with Borderline Personality Disorder are detained and are usually managed successfully in the community.

As a result of the ongoing question of crime and people with mental disorders legislation is put in place to ensure the public's safety and the wellbeing of the individual with the mental disorder. Washington State, USA, legislation is as follows:

* Prevent inappropriate, indefinite commitment of mentally disordered people and to eliminate legal disabilities that arise from such commitment.
* To provide prompt evaluation, timely and appropriate treatment of persons with serious mental disorders.
* To safeguard individual rights.

* To provide continuity of care for persons with serious mental disorders.

* To encourage to full use of all existing agencies, professional personnel and public funds to prevent duplication of serious and unnecessary expenditures.

* To encourage, whenever appropriate, that services be provided within the community.

* To protect the public safety.

United Kingdom legislation is as follows:

The Mental Health Act 1983

The 1983 Mental Health Act is the current principal Act governing the treatment of people with mental health problems in England and Wales. Its primary role is protective. Whilst the Act outlines a range of responsibilities and duties, its power to enforce the compulsory detention of a person with a mental disorder in a psychiatric hospital is one of its best known functions. There are plans to review the Act at a future date.

Compulsory admission under the Act may take place when the patient is:

* suffering from mental disorder **and**
* detention is necessary in the interests of his or her own health **or** safety **or** for the protection of others. Only one of these latter

grounds needs to be met and a person need not be behaving dangerously to be compulsorily detained (**52**).

There are three admission procedures under the Act which result in compulsory detention:

        * emergency admission for assessment for up to 72 hours (**Section 4**)

        * admission for assessment with or without treatment for up to 28 days, which is not renewable (**Section 2**)

        * admission for treatment for up to six months, renewable for a further six months, and thereafter for periods of up to 12 months at a time (**Section 3**).

These procedures are called 'sections' as they refer to specific sections of the Act. A patient can only be admitted under section 3 if the necessary treatment cannot be provided without detention in hospital. Patients who are discharged from a Section 3 are automatically the subject of Section 117, which requires health and local authorities to arrange a package of 'aftercare'. The purpose of this is to enable a patient to return home and re-engage with activities of daily living. It aims to minimise the risk of readmission. (See **Mental Health Act: Key sections and grounds for detention** for further details of these orders and specific grounds for admission.) An additional section of the Act, Section 7 (2), deals with 'guardianship'. It provides a mechanism whereby a person over 16 can have 'their interests protected and be under some control' of the local authority or a guardian appointed by the local authority. Its purpose is to ensure that a patient receives support and community care where it cannot be provided without the use of compulsory powers. It has rarely been applied to older people as its use widely varies between authorities. Last year, it was applied in 932 cases, ranging from 63 times in Lancashire to none at all in 12 London boroughs and 11 other councils.

Only a small number of professionals are involved in applying the Act. These are primarily approved social workers, GPs and doctors approved under Section 12 of the Act - either psychiatrists or others with specific training in mental health. Each professional performs an assessment of the patient's mental health and circumstances. If any one of them considers that there is insufficient evidence to warrant compulsory admission, the person cannot be detained under the Act. The patient's 'next of kin' can also 'apply' for their relative to be detained under the Act and has the power to formally request an assessment under the Act in certain circumstances.

Patients' rights

The Act provides the following safeguards for

those subject to detention:

> * They have to be informed as soon as practicable after admission of the reasons for their detention and rights of appeal.

> * People who have been detained for more than a few days have the right to appeal against their detention to a Mental Health Act Review Tribunal, an independent committee comprising medical, legal and lay people, which has the power to discharge patients in certain circumstances. Patients are entitled to free legal representation in such appeals.

> * The Mental Health Act Commission is a government body established to monitor the care of people who are detained, and to ensure that their rights are upheld. The commissioners make regular visits to all hospitals, and will also respond to individual requests for visits. Most hospitals also have an independent hospital managers' committee to protect the rights of detained people

These safeguards are not available to informal patients.

Mental Illness and Imprisonment

Once again a number of questions arise when considering imprisonment for people with mental disorders.

> * What types of behaviour should fall into the Criminal Justice System.

* Not all undesirable behaviour can be classified as a crime.

* Most people with mental illness/ disorder do not commit serious crime. They usually fall under the category of poor, homeless and/or substance abuse and fall in and out of help services.

The cost of imprisonment also needs to be taken into consideration and the fact that mental health and substance abuse treatments in the community are cheaper than imprisonment. research has shown that imprisonment for these types of individuals is ineffective although the use of imprisonment is rising which only adds to the problem of overcrowding in prisons as well as the safety and stability of the prison population and does not contribute to public safety. Prison may also be used because there is a lack of services available in the community or the individual may be considered as unmanageable. Overall it is valid to say that the general view of people with mental disorders are more likely, because of their state of mind, to commit criminal and violent behaviours to themselves, family members, friends and the public than those who do not suffer from any form of defined mental illness/ disorder.

In 2007 the Mental Health Act 1983 was

amended, (Mental Health Act 2007) which gives health professionals the powers in certain circumstances to detain, assess and treat people with mental disorders in the interest of their safely or for public safety. Powers set out in the 1983 Act allow for both 'civil' admissions to hospital and criminal justice admissions from the courts or prisons. Within the amendment are provisions to safeguard patients to ensure they are not inappropriately treated. But, if someone is considered to be detained because they are deemed to be a danger to the public there are very little guidelines on what types of behaviour are considered as being a danger to the public. The little guidelines there are generally means a defined mental disorder. The Mental Health Act 1983 has ten sections which have sub sections to them, there are 149 in total, within this mental disorder is defined as, 'any disorder or disability of mind' but this does not correspond with the mental disorders covered in the DSM-IV.

There has, and will continue to be, much research done into the subject of mental health and violence. Much of the research done in recent years has been based on the psychological system of mental disorders as a way of explaining violent and criminal behaviour. Much of the research has been based on incarcerated offenders, psychiatric patients as well as the general public and babies. Teasdale (2009) states that the predictors for violence among people with mental disorders are the psychological systems of hallucinations, delusions, medication compliance and the continuation of treatment. He also noted that women and men respond differently to the psychological systems and in turn their participation in violent acts. Siler et al (2008) disagrees with this and states that drug and alcohol abuse are prominent in controlling violence because of their strong link to mental health and violence. John Bradford (2008) suggests that comorbidity (the simultaneous presence of two chronic diseases or conditions in an individual) is a common factor with mental disorders and violence. He also states that improvements can be made with improved risk assessment and treatment intervention.

Certain disorders such as schizophrenia and affective disorder (another term for a mood disorder) have also been the subject of research and it was found that many of both categories had criminal records and some level of substance abuse. The studies conducted by Modestin and Wuermle (2005) found that those with schizophrenia without comorbid substance abuse were at an increased risk of violent criminality than those with affective disorder. In conclusion this shows a link between psychopathology, mental illness and violence. According to Frank Sirotich (2008) it does not necessarily predict violence if someone suffers from hallucinations commanding them to do certain acts but the likelihood of someone committing a violent act is increased when they suffer auditory hallucinations involving command of violent acts (Frank Sirotich 2008). He also states that another significant factor in relation to violence and criminality is that of a history of delinquency prior to adulthood, as well as factors such as family criminality and parental violence. He concludes by saying that among mentally disordered people early arrests at a young age and juvenile delinquency are strong indicators of violence and criminality among mentally disordered people. It is clear that much further research needs to be done around the subject of the relation between criminality and violence among mentally disordered people taking all factors into account including, family, social status, background and geographic factors.

Broadmoor and It's Residents

In the 1860's the hospital 'Broadmoor Criminal Lunatic Asylum' was built and it covered 210,000 square meters with a secure perimeter. The first person to be admitted to Broadmoor was a woman who committed infanticide (killing own children) on the 27th May 1863. The first male patient to be committed to Broadmoor was on 27th February 1864. Broadmoor had five blocks for men and one block for women. The whole Asylum was not completed until 1868. In 1902 an additional male block was added. As soon as Broadmoor was opened it began to fill up rapidly and became overcrowded quickly so a branch asylum was opened called 'Rampton Secure Hospital'. It opened its doors in 1912. Rampton only remained open until the end of 1919 but it was later reopened as an 'institute for mental defectives' rather than an asylum for lunatics. During the first world war block one at Broadmoor was used as a prisoner of war camp and was known as 'Crowthorne War Hospital' for the mentally ill German soldiers.

In 1952 an inpatient called John Straffen escaped from Broadmoor and went on to murder a local child. After this happened Broadmoor set up an alarm system so if anyone escaped the alarm would be sounded to warn people in the immediate vicinity and also to warn people in the surrounding towns that a dangerous patient had escaped. Once the alarm had been activated, which sounded similar to an air raid siren, there was a procedure to be followed by the surrounding towns and local residents. All schools in the area must make sure no child was ever out of the direct supervision of a teacher or a member of staff.

The alarm was tested every Monday morning at 10am for two minutes, with a two tone sound, then a single tone representing 'all clear' this would be sounded for a further two minutes. The sirens were located at different sites, schools, colleges and council depots.

Broadmoor Criminal Lunatic Asylum later changed its name to Broadmoor Hospital. This change reflected changing attitudes towards the word asylum, criminals and mental illness. Despite the public's perception of Broadmoor being a prison, it is a hospital. This misconception could be partly put onto the media's representation of Broadmoor and because it houses some of the most notorious serial killers and violent criminals and also to the fact that nearly all the staff are members of the Prison Officers Association. Broadmoor is not only a place where patient care is provided it is also a place for training and research. Eventually three main secure hospitals were in operation, Broadmoor, Rampton and Ashworth. Each of these hospitals were responsible for their own security policies. In 1999, following the Peter Fallon QC inquiry into Ashworth there was serious concerns about the security and the abuse that came about from the poor management with the decision being to review the security at all three hospitals. The Chief Executive of the National Health Service at this time was Sir Alan Langlands and the responsibility of the review was his. The security at Broadmoor was improved.

The Well Known Residents

Broadmoor Hospital has become a high-security psychiatric hospital at Crowthorne in the Borough of Bracknell Forest in Berkshire, England. It is the best known of the three high-security psychiatric hospitals in England. The hospital has seen some prolific inmates since it's opening, here is a description of some of its most famous tenants.

Robert Napper - Robert Clive Napper is a convicted British murderer and rapist who was remanded in Broadmoor Hospital indefinitely on 18 December 2008 for the manslaughter of Rachel Nickell. He is a paranoid schizophrenic who has also been diagnosed with Asperger's syndrome. The marriage of Napper's parents was violent; Napper witnessed violent attacks on his mother which ended in divorce when he was 10. Napper and his siblings (two brothers and a sister) were placed in foster care and underwent psychiatric treatment. Meanwhile, Napper underwent a personality change after a family friend assaulted him on a camping holiday when he was 12. The offender was jailed, but Napper became introverted, obsessively tidy and reclusive according to his mother.

He also bullied his siblings and spied on his sister while she undressed.

Napper's convictions include an offense with an air-gun, stabbing a young mother forty-nine times in front of her two year-old son, killing then sexually assaulting a woman and smothering her four-year-old daughter, and admitted to two rapes, but it is believed he is the 'Green Chain Rapist' who carried out at least 70 savage attacks across south-east London over a four-year period ending in 1994

Graham Young - Graham Frederick Young is notable for his obsession with the use of poison, and for having been imprisoned for murder in his teens, only to kill again after his release. Born in Neasden, north London, he was fascinated from a young age by poisons and their effects. In 1961 at 14 he started to test poisons on his family, enough to make them violently ill. He amassed large quantities of antimony and digitalis by repeatedly buying small amounts, lying about his age and claiming they were for science experiments at school. In 1962 Young's stepmother Molly died from poison. He had been poisoning his father, sister, and a school friend. Young's aunt Winnie, who knew of his fascination with chemistry and poisons, became suspicious. He might have escaped suspicion as he suffered the same nausea and sicknesses as his family, however he sometimes forgot which foods he had laced. He was sent to a psychiatrist, who recommended contacting the police. Young was arrested on May 23, 1962. He confessed to the attempted murders of his father, sister, and friend. The remains of his stepmother could not be analyzed because she had been cremated. Young was sentenced to 15 years in Broadmoor but was released after nine years, having been deemed "fully recovered". After release from hospital in 1971, he began work as a storekeeper at John Hadland Laboratories, which manufactured thallium bromide-iodide infrared lenses used in military equipment. Soon after he began work, his foreman, Bob Egle, grew ill and died. Young had been making tea laced with poisons for his colleagues. A sickness swept through his workplace and, mistaken for a virus, was nicknamed the Bovingdon Bug. These cases of nausea and illness, sometimes severe enough to require hospitalization, were later attributed to Young and his tea. Young poisoned about 70 people during the next few months, although none fatally. Young is the subject of an extremely good film called The Young Poisoner's Handbook

Kenneth Erskine - Kenneth Erskine is an English serial killer who became known as the Stockwell Strangler. During 1986, Erskine murdered seven elderly people, breaking into their homes and strangling them; most often they were sexually assaulted. The crimes took place in London. A homeless drifter and solvent abuser, Erskine was 24 years old when he committed the crimes, but had the mental age of a 12-year-old. Police suspected Erskine of four others murders but Erskine has never been charged with any of these murders. Erskine was sentenced to life imprisonment with a recommended minimum term of 40 years, but has since been found to be suffering from mental disorder within the meaning of the Mental Health Act 1983, and is therefore now held at Broadmoor. He is unlikely to be freed until at least 2028 and the age of 66. Some 20 years later, the trial judge's recommendation is still one of the heaviest ever handed out in British legal history.

In February 1996, Erskine was again in the news, this time for preventing the possible murder of Peter Sutcliffe (see below), by raising the alarm as a fellow inmate, Paul Wilson, attempted to strangle Sutcliffe with the flex from a pair of stereo headphones.

David Copeland - David John Copeland is a former member of the British National Party and the National Socialist Movement, who became known as the "London Nail Bomber," after a 13-day bombing campaign in April 1999 aimed at London's black, Bangladeshi and gay communities. The bombs killed three, including a pregnant woman, and injured 129, four of whom lost limbs. No warnings were given. After his arrest, he told psychiatrists that he had started having sadistic dreams when he was about 12, including dreams or fantasies that he had been reincarnated as an SS officer with access to women as slaves. Copeland wrote to BBC correspondent Graeme McLagan, denying that he had schizophrenia, and telling McLagan that the "ZOG," or Zionist Occupation Government, was pumping him full of drugs in order to sweep him under the carpet. He wrote, "I bomb the blacks, Pakis, degenerates. I would have bombed the Jews as well if I'd got a chance". When asked by police why he had targeted ethnic minorities, he replied: "Because I don't like them, I want them out of this country, I believe in the master race.

Although Copeland was diagnosed by five psychiatrists as having paranoid schizophrenia, and a consultant concluded he had a personality disorder, his plea of diminished responsibility was not accepted by the prosecution, which was under pressure not to concede to his pleas of guilty to manslaughter. He was convicted of murder on June 30, 2000, and given six concurrent life sentences.

Peter Sutcliffe - Peter William Sutcliffe is an English serial killer who was dubbed The Yorkshire Ripper. Sutcliffe was convicted in 1981 of murdering 13 women and attacking several others. He is currently serving life imprisonment in Broadmoor. Reportedly a loner at school, he left at the age of 15 and took a series of menial jobs, including two stints as a grave digger during the 1960s. He frequented prostitutes as a young man and it has been speculated that a bad experience with one (during which he was allegedly conned out of money) helped fuel his violent hatred against women.

In 1981, Sutcliffe was stopped by the police with a 24 year old prostitute. A police check revealed the car was fitted with false number plates and Sutcliffe was arrested for this offence and transferred to Dewsbury Police Station, West Yorkshire. At Dewsbury he was questioned in relation to the Yorkshire Ripper case as he matched so many of the physical characteristics known. The next day police returned to the scene of the arrest and discovered a knife, hammer and rope he discarded when he briefly slipped away from police during the arrest. After two days of intensive questioning, on the afternoon of 4 January 1981 Sutcliffe suddenly declared he was the

Ripper. Over the next day, Sutcliffe calmly described his many attacks. Weeks later he claimed God told him to murder the women. He displayed emotion only when telling of the murder of his youngest victim, Jayne MacDonald.

At his trial, Sutcliffe pleaded not guilty to 13 counts of murder, but guilty to manslaughter on the grounds of diminished responsibility. The basis of this defence was his claim that he was the tool of God's will. Sutcliffe first claimed to have heard voices while working as a gravedigger, that ultimately ordered him to kill prostitutes. He claimed that the voices originated from a headstone of a deceased Polish man, Bronislaw Zapolski, and that the voices were that of God.

In the years of Sutcliffe's incarceration, there have been numerous attempts on his life from other inmates. The first was during his stay at HMP Parkhurst when James Costello, a 35-year-old career criminal from Glasgow plunged a broken coffee jar twice into the left side of Sutcliffe's face. Whilst at Broadmoor he was subject to an attempted strangulation (thwarted by Kenneth Erskine, above) and lost the vision in his left eye after being attacked with a pen.

John Thomas Straffen - John Thomas Straffen was a British serial killer who was the longest-serving prisoner in British legal history. Straffen killed two young girls in the summer of 1951. He was found to be unfit to plead and committed to Broadmoor; during a brief escape in 1952 he killed again. This time he was convicted of murder. Respited due to his mental state, his sentence was commuted to life imprisonment and he remained in prison until his death more than 50 years later.

Aged 8, Straffen was referred to a Child Guidance Clinic for stealing and truancy. In 1939 he first came before a Juvenile Court for stealing a purse from a girl, and was given two years' probation. His probation officer found that Straffen did not understand the difference between right and wrong, or the meaning of probation. The family was living in crowded lodgings at the time and Straffen's mother had no time to help, so the probation officer took the boy to a psychiatrist. As a result, Straffen was certified as a mental defective under the Mental Deficiency Act 1927. A report was compiled on him in 1940 which gave his Intelligence Quotient as 58 and placed his mental age at six. When Straffen was 14, he was strongly suspected of being responsible for strangling two prize geese owned by one of the officers of his school; however, no proof was found and it was not noted on his records. At the age of 16 the school authorities undertook a review which found his I.Q.

was 64 and his mental age 9 years 6 months and recommended his discharge.

In 1951, Straffen killed two young girls for which he was sent to Broadmoor. In 1952 whilst cleaning some outbuildings, he escaped over a perimeter wall, and within 2 hours had killed another young girl. It was this escape and subsequent murder that urged the government to install an alarm system. To this day, the alarm is tested every Monday morning at 10am for two minutes, and then sounded again to give the 'all clear'. With hooters located in several locations around Surrey and Berkshire, the alarm can be heard for up to 15 miles in each direction from Broadmoor.

Charles Bronson - Charles "Charlie" Bronson (born Michael Gordon Peterson) is an English criminal often referred to in the British press as the "most violent prisoner in Britain". Born in Luton, England, Michael often found his way into fights before he began a bare-knuckle boxing career in the East End of London. His promoter was not happy with his name and suggested he change it to Charles Bronson.

In 1974 he was imprisoned for a robbery and sentenced to seven years. While in prison he began making a name for himself as a loose cannon often fighting convicts and prison guards. These fights added years onto his sentence. Regarded as a problem prisoner, he was moved 120 times throughout Her Majesty's Prison Service and spent all but 4 years of his imprisoned life in solitary confinement. What was originally a seven year term stretched out to fourteen year sentence that resulted in his first wife Irene, with whom he had a son, leaving him. He was released on October 30, 1988 but only spent 69 days free before he was arrested again. Bronson has spent a total of just four months and nine days out of custody since 1974. Known as one of the hardest criminals in England, Bronson has written many books about his experiences and famous prisoners he has met throughout his internment.

Bronson has been involved in over a dozen hostage incidents, one of which includes taking hostages and staging a 47-hour rooftop protest at Broadmoor in 1983, causing £750,000 (nearly $1.5m) worth of damage. Bronson has spent time at all three of England's high-security psychiatric hospitals.

Richard Dadd - Richard Dadd was an English painter of the Victorian era, noted for his depictions of fairies and other supernatural subjects, Orientalist scenes, and enigmatic genre scenes, rendered with obsessively minuscule detail. Most of the works for which he is best known were created while he was incarcerated in

Broadmoor hospital.

In 1842, Sir Thomas Phillips, the former
mayor of Newport, chose Dadd to accompany him as
his draftsman on an expedition through Europe to
Greece, Turkey, Palestine and finally Egypt. In
November of that year they spent a grueling two
weeks in Palestine, passing from Jerusalem to Jordan
and returning across the Engaddi wilderness. Toward
the end of December, while traveling up the Nile by
boat, Dadd underwent a dramatic personality change,
becoming delusional and increasingly violent, and
believing himself to be under the influence of the
Egyptian god Osiris. His condition was initially
thought to be sunstroke. On his return in the spring
of 1843, he was diagnosed to be of unsound mind and
was taken by his family to recuperate in the
countryside village of Cobham, Kent. In August of
that year, having become convinced that his father was
the Devil in disguise, Dadd killed him with a knife and
fled for France. En route to Paris Dadd attempted to
kill another tourist with a razor, but was overpowered
and was arrested by the police. Dadd confessed to the
killing of his father and was returned to England,
where he was committed to the criminal department
of Bethlem psychiatric hospital (also known as
Bedlam). Here and subsequently at the newly created
Broadmoor, Dadd was cared for and encouraged to

continue painting. Dadd probably suffered from a form of paranoid schizophrenia. He appears to have been genetically predisposed to mental illness; two of his siblings were similarly afflicted, while a third had "a private attendant" for unknown reasons.

Daniel M'Naghten - Daniel M'Naghten (pronounced, and sometimes spelled, McNaughton) was a Scottish woodturner who assassinated English civil servant Edward Drummond while suffering from paranoid delusions. Through his trial and its aftermath, he has given his name to the legal test of criminal insanity in England and other common law jurisdictions known as the M'Naghten Rules.

In 1840 M'Naghten sold his wood turning business and spent two years in London and Glasgow. Whilst in Glasgow in 1841 he complained to various people, including his father, the Glasgow commissioner of police, and an MP, that he was being persecuted by the Tories and followed by their spies. No-one took him seriously, believing him to be deluded. In January 1843, M'Naghten was noticed acting suspiciously around Whitehall in London. On the afternoon of 20 January the Prime Minister's private secretary, civil servant Edward Drummond, was walking towards Downing Street from Charing Cross when M'Naghten approached him from behind, drew a pistol and fired at point-blank range into his back. M'Naghten was overpowered by a police constable before he could fire a second pistol. M'Naghten appeared at Bow Street magistrates' court the morning after the assassination attempt. He made a brief statement in which he described how persecution by the Tories had driven him to act: "The Tories in my native city have compelled me to do this. They follow, persecute me wherever I go, and have entirely destroyed my peace of mind... It can be proved by evidence. That is all I have to say"

Ronald Kray - Ronald Kray along with his twin brother Reginald, were the foremost perpetrators of organized crime in London's East End during the 1950s and 1960s. Ronald, commonly referred to as Ron or Ronnie, suffered from paranoid schizophrenia. The Krays were involved in armed robberies, arson, protection rackets, violent assaults including torture and the murders of Jack "The Hat" McVitie and George Cornell. As West End nightclub owners they mixed with prominent entertainers including Diana Dors, Frank Sinatra, Judy Garland and politicians, which gave the Krays a veneer of respectability. In the 1960s they became celebrities in their own right, being photographed by David Bailey and interviewed on television.

The Kray twins became famous locally for their gang and the mayhem they caused. They narrowly avoided prison several times and in early 1952 they were called up for National Service. They deserted several times, each time being recaptured. It was during this period that Ron started to show the first signs of mental illness. He would refuse to eat, shave only one side of his face and suffer wild mood swings, sitting still for hours before erupting into a violent frenzy. On one occasion, Ron climbed into the prison rafters and, according to one guard, refused to come down for some six hours in spite of brother Reggie's pleas. It is not clear whether at this stage it was another prank to annoy their guards, or if Ron had become unbalanced. Guards at the Canterbury military holding prison were convinced he was dangerously psychotic.

They were arrested in May 1968 and convicted in 1969 by the efforts of a squad of detectives led by Detective Superintendent Leonard "Nipper" Read, and were both sentenced to life imprisonment. Ronnie was eventually certified insane and lived the remainder of his life in Broadmoor, dying on 17 March 1995 of a massive heart attack, aged 61. His funeral on 29 March 1995 was a huge event with people lining the streets. Reggie was released from prison on compassionate grounds in August 2000, a few weeks before his death from cancer.

Oakridge and Experimental Therapies

Oakridge was a maximum security hospital in Penetanguishene, Ontario, USA for male patients. It was opened in 1933 as a hospital for the criminally insane for 150 patients which went up to 304 in 1958. People were referred here from other institutions and after their time here they would be returned to the former institutions in preparation for being released back into the community. Oakridge became famous and attracted much attention for the therapeutic programmes it provided. Many scientific and research paper have come from the staff at Oakridge.

Oakridge was divided into two units which had four wards each. There was the Activity Treatment Unit and the Social Therapy Unit. In the Activity Treatment Unit the patients have a wide number of behavioural problems with a large range of severity. Its main focus is on the patients who do not respond well to verbal forms of therapy and behaviour modification. Each ward has it own function, for example, one ward is aimed at reducing assaultive behaviour, teaching the patients basic hygiene skills and work habits. Another ward is for admittance and initial assessment and another ward for structured, individualised programmes for patients who are long term. Patients are moved from one ward to another as the progress with their treatment.

The Social Therapy Unit is in the maximum security building of Oakridge. Most patients in this unit have some variation of personality disorder and most with a long history of anti social behaviour. Oakridge used a number of experimental therapies to treat the patients. Years later there was much concern about the therapies used which ended in a court case.

Experimental Therapies used at Oak ridge

Defence Disruptive Therapy - This experimental programme was developed in the mid 1960's by Dr Baker. This is where patients would be injected with drugs that had been suggested to the psychiatrists by the other patients. The drugs suggested included amphetamines, LSD and Ritalin. These drugs were also mixed with alcohol creating a toxic and hallucinogenic mix. It was no surprise that by late in 1967 the inmates who had received this treatment had an increased risk of suicide and homicide.

M.A.P The Motivation, Attitude, Participation Program - This experimental program involved rotating groups of men between four and eight. These men were forced to sit on a cold hard floor for around eight hours a day. The group were only allowed no more than two moves and were not allowed to stand. Failure to comply with the rules resulted in the inmate being confronted verbally, then heavily sedated and put into restraints or sent to solitary confinement.

Total Encounter Capsule Program - In the program the 'capsule' is a windowless small room, no bigger than 8' x 10'. This small room was always lit so the men could not distinguish day from night. This caused to men to become disorientated and confused and major confrontations would arise between the men. The situation was made worse by the fact that the men would be stripped naked and could be locked in the small room for up to two weeks. The only food that these men were provided with was in liquid form and would be fed to them through straws pushed through holes in the capsule wall. During their two weeks in the capsule the men would also be fed different drugs, usually hallucinogens. They did not have beds in the capsule and were forced to sleep on a rug over a foam mat on the cold hard floor. The only other facilities in the room was an open toilet and a sink. Other psychiatric patients would be constantly observing them through a one way mirror in the ceiling or CCTV. The experimental program ran from August 1968 all the way to 1979.

The LSD Experiments - These experiments

were conducted by Dr Baker as part of the Defence Disruption Therapy program. This involved stripping the men and confining them to the capsule in various drug induced states. At time they were given massive doses of not only LSD but LSD combined with methamphetamine. As a result of these experiments it was documented that the patients suffered from long lasting effects including homicide, suicide, sever depression, extreme anxiety, paranoid psychoses and schizophrenic reactions.

In October of 2001 a lawsuit was taken against The Ontario Government, Dr Elliot Baker and Dr Gary Maier for the breach of basic human and civil rights of all the patients who endured the experimental therapies.

Insanity Plea Used as Defence

The first thing that must be noted when discussing the insanity defence is that insanity is a legal concept and it is not a medical or psychiatric term. The insanity defense refers to a defendant's plea of not guilty by reason of insanity, meaning that at the time of the offence they did not have the mental capacity to realise that they were committing an offence or they did not know that what they were doing was wrong. One of the earliest known case of the use of the insanity plea was in February 1859 when Daniel Sickles knew that his wife had been having an affair and saw a man crawling up the side of his house into his wife's bedroom. In a fit of rage he took two handguns from his bedroom and, while screaming 'you must die' he shot the man in the thigh and other leg. While the man was lying on the floor he begged Daniel not to kill him but, still in a rage, Daniel shot him in the chest and he died. When the case came to court Daniel's solicitor claimed that he could not be held responsible for killing the man because knowing his wife was seeing another man had driven him insane. He was acquitted.

The insanity plea is not used in many cases and only a small number of those are judged to be insane. An offender found not guilty by reason of insanity are committed to mental institutions are are much more likely to spend considerably more time in the mental institution than in a prison. Overall the insanity defence is not very successful and the chances of an offender being found not guilty due to insanity are very slim.

Cognitive insanity is another form of the insanity defence. This is where the offender is considered as not truly insane but is so mentally impaired that they were unaware of the true nature of their act. Incompetency is not covered by this umbrella. Incompetency is when the offender is considered not fit to stand trial. In this situation the offender will be held in a mental institution until they are considered fit to take part in the trial.

Another form of insanity is, more commonly know as, 'irresistible impulse' but is also known as 'volitional insanity'. This describes an offender who is fully aware of right and wrong and capable of distinguishing between the two but, for some reason, they were temporarily unable to control their actions. A crime of passion is a good example of this or a crime of vengeance is another good example. For example, if someone brutally assaulted a child and the father or mother of that child killed the offender. The argument in court would be along the lines of, that the parent was so angry it brought on mental illness and they were unable to control their actions even though they still knew it was wrong to do so.

In some states in America they have the 'Guilty but Mentally ill' verdict. This can raise problems when in court because the jurors have two chances to find the offender guilty and only one to find them innocent. This can also result in the misconception that the offender will get the same treatments in prison as they would receive in hospital and may be sent to prison when a hospital would be more appropriate. It also means that an offender can be sent to a mental hospital and when they are

considered 'normal' again, then sent to prison or their
is a risk of an offender being released from a mental
institution before they are stable enough to do so
which can result in devastating events.

In 1843 the most influential trial in British
history was that of Daniel M'Naughton. M'Naughton
believed that in order to protect his own life he had to
kill the Prime Minister, at that time, Sir Robert Peel.
In his attempt he shot and killed Sir Robert Peel's
secretary Edward Drummond. During his trial a
number of experts testified that M'Naughton was of
unsound mind and clearly delusional and he should be
considered to be legally insane. The judge then gave
the following instructions to the jury:

> "If he was not sensible at the time he committed
> that act, that it was a violation of the law of god
> or of man, undoubtedly he was not responsible
> for that act, or liable to any punishment
> whatever flowing from that act I cannot help
> remarking, in common with my learned
> brethren, that the whole of the medical evidence
> is on one side, and that there is no part of it
> which leaves any doubt on the mind. It almost
> unnecessary that i should go through the
> evidence.....but if on balancing the evidence in
> your minds you think the prisoner capable of
> distinguishing right and wrong, then he was a

responsible agent and liable to all the penalties the law imposes.

(The Queen Against Daniel M'Naughton, 1843, p.73)

M'Naughton was found not guilty on the grounds of insanity. This conclusion was reached without the jury retiring for deliberation and was based on M'Naughton's delusional thoughts. M'Naughton was sent to Bedlam. The acquittal brought immediate and intense public outrage, to the point, Queen Victoria even wrote to Sir Robert Peel complaining about the verdict. The main concern was that the judge had interrupted the trial and instructed the jury to find him not guilty on the grounds of insanity. This called for reform and a consensus to be set as the current standards for insanity defense was vague and inconsistent. The conclusion by the House of Lords was the 'M'Naughton Standard'. The criteria to establish an insanity defence were set as follows:

The accused was labouring under such a defect of reason, from disease of the mind, as not to know the nature and quality of the act he/she was doing or if he/she did know it, that he/she did not know what he/she was doing was wrong. This must be clearly proven at the time of committing the offence.

(House of Lords Debate, 1843, p.75)

This new standard restricted legal insanity to the aspects of the 'cognitive prong' not knowing the nature and quality of the act and the 'moral incapacity' the inability to know the act was wrong 'right-wrong' test. It must also be noted that the legal definition of insanity can vary from country to country or state for state in America. In America the states of Utah, Montana, Kansas and Idaho do not allow the insanity defense at all. In summary, the M'Naughton rule states that an individual is assumed sane and in order to establish an insanity defence the accused individual must have been suffering from some form of defect of the mind which prevented them from knowing that the act they were doing was wrong, both legally and morally wrong. The 'irresistible impulse' test was a test which determined if the offender was capable of choosing between right and wrong and if they were able to control their impulses. Views regarding the insanity defence differ greatly. Many views it as a legitimate defence whereas others feel it serves no real purpose and should be abolished. It is also considered by some as an easier option and a way of receiving less severe consequences for their crimes, but, as we have already discussed, most of those whose insanity defence is successful are sent to mental institutions for a longer period of time then they would have spent in prison.

Example Cases

Before the M'Naughton case, in 1724 the Right Honorable Lord Onslow was shot by Edward Arnold, according to the records available, earlier that day Arnold had enquired about where Onslow was and at some point that day had tried to buy a larger shot for his gun. When Onslow returned from a fox hunt Arnold walked up to him and shot him. Onslow was not fatally wounded and Arnold struggled to attack him again but he was held back by others who had also been on the hunt. When it came to the trial there was no question Arnold had shot Onslow as there was many witnesses but the question of Arnold's sanity was at the forefront of the trial. Arnold claimed that Onslow had sent imps who were constantly plaguing and disturbing him. During the trial even Arnold's brothers and sisters-in-law said that he was nonsensical, ill natured and claimed that he was a madman. They also stated that he had been that way for many years. On the other hand, people who had been there on the day of the shooting claimed that they had seen Arnold and he did not seem as though he was mad to them. Concluding the trial, Justice Robert Tracy gave the jury the following instructions when deciding the verdict:

> "The shooting of Lord Onslow, which the fact for which this prisoner is indicted, is proved beyond all manner of contradiction; but whether this shooting was malicious, that depends upon the sanity of the man. That he shot, and that willfully [is proved]: but whether maliciously, that is the thing, that is the question; whether this man hath the use of his reason and sense? If he was under the visitation of God, and could not distinguish between good and evil, and did not know what he did, though he committed the greatest offence, yet he could not be guilty of any offence against any law whatsoever...If a man be deprived of his reason, and consequently of his intention, he cannot be guilty; and if that be the case, though he had actually killed my Lord Onslow, he is exempted from punishment; punishment is intended for example, and to deter other persons from wicked designs; but the punishment of a madman, a person that hath no design, can have no example. This is on one side. On the other side, we must be very cautious... When a man is guilty of a great offence, it must be very plain and clear, before a man is allowed such an exemption; therefore it is not every kind

of frantic humour or something unaccountable in a man's actions, that points out to be such a madman as it is to be exempted from punishment. It must be a man that is totally deprived of his understanding and memory, and doth not know what is doing, no more than an infant, than a brute, or a wild beast, such a one is never the object of punishment" (p. 764)

This test became known as the 'wild beast' test which establishes that in order for an offender to be found insane and not held responsible for their crimes he/she must be 'totally deprived' at a level of an infant, a brute or a wild beast. Arnold was found guilty of the crime and sentenced to death but Lord Onslow intervened and instead of being put to death Arnold was sent to prison.

James Hadfield was a former soldier who attempted to assassinate King George III by shooting him while he was in the theatre. He was charged with high treason. Hadfield was delusional and thought that he had contact with god. He thought that the world was going to end and the only way to save the world was to sacrifice himself. He believed that he could not simply commit suicide because this would not give salvation.So Hadfield decided to attempt to kill the King in order for him to be put to death. He claimed the attempt was a deliberate failure. It was discovered that Hadfield had served in the English military and he had suffered repeated blows to the head and neck by an enemy's sword, as a result of this hadfield became mentally disturbed. This could have been the result of his head injuries or as a result of the trauma of the event. When Hadfield came to trial his lawyer, Thomas Erskine, was aware that Hadfield would not pass the 'wild beast' test so he made the proposal of a new test called the 'irresistible impulse' test. He claimed that because Hadfield suffered from delusions, these delusions gave him the irresistible impulse to attempt to kill King George. He also claimed that Hadfield could not control his actions because of the severe mental illness he suffered. Erskine used expert witnesses to back up his claim that his injuries had caused his mental illness and therefore his delusions. After several witnesses testified of Hadfield's delusional personality, Lord Kenyon, the judge in the case, stopped the trial and asked if the prosecution would accept a not guilty plea. The entire court was convinced of Hadfield's insanity and the jury found him not guilty by 'being under the influence of insanity at the time the act was committed' (hadfield's Case, 1800. p. 1356) Hadfield was sent to Bedlam where he died in 1841. This case saw the precedent for the 'irresistible impulse' test and the end of the 'wild beast' test.

This case was yet another failed attempt of an assassination of a royal member. This time the target was Queen Victoria. As she took her evening carriage ride Oxford shot two shots at her but was quickly apprehended by a witness and taken into custody. (The Queen Against Edward Oxford, 1840). The main question in his case was of his mental state at the time of the offence. Oxford's family members and friends testified at the trial that, as well as Oxford himself, his father and his grandfather all displayed odd and violent behaviour. They claimed that none of them were in 'their right minds'. Oxford had no clear motive for the attack which lead to two physicians testifying that he was of unsound mind. Dr Connolly, who was in charge of the Hanwell Lunatic Asylum interviewed Oxford and noted that he had a 'total inability to reason' and 'an apparent incapacity to comprehend moral obligations, to distinguish right from wrong' (Oxford's Case, 1840, p.540) The judge in the trial, Lord Denman, instructed the jury that if Oxford was in

> "that state of mind that you cannot say he was a free agent, but that some controlling disease was the acting power which he could not resist, he would not be guilty, and would be entitled to be acquitted." (Oxford's Case, 1840, p. 551)

Further to this he stated:

> "A man charged as a criminal is not responsible for the act, who, in the language of the law, is non compos mentis, or not able to distinguish between right and wrong. The meaning of it is that he, from a diseased state of mind, is wholly unconscious that it is wrong in him to do the act charged upon him." (Oxford's Case. 1840, pp. 551-552)

This represents the 'cognitive prong' of the definition of insanity. Meaning the inability to know that the behaviour is wrong. This is used in many countries to determine legal insanity. Oxford was found not guilty on the grounds of being insane at the time of the offence. He was sent to Bedlam.

The Model Penal Code is another test used in most modern courts today as a means of testing the defendant's sanity.

Today, depending on the country and jurisdiction, courts use one or a combination of the following tests for legal insanity:

    * **The "M'Naghten Rule"** - Defendant either did not understand what he or she did, or failed to distinguish right from wrong, because of a "disease of mind."

    * **The "Irresistible Impulse"** Test - As a

result of a mental disease, defendant was unable to control his impulses, which led to a criminal act.

* **The "Durham Rule"** - Regardless of clinical diagnosis, defendant's "mental defect" resulted in a criminal act.

* **The "Model Penal Code"** Test for Legal Insanity - Because of a diagnosed mental defect, defendant either failed to understand the criminality of his acts, or was unable to act within the confines of the law.

Chapter 9
Crime and The Media

The Problem of Crime and The Media

The main source of the public's perception of crime comes from the different media sources that are available to most these days, news reports on television, the internet, newspapers and magazines. It not only derives the public knowledge of crime it also gives us a perception of the police and the Criminal Justice System. What the media publishes influences our attitudes towards crime and punishment. Crime related stories are the most widely covered type of news article and are more so covered by newspapers, the most common source of information that is crime related. In order to sell their newspapers they often 'sensationalise' a story and will use an attention grabbing headline to do so. Unfortunately, these headline stories do not alway represent the true facts of the story. What these attention grabbing headlines and the sensationalisation of a story does is needlessly fuels the public's fear of crime. You need only pick up two or three of the leading newspapers and the main story will be shocking in some way.

The Fear of Crime

The fear of crime was defined by Garofalo

(1981) as an 'emotional reaction characterised by a sense of danger and anxiety, produced by the threat of physical harm, elicited by perceived cues in the environment that relate to some aspect of crime'. although this is a good overall description of the fear of crime the level of the fear of crime can differ from each individual's own personal definition related to their own personal experiences of crime. This individual level of fear will be influenced by many factors, one of being repeatedly victimised or if someone knows of someone who has been repeatedly victimised in their own neighbourhood, they are likely to have a higher fear of crime. Some studies into the fear of crime, conducted by the Beth Johnson Foundation, on people over the age of fifty showed that those who had been mugged or burgled had high levels of fear of crime resulting from these previous experiences, but this study only included a small target population and called for further research including a much wider demographic of people and including all age groups. In 2010 Jewkes acknowledged that people would be more fearful of crime after personal experiences and knowing people in their community with personal experience but he states that many more people will experience fear of crime as a result of indirect contact with crime. The actual amount of crime can be a contributing factor to the fear of crime, as well as this, an individual's neighbourhood can also be perceived as fearful because their immediate environment is perceived as threatening through thing such as, broken windows, teenagers hanging around the streets and a general noisy neighbourhood, (Baumer 1985)(Hunter and Baumer 1982). In 1988 Box, Hale and Andrews identified several factors which contributed to the fear of crime. These are:

* Perceptions of personal risk.
* Seriousness of various offences.
* Confidence in the police.
* Confidence in the Criminal Justice System.
* Personal knowledge of crime.
* Victimisation.
* Vulnerability.
* Environmental clues.
* Environmental conditions.

They suggest that this type of research should be conducted in households in close proximity to each other, therefore the environmental factors should be similar but other factors should be very different from each other.

The British Crime Survey

The British Crime Survey began in 1982 and

can show a good indication of the public's perception of crime. The British Crime Survey conduct face to face victimisation surveys in England and Wales. The individuals are asked about their personal experiences of crime within the last twelve months. The British Crime Survey of 2009 to 2010 showed that 66% of people believed that crime had risen across the country in the past few years, when the Home Office statistics of 2010 show a decrease in a large number of crimes between 2002 and 2010. As crime has, according to the Home Office, decreased every year for the past eight to nine years. It would suggest that the public's fear of crime is not accurate and the public's perception of high levels of crime is contributed to by the media.

Crime and the media has been, and will continue to be, an ongoing debate around the suggestion that the media exaggerate the extent of crime through television, radio, newspapers and crime fiction, all of which have an impact on the public's perception of crime and the fear of it. Previous research has shown that the media is the most influential source of fueling the public's fear of crime. Jewkes (2010) states that, 'numerous writers have examined the proposition that the media present crime stories, both factual and fictional, in ways which selectively distort and manipulate public perception, creating a false picture of crime which promotes stereotyping, bias, prejudice and gross oversimplification of the facts. Their conclusion is that it is not just official statistics that misrepresent the picture of crime but that the media are also guilty of manipulation and fueling the public's fear'. (Roberts and Doob 1986). To add to this Surette (1998) states that 'the public's perception of victims, criminals, deviants and law enforcement officials is largely determined by their portrayal in the mass media', further adding to the above statement is research indicating that most of the public's knowledge about crime and justice is obtained from the media. It can be said that the mass media plays a huge part in the construction of criminality and the Criminal Justice System by focusing in on the public's fascination with crime and talk of crime with books, films, newspapers, television, magazines, radio etc.

Moral Panics

A subject that often comes to the forefront when discussing the influence of the mass media on the crime levels and the fear of crime is that of 'moral panics'. This theory was first introduced by stanley Cohen in the 1970's with his publication of the book 'Folk Devils and Moral Panics: The Creation of Mods and Rockers' which refers to the idea of the public and political reactions to certain groups of people or individuals who appear to be some kind of threat to the overall consensual values and interests of the general public. This is a process of labelling certain individuals or groups as deviant without giving the main facts of the story and at the same time extensively covering crime stories. A good example of this is the 'goth' culture. This group of people who have chosen to dress a certain way and listen to a certain type of music and have their own codes of conduct etc have been labeled by society as a group of people to be feared and are perceived as some kind of threat to the consensus of society.

The media tends to sensationalise and amplify what could be considered as, concerning but not major events. On example would be the fashion trend of wearing 'hoodies' by the youth. Some incidents were reported of youths committing crime who were wearing hoodies and through the press and media it was portrayed that anyone wearing a hoodie was to be feared and suggested they were from a criminal culture.

The Demonisation of Children

New Strand Shopping Centre in Bootle, Merseyside is where two year old James Bulger was taken on 12th February 1993 by Robert Thompson and Jon Venables both aged ten years old at the time.

His mutilated body was found on a railway line two-and-a-half miles away two days after his murder. He had been tortured and murdered by the two ten year old boys. The details of the crime were horrific and shocked the public as well as everyone involved in the case. This then sparked a major widespread debate on how to handle the young offenders. It was such a shock to everyone that two so young boys could carry out such a horrendous crime on such a defenceless infant. This led to a change in the way the general public viewed children. They no longer saw them as innocent playful children but as children who were capable of committing terrible acts of violence and therefore should be feared or at least be warey of. This process is known as demonisation.

Violence, Video Games, TV, Film and Media

The vast majority of homes in most countries across the world have TV and a video games console as well as, incorporated into these, smart devices and applications. This enables a vast amount of people to gain access to video games and films, both of which have been under discussion with regard to the part they play in societal violence and culture. Several individual games and films have come under scrutiny with claims that they are responsible for the encouragement, normalisation and desensitisation of violence and antisocial behaviour. Video games have been criticised for being misrepresentative of real demographics, as well as the misrepresentation of minorities in certain games like 'Grand Theft Auto'. This game has also be accused of promoting race violence. The University of Central Florida conducted a study into video games and their representations of females. They found that in their study of 33 leading games:

* 21% portrayed violence against women.
* 41% contained no females.
* 30% misrepresented females in terms of their body as well as their positions as 'damsels in distress' or insignificant participants.
* 28% portrayed women as sex objects.

(Dietz 1998)

Therefore the question arises of, do these video game manufacturers have a social responsibility to portray population demographics as accurately as possible. Bearing this in mind, would this limit their ability to make exciting and riveting games. Jack Thompson, a video game activist, had labelled violent video games as 'murder simulators' and he has campaigned to limit the amount of violence in video games. The gaming industry makes claim to the more realistic the gameplay is the better the gamers experience. It has been said that video games can be perceived as how to react when confronted by the same or similar situation in real life, which would be with violence. Violence in the video games is considered by many to be worse than violence in films and music videos because people can interact with the video games. It has also been claimed that continuous video game playing will gradually desensitise and emotionally harden the player to the extreme and graphic violence within the games.

Chapter 10
Punishment, Execution and Social Control

Justifying Societal Control

Punishment need to be justified because it involves the infliction of harm and suffering upon some members of society by other members of society. Punishment is defined by the Oxford dictionary as, the action of punishing or the state of being punished and, informally, rough treatment. It is clear that 'rough treatment' needs to be justified in order to uphold its legitimacy as legitimacy has to be perceived as morally justified which arises problems from the onset. How can punishment be morally justified when we are all taught through social institutions such as school and family that it is morally wrong to deliberately inflict pain, harm and/or suffering upon another person. On the other hand, punishment and its justification, could be considered as socially constructed. A sign of changing moral values throughout time combined with changing ideologies. Moral values have changed in line with new ideologies and new ways of justifying punishment.

We have a criminal justice system which exists to punish people who have committed a pre-defined criminal offence. What constitutes as a criminal offence depends upon the ideologies of the majority or the ruling bodies at any given time in history and the present. The criminal justice system includes a number of other institutions grouped together to create the criminal justice system. These institutions include the penal system, the police, the prosecution authorities and the courts. One way our criminal justice system attempts to rationally justify punishment is to relate it to the beneficial social consequences which arise from it. A rational justification of punishment must give good reasons for believing that punishing offenders is the more effective means of achieving a goal or manageable level of offending. Therefore it can be shown that punishing offenders is a rational thing to do. In contrast to this is classical consequentialism which changes the rational justification of punishment into a moral justification by adding the grounds to achieve keeping the rate of offending to a manageable level is the best possible means of maximising satisfaction or well-being which is morally desirable. These concepts can be traced back to pre-industrial or, in Durkheim's terms, 'organic' societies. In these organic societies, according the Emile Durkheim (1858-1917) exist a collective conscience, a group of beliefs, morals and social values held by small, close knit communities. In these societies punishment took the form of harsh public displays of which could be justified as a form of upholding the collective conscience for the good of the rest of the society and also to set an example to the rest of the community justifying the punishment as a deterrent effect.

Deterrence is defined in two forms, general deterrence and individual deterrence. Deterrence can be seen as both a retributive and reductive. Retribution and reductivism are the two most frequent justifications for punishment. Retributivism claims that the punishment is deserved by the offender and this is their justification. Reducing the incidence of crime with reductivism justifies the punishment. Relating this back to Durkheim's concept of organic societies and the collective conscience general deterrence would take the form of the offender being subject to some form of public punishment, being excluded from the community, to be isolated and condemned as an example to others, justified not only because the offender deserves the punishment and to set an example to others but also justified on moral ground relating to religion. Industrialisation and the movement away from religion and towards more scientific explanations of human behaviour makes it more difficult to justify punishment with moral justifications. The justification of general deterrence provides encouragement to others in the community to uphold the social values and maintain the status quo. The idea of an individual being punished to set an example to others appears unjust and severely lacks a humanitarian standpoint. Individual deterrence occurs when an individual commits a crime and the punishment they receive is so unpleasant and harsh the offender refrains from re-offending because of fear of the same punishment or worse.

Retributivism states that the punishment should be in proportion to the offence committed or that offences should be balanced out with equivalent penalties, as the saying from the Old Testament, 'an eye for an eye and a tooth for a tooth'. This direct equivalent in our modern societies would be considered barbaric, it would not be acceptable to rob a robber or rape a rapist, so arises the question of what is meant by 'balanced out'. We are all taught that two wrongs do not make a right, if a murder has taken place then there is no sentence that can put that right. To give a meaningful sense of 'balancing out' we must look at it from a societal viewpoint which would be offences have to be punished to prevent offenders from enjoying their ill-gotten gains assuming that the offender has gained from their crimes. Retributivism justifies punishment by assuming an offender has willingly broken the law and deserves to be punished for it. Retribution was revived in the 1970's and the central concept is one of deserts, central to the notion of justice and 'just deserts'. During the 1980's under Thatcher's conservative government it took the form of short, sharp, shock detention centres. Hard labour and strict military style regimes were intended to produce individual deterrence. These new harsh detention centres proved to be unsuccessful in terms of the reduction rates and in comparison to the detention centres without the new harsh regimes. The notion of the 'just deserts' is a strategy. A philosophy of law and order. This is a categorisation of criminal justice policy which attains that offenders should be dealt with as severely as possible. This government strategy was to make every stage of the criminal justice system harsher and more punitive (Cavadino and Dignan 2002). Within this ideology is embedded an 'exclusionary' approach. This rejects the individual from the community as with Durkheim's idea of exclusion from communities to uphold the dominant collective moral values. But rather than the dominant values held by a community, in contemporary societies the dominant ideologies are maintained by governmental ideologies. Moral values and justifications are determined by government policies made by the most powerful and more dominant group or class.

Retributivist justifications can sound weak

when simply stating that the punishment is justified because the offender deserves it. It does not provide the basis alone for a good argument. It improves its position when backed up by the notion of 'just deserts'. The offender should be punished as severely as they deserve. For example, minor punishments for minor offences and severe punishments for more serious crimes. Incorporated within retributivism is a 'tariff' which is a set of punishments which are matched to how serious the offence committed is. Retributivism is often mistaken for being a strategy A policy because it is often mistaken for inflicting the harsher punishments. The punishment has to be deserved and proportionate. Most people want to see criminals get what they deserve. What some people consider as deserved punishment can often be harsh and different people have different ideas of what is considered harsh. Retribution is actually more humane than some other strategies. To retributionists like cases should be treated alike meaning similarly deserving. One of the main features of retributivism is that both the offender and the victim have rights, resembling a strategy C approach to protect and uphold human rights of all.

Deterrence is also included within a reductivist approach along with incapacitation. This means that the offender is prevented from committing further offences by the punishment they receive, which is usually a physical punishment. According to Michael Howard in 1993 'prison works'. It not only works as a deterrent but it also protects the public from murderers, robbers and rapists etc. In some societies execution ensures the offender never re-offends. A more extreme example of this is cutting of a thief's hand to make sure they never steal again. Long prison sentences can also have an incapacitative effect but only for the duration of the sentence. Life in prison does not mean for the rest of the prisoner's life, life means, for a set minimum length of time and then only when the offender proves to be no longer a risk to society. This can be problematic because it is very difficult to predict whether an offender will re-offend or not or how serious the offence will be. This can only be done by psychological testing or just pure guesswork. Incapacitation can be justified as a form of punishment in other forms such as driving offences. The disqualification from driving prevents the offender from re-offending but only if they abide by the disqualification, making it difficult to enforce. The use of attendance centres can be used to prevent offenders from committing certain offences and predicted times, such as football matches. Incapacitation is very difficult to justify as it usually involves harsh forms of inhumane punishment and overly long prison sentences only to add to the current penal crisis. In the US they have a 'three strikes and you're out' law. In this case the offender is automatically given a life sentence for the third offence no matter how trivial the offence may be. This 'three strikes and you're out' principle was adopted by the English Crime (Sentences Act 1997. This included semi-mandatory prison sentences for adult domestic burglars and drug dealers convicted for a third time (Cavadino and Dignan 2002). The Criminal Justice Act 1991 introduced the permission of extra severe prison sentences for violent and sexual offences if the court thinks the public needs protecting from serious harm.

As well as deterrence and incapacitation, reform and rehabilitation are also incorporated within the reductivist approach. Humanitarian approaches, strategy C approaches include 'inclusiveness'. Some supporters of strategy C approaches are in favour of rehabilitating and reforming offenders and some prefer restorative justice which aims for the offender to repair the damage done to the victim and the community.The notion of 'just deserts' incorporated into retribution, the idea that the offender gets what they deserve, falls apart at the notion of remand. It does not appear fair or morally right or deserving to keep an unconvicted or innocent individual detained in prison while awaiting trial and does not help to support the idea of reductivism. While on remand the innocent are in danger of recidivism and labelling. Any form of punishment produces a labelling effect which also should be justified. Labelling an individual a criminal can have the effect of permanently excluding them from a group or a community with detrimental effects such as further employment, access to education and acceptance from new people. The production of labelling can be justified from a utilitarian viewpoint. It would be beneficial to the community or a society to sacrifice the few for the greatest happiness of the greatest number, but this is a rational justification and justifying it morally is far more problematic. It is difficult to justify when considering soldiers at war. It is morally wrong to kill but this does not apply when it comes to war.

The notion of 'just deserts' was to reduce the prison population. The Criminal Justice Act 1991 incorporated along with a strategy B aim to make prison and the population more manageable. More offenders should be punished in the community.

Reductivism justifies its punishment by its 'future consequences'. There is less chance of an offender re-offending if they are punished for the offence. Reductivism is supported by utilitarianism (Jeremy Bentham) 'the greatest happiness by the greatest number of people'. If an offender is punished the pain and discomfort of the offender outweighs the benefit to society by preventing further offending. Utilitarianism could be used for the justification of killing during war.

Rehabilitation and reform supports the idea that punishment can reduce the incidence of crime. It aims to improve the offender's character and behaviour so they will be less likely to re-offend. This is its justification. This suggests that offending is an illness which can be treated and does not deserved to be punished. For reform, punishment is an opportunity for treatment and re-training. Statistics can suggest otherwise. During the early 1970's research showed that measures intended to reform offenders were no more effective than harsher measures. From this came the notion that 'nothing works'. Kershaw (1999) found that when considering different characteristics of offenders sentenced to custody or community sentences or any other type of punishment made no difference to whether they re-offend or not. Reform is now looked at as measures to enable or assist offenders to improve their behaviour termed 'facilitating change'. Reform does not hold strong as a justification for punishment.

A Marxist analysis of punishment as a justification could be viewed as a strategy B approach.

A managerialist strategy which attempts to apply bureaucratic and administrative mechanisms to criminal justice to make the system run smoothly and cost effective, It can be seen as justifying methods of control and justifying punishment by means of the economy. Society will always demand that offences, some more than others, to be punished, so in a Marxist perspective punishment is managed to be cost effective. For example, during the time when transportation was a popular form of punishment the labour of prisoners was needed to develop the land. Offenders were put to work to produce goods and labour at a minimum of cost. After Durkheim's move from organic societies to mechanical societies, after industrialisation and specialisation, the imprisonment of offenders served to supply a workforce during times of demand. At a time when there was no longer a need for a workforce fewer offenders would be imprisoned. Punishment was managed in terms of economy and the need for labour. This view reflects the ruling class's dominant ideologies, producing goods at a little cost, maintaining the ruling class ideologies and maintaining the oppression of the working classes by the ruling class. A modern example of this can be seen with the opening of training centres at a prison in Doncaster where the inmates are taught a trade within the construction industry. This has been derived from a shortage of skilled workers within the construction industry.

One conclusion that we can come to is that desire for retribution is at the heart of our concept of justice and little effort is put into reform and rehabilitation. It is difficult to justify punishment from any point of view. The practice of punishing offenders is confused by the wide range of rational and irrational, moral and non-moral values such as blaming, resentment, love and so on. Punishment cannot be understood solely in terms of its beneficial social consequences or ruling ideologies because societies can make demands and hold protests. If we took the idea that punishment does not work and prison does not work then what would we do with the murderers, robbers, rapists and child abusers. Society would demand punishment even if that meant taking it into their own hands. Therefore perspectives of punishment do not lie solely in the hands of the dominant, whether that is a dominant class or the dominant members of a group or a society. There is no answer as to what justifies punishment. What may be justification to one may not be to another it depends solely on our own personal morals, beliefs and values shared with some and not with others.

Hanging - This type of execution has been used in

England since Saxon times. Two men were hanged on the same day in 1964, this was the last hangings in Britain, the following year the death penalty was abolished for murder in Britain for a trial period of five years and was then permanently abolished in 1969. It was once common for hangings to take place in public and this was attended by many, almost like a family day out, but it was also used as a form of deterrence. The saying 'money for old rope' comes from the days of public hangings where the hangman would cut the rope used to hang the offender into sections and sold to the public as a souvenir. The more famous or higher status the hanged person was the more the hangman could charge for the rope helping to top up the hangman's income. The last public hanging was in 1868.

One of the most famous hangmen was Albert Pierrepoint. When he was a young boy he already had a father and an uncle who were hangmen so it was no surprise when he told his school teacher he wanted to be a hangman when he grew up. When he was just twenty six years old in 1931 he applied to become an executioner. A year later he became the assistant of his uncle. He did not become a hangman until nine years later when he hung a famous gangland murderer. After this he became known as a quick, efficient good hangman and went on to hang a further thirty people during the second world war.

In July of 1955 he hanged Ruth Ellis who was the last woman to be hung in this country. Two more executions followed after this one the hanging suddenly stopped. This was around the time he was due to retire. It has been documented by some sources that the job of hangman had got to him and it was not uncommon for hangmen to turn to drinking as a way of coping with the stress of the job. It is believed that Pierrepoint executed at least 400 people but some text suggests that this would be in the region of 600. 200 of the hangings he carried out were people convicted of war crimes. He resigned in 1956 and went on to become a pub landlord.

Electric Chair - The electric chair was first used in 1890 in America to execute William Kemmler. At this time the chair did not work as efficiently as was expected and it took a while to eventually kill William Kemmler. Over the years adjustment to the electric chair made it more efficient and this became a very popular form of execution in America. There was much debate around the subject of the use of the electric chair and if this was a humane way to execute with regards to the amount of pain suffered by the offender.

Lethal Injection - This form of execution was once again seen to be a more humane way of killing an offender and has become the most common form of execution in America since the first use in 1982. Lethal injection was first proposed in 1888 as it was considered to be a cheaper method of execution than hanging. It was first developed in America. Three drugs are used in the process of the execution. Firstly, Sodium Thiopental or also known as Pentobarbital is administered to induce unconsciousness. Secondly, Pancuronium Bromide or also known as Pavulon is used to induce respiratory arrest and muscle paralysis. Then finally, Potassium Chloride is administered to stop the heart. This form of execution was used because it was considered as a painless form of execution but this has always been under debate. Therefore, the export of the drugs used was banned by the European Union in 2011.

Types of Punishment Throughout Time

Banishment - Since Ancient Times banishment has been used as a form of punishment. This would be for a fixed length of time or permanently. Because communities were relatively small and close knit at the time, banishment from the community could have devastating effects on the offender. People often relied on each other for food, materials and for overall survival so it would be very difficult for a banished offender to survive outside the community on their own. This form of punishment can still be seen in the form of social exclusion for offender with certain types of offences such as offences against children and sexual offences but is administered by the community. It is also used in schools in the form of isolating for disruptive behaviour and suspension from school for a fixed period of time.

Bastinado - This type of punishment was commonly used in parts of Asia and involved the offender being beaten on the soles of their feet with a stick. It was documented as being very painful.

Beheading - Beheading is another form of punishment that has been used since ancient time and was usually done with a sword or an axe. It wasn't always a swift execution as sometimes it would take several blows to sever the head completely. Beheading was usually reserved for the more wealthy in England. The last person to be beheaded in England in 1747 was a scottish man named Simon Fraser.

Birching - As the name suggests this punishment involved birch branches which were used to beat the offender across the behind. It was usually used for minor offences but was once a common punishment used in schools. Birching was used in prisons in

England until 1962 but it was abolished as a punishment for minor crimes in 1948.

Boiling Alive - In 1531 a law was passed in England which allowed being boiled alive to be used as a form of execution. One can only imagine how horrific this form of execution would be luckley this law was repealed in 1547.

Branding - It is not clear how far back in time this form of punishment goes but it is believed it is a very old form of punishment. It involved using red hot irons to brand people. This was abolished in 1829. Today branding is considered by some as a form of body art.

Breaking on the wheel - This type of punishment, or rather execution, was used in parts of Europe but seemed to be used much more commonly in Germany and France. Breaking on the wheel consisted of the offender being tied to a wheel, then a hammer or iron bar was used to break their arms and their legs in several places. Strangulation or a heavy blow to the chest would be used to end the execution but he could also be left to die on the wheel. In 1827 Germany abolished this type of execution.

Burning - This form of execution is also a very old and is commonly associated with the burning of witches in the 16th and 17th centuries although in England they were usually hanged, it was more common in Scotland and most of europe to burn women suspected of being a witch and in the 18th century more common in England if a woman was found guilty of murdering her husband. It is also know that some offenders were strangled before being burned showing compassion and reducing their suffering. In 1401 a law was passed in England making the punishment for nonconformity (heresy) burning. Almost 300 people were burned to death in the 16th century in England for the offence of heresy.

Cactus Needles - The Aztec children were punished by having cactus needles forced into their skin.

Cane - In the 16th century it was common for boys to be punished with the use of birch twigs, jumping forward to the 19th century a bamboo cane became more popular for the punishment of both girls and boys. Later in the 20th century this type of punishment was used in both primary and secondary schools but this was abolished in most primary schools by the end of the 60's and the early 70's but it wasn't until 1987 that the cane was abolished as a form of punishment in state funded secondary schools in England and was not abolished until 1999 in private schools.

Cangue - This was a form of punishment preventing an offender from feeding or drinking without help. It was a form of Chinese punishment and consisted of a wooden board locked around the offender's neck so they could not reach their mouth with their arms.

Cold Shower - Forcing a child to have a cold shower was a form of punishment used in some schools in the 20th century.

Crank - The crank was simply forcing an offender to turn a handle over and over. The offender would be made to turn the handle thousands of times before they were aloud to eat.

Crucifixion - This type of punishment is well known and the Roman Empire banned it in 337 AD. The offender was forced to carry the cross, made of wood, to the place where the execution was taking place. The offender's hands were tied or nailed to the cross. A block of wood was usually placed at their feet ensuring that their weight did not tear the hands. Their feet was also nailed or tied to the cross. This punishment is extremely harsh, not only because of the nailing to the cross but they would be left there in the hot sun which attracted flies and other insect. As time went on it would become more and more difficult for them to breath so they would often die of suffocation. Sometimes this agonising death could drag on for days. It is known for some offenders to have their legs broke in order to hurry the process along.

Drowning - In the middle ages this was sometimes

used as a punishment for murder and the Anglo-Saxons also used this as a form of punishment. Surprisingly drowning was not a commonly used form of execution. During the French Revolution it was used as a way of killing large numbers at once on ships with trapdoors which were sunk with all the offenders on it. It was also used in the 13th century in England on the king's ships as a punishment for murder. The offender would be tied to the victim's body then thrown over board. Around this time it was known for female murderers to be tied to a post at the harbour and left to drown as the tide came in.

Ducking Stool - The ducking stool was a wooden seat attached to a long wooden pole and was used at a time when women could be convicted of scolds (a woman who nags or grumbles constantly) or gossips, they were usually ducked in the local river or pond. 1809 saw the last woman to be ducked in England. This gradually died out but the textile mills of the early 19th century would duck the heads of children considered lazy. Today this is used as a form of entertainment at fairgrounds.

Fines - Forcing people to pay money as a form of punishment has been used since ancient time. It may also have been in the form of goods such as cattle. It is still used today for a large number of different offences.

Firing Squad - The first guns were not very accurate so firing squads did not become common until further development in guns accuracy. This type of execution was not used for the general public and was a military used punishment. Although in 1977 Gary Gilmore was executed by firing squad. He was a convicted murderer of two people in Utah. He was the first person to be executed in America for ten years.

Flogging - This type of punishment was usually used for minor crimes and was abolished in 1881. It was used in England from the middle ages but during the 18th century it was a common punishment used by the military.

Garroting- -This type of execution is known to be used in Spain. It is basically a form of strangulation. This was a post with a metal collar attached which was slowly tightened.

Gas Chamber - This is a cyanide gas filled room while the offender is strapped to a chair, they then used powerful fans to remove the gas once the offender was dead. America in 1924 saw the first use of the gas chamber.

Guillotine - The guillotine is often thought to have been invented in France but it was actually invented in Halifax England. This misconception is probably because it was very popular in France during the French Revolution but it was also used in part of

Europe before the French Revolution, possibly as early as 1307. This form of execution saw a movement towards creating a more humane way of executing offenders by Joseph Ignace Guillotin (1738 - 1814). Thomas Schmidt was given the job of building the first guillotin. 1792 saw the first use of the guillotine with the execution of Nicolas Jacques Pelletier. France abolished the death penalty in 1981 but the guillotine was last used in France in 1977.

Hanging, drawing and quartering - This was a gruesome form of execution and was used for treason in England. First the offender was taken by horse and hurdle (a portable wooden frame) to where the execution was to take place. He would be hanged but cut down before death then the executioner would cut him open and pull out his intestines and/or internal organs, he was then beheaded and his body cut into four parts. In 1814 this was changed to the offender being hung until he was dead and then beheaded only. Hanging, drawing and quartering was not officially abolished until 1870 and the last case was in 1820.

Hard Labor - Offenders could be sent to prison with hard labour, very hard physical work. This form of punishment was abolished in 1948 in Britain.

Horse - Another very painful punishment where the offender was made to sit on a wooden construction called a 'horse' with his hands tied behind his back and legs at each side. Weights were then tied to his legs.

Hulks - Hulks were old ships used as prisons. This was because before 1776 some British prisoners were transported to North America but due to rebellion in the same year, the Hulks were used to house prisoners. Transportation to Australia began in 1787 but offenders were held on hulks before transportation. These were abolished in 1857.

Jougs - This was a metal collar attached to a wall with a chain which was fastened around the offender neck. This was an old Scottish punishment.

Keelhauling - This was used in the Dutch Navy and involved tying a man to a rope and dropping him into the sea where he was pulled under the keel of the ship. The Barnacles attached to the ship would shred the offender skin, he may also drown.

Lock-up - These were just a simple bare cell that was used to detain drunkards in many English villages.

Mutilation - Another gruesome and inhumane form of punishment. In England in the 16th and 17th centuries saw the cutting off of ears as a form of punishment but mutilation was used in Saxon England and throughout the Middle Ages as a punishment for poaching and stealing. Mutilation could include horrific acts such as cutting out the tongue, cutting off noses, ears and hands and even blinding.

Oubliette - Oubliette comes from the French word 'oublier' which means to forget. There was a pit at the bottom of dungeons where prisoners would be thrown into and forgot about.

Picket or Piquet - This was used in the 17th century and was a military punishment. It involved a wooden stake which was pointed but not sharp and the offender would be hung by the wrists with one foot on the pointed wooden stake. When his wrists became tired he would have to support his weight on his foot which soon became very painful. This form of punishment died out because the soldiers could not march after it.

Picking Oakum - Offenders and people in workhouses were made to pick oakum because it was a very unpleasant job. Oakum was ropes from ship that were covered in tar. These ropes had to be recycled by being pulled apart by hand which would make their hands blister and their fingers bleed.

Pillory and Stocks - The stocks were wooden frames with hole in it for the offenders feet. This was a way of humiliating the offender and sometime unpleasant things would be thrown at them. The pillory was similar but had holes for the head and hands. The stocks were abolished in 1872 and the use of the pillory in 1837 in Britain. This was another method of punishment which can now be seen as a form of entertainment.

Poison - Socrates was forced to drink hemlock to kill him but this method is known to have been rarely used as a form of execution.

Pressing - Pressing was used in England to punish an offender if they refused to make a plea, guilty or not guilty. This was performed by placing a wooden board on top of them and then adding weights until the offender made a plea or they would be crushed to death. The last known pressing in England was in 1735.

Prison - Prison were not used as a punishment before the 19th century. They served the purpose of holding an offender until their trial. Similar to the remand centres we have these days. Being sent to prison was often a death sentence in itself because the prisons were so dirty and overcrowded and disease was rife. Typhus was a common disease in prisons therefore it was called jail fever. During the 19th century although the prison conditions were improved there was a very harsh regime.

Scold's Bridle - This was last used in Britain in 1824. It was used in Scotland in the 16th century and in England in the 17th century. This was used for women guilty of heresy. A metal frame with a bit that stuck into the mouth was placed over the woman's head to prevent her from talking. It was also called the branks.

Slavery - In the Roman Empire certain crimes could be punished by being made a slave but most slaves were prisoners of war in Ancient times.

Stoning - This was common in the Middle East and is still used in some regions today. It is simply stones being thrown at the offender until they are dead.

Sweatbox - In hot countries a sweatbox was a cramped cell where the prisoner would sweat until he felt the effects of dehydration.

Transportation - North America was the first place used for transportation in the 17th and early 18th centuries. This ended due to the American Revolution in 1775 so transportation to Australia began in 1787 until 1868.

Treadmill - The treadmill was a device used for driving machinery. It was a large wheel with steps. It was first invented in 1817 and came into prisons soon after. In 1898 it was abolished in British prisons.

Whirligig - This was a military punishment. It was a wooden cage on a pivot. The prisoner was shut inside and then it was spun around until the prisoner became nauseous and vomited. A word that is now commonly used for a rotating washing line on a pole.

Chapter 11
Policing and Crime Prevention

History of The Police

The Metropolitan Police Force was established in 1829 by Sir Robert Peel when he passed the first Metropolitan Police Act. Before this act came into force the London area, but no the actual city, was covered by the local 'Watch'. Other areas were controlled by establishments set up during the eighteenth century which were still in force after the first establishment of the Metropolitan Police Force. These consisted of the Bow Street Runners which were men who conducted street patrols either on foot or on horseback. The were originally called the Bow Street Patrols. The Magistrates controlled the offices which deployed Police Office Constables and there was River Police or Marine Police. It took ten years for all these separate establishments to be brought under the umbrella of the Metropolitan Police Force. In the same year The City of London Police Force was established as an independent force and remains that way today. During the 18th and 19th centuries London expanded considerably and maintaining order and upholding the law had become a matter of public concern because of the lack of organisation within the force. By 1826 Sir Robert Peel was formulating a plan for six police districts to cover a ten mile radius from St Paul's but the City of London was not included. The committee was not set up until 1828 that paved the way for the police Bill. This lead to the setting up of an organised police force in London. 29th September 1829 saw the establishment of the Metropolitan Police Force by Sir Robert Peel and put Col. Charles Rowan and Richard Mayne in charge of the force at which, Richard Mayne and commissioner Peel stated that the main duty of the police would be crime prevention rather than the detection of crime. Peel proposed that all senior uniformed ranks should not be filled with people from higher social classes and should be filled with those from the lower classes, and that it would be a low paid job as to ensure that the police did not feel superior to the job or his colleagues. In the Metropolitan Police Act 1829 was the definition of the original Metropolitan Police District which covered approximately a seven mile radius of Charing Cross but within a year seventeen divisions were set up with three more following in 1865 and another in 1886.

In 1836 the Bow Street Horse Patrol was incorporated into the force and operated in the outlying Metropolitan divisions. The River Thames force was converted into the Thames Division in the second Metropolitan Police Act 1839 it absorbed the

Bow Street Foot Patrol and extended the Metropolitan Police District to a fifteen mile radius. There was attempts to incorporate the City of London police but they were unsuccessful and it had remained independent to this day.

Each division had a structure of a superintendent, four inspectors and sixteen sergeants. Regulations were set for new recruits which consisted of, being at least five foot and seven inches in height, literate, of good character, be well built and be under thirty five years old with the minimum age usually twenty. These officers were expected to work seven days a week and bearing in mind they were on a wage no more than a farmer would have at that time. During this time women were not employed in the police force as they were expected to stay at home and take care of the home and family although the wives of officers could be asked to come into the station to deal with female offenders mainly to search them and supervise them while they were in custody. In 1889 fourteen women were employed by the Metropolitan police to deal with women and became known as 'matrons'. (Dell 2010).

The view of women began to change in 1897 with the establishment of the Union of Women Workers in order to show that women were capable of other jobs besides keeping house and looking after children. The women who joined the Union of Women Workers usually did so voluntarily and mainly in the social sector. This was still a low key and hardly recognised. During the First World War 1901-1914 many of the officers were called to duty and this left a lack of officers enabling women patrols to operate. This generated a movement in the communities views on what women were able to do. These new views were reinforced by the Chief Commissioner of the Metropolitan Police at the time, Sir Edward Henry, also endorsed by Mr McKenna, the Home Secretary, who signed the women's passes to authorise them to patrol public places and the streets and were expected to do the job of a police officer, male or female. After a meeting with Sir Edward Henry, Margaret Dawson pursued him to recruit women, train them and allow them to patrol the streets in uniform, these women were not paid for this. From this the Policewoman Volunteers was set up and were separate from the patrols. The Women Police Volunteers took up the problem of sexualy transmitted infections, which had resulted from the coming and goings of soldiers, by informing them of the consequences of infidelity. Nina Boyle had been told by Sir Edward Ward that although it would make sense for women to replace the male officer while they were away at war, women were simply not suitable to do a man's work. As a result of this Margaret Dawson made her deputy of the Women Police Volunteers. Their plan was to do as well as possible at the job while the men were away in hope that it would change the public's view on women and the police force and they would be kept on after the war and the men returned.

In an attempt to change views and in order to show they were the same as the male officers they changed their name to the Women's Police Service. Every member of the Women's Police Service would be given a uniform and and would have strict rules to abide by becoming more inline with the male officer's role. This lead to them been given I.D cards and the power to patrol the streets. As a result of this the Metropolitan Police started to allow women to become sergeants and inspectors but their duties were limited and still mainly related to women offenders. The first 'proper' policewoman in Britain was Edith Smith who had the full powers of arrest, showing a significant change in the attitudes towards women in the police force. The Bishop of Grantham had followed Edith's work and made a call for a National Women's Service. In December of 1915 official women police were appointed. In 1916 the Women's Police Service was asked to patrol the munitions factories where they received a wage for this. At this time also saw women officers being trained in London, Bristol, Glasgow and Liverpool. These training facilities became known as the federated schools for police women and patrols U.K.

What was now known as The Ministry of Munitions Women Police Service (MMWPS) had decided to train and equip women police to patrol the factories. July 1916 saw the first agreement being signed between the Women Police Service and the Ministry of Munitions, called the Queen's Ferry Agreement and then later in 1916 a second agreement was signed called the Gretna Agreement. This lead to other agreement signed to patrol other munitions factories. By 1918 London had its own womans force. Nevil Macready appointed a Mrs Stanley of the Women's Patrols as superintendent of the Metropolitan Women Police Patrols, upon this she appointed twentyfive other women, although they had no powers of arrest they still took their orders from New Scotland Yard. Out of the 126 women that were now employed only 33 of them held the same powers as men.

In 1920 Dame Helen Gwynne-Vaughan made recommendations regarding the women police, these were

* That all police women should be sworn in, given full powers of arrest and ranked with the male police officers, forming an integral part of the police force and being trained and appointed by the Chief Constables.

* That their pay should be standardised and approximated to that of men and that their allowances should be the same.

* That their hours should be seven daily.

* That marriage should be no bar to service.

* That their pensions should be granted on a scale slightly lower than of men, but gratuities for dependent children should be the same for both sexes. (Dell 2010)

Unfortunately these recommendations were not taken very seriously with the exception of that of pay.

The next major change did not come about until 1968 when Sislin Fay Allen was the first black officer. By 1973 the Women's Service became fully integrated into the Metropolitan Police and the role of women in the police force was redefined during 1970-1975 with the introduction of the Equal Pay Act 1970 and the Sex Discrimination Act 1975. Overall, the public's expectation of the police remains the same. Criminals should be caught and punished and the public want to see the police within the communities doing their job.

Policing and Crime Prevention: Possible Bias within the Police Force

At the beginning of the nineteenth century the 'authorities' at the time were faced with a rising crime rate in London. Over time this rising crime problem was widespread to every part of the UK. During the nineteenth century to role of policing was to enforce control over the crime rates which were continually rising due to industrialisation and the rising number of people living in poverty and unemployment.

Reith (1938) argued for the need to establish an organised police force which would become known as the Metropolitan Police. During this time prisons were reformed and the police were established. In 1829 Sir Robert Peel created the Metropolitan Police Force. Before the establishment of the police magistrates, night watchmen and parish constables were responsible for policing. London was still at the centre of the development of the Metropolitan Police where the problem of crime and the fear of crime continued to grow along with the vast increase of London's size and population. The expanding slum areas added to the problem of crime and disorder. There were several different models of police throughout England by the middle of the nineteenth century. These ranged from parish constables who, due to reform, were now supervised by superintendents to the Metropolitan Police in London.

In 1856 the County and Borough Police Act produced legislation making it compulsory for all boroughs and counties to set up a uniformed ranking system of police forces. In 1854 Palmerston, who served briefly at the Home Office brought forward a bill proposing that the Home Secretary drew up police regulations and some smaller forces merge with surrounding counties. These were not received favourably and were dropped two years later although the merging of forces happened anyway. After the development and establishment of the new police some groups and individuals continued to do what was considered police work. Some parish constables were still employed until well into the twentieth century. Private property owners still employed gamekeepers and watchmen. Places like the docks had their own police and were later incorporated into new local town forces. In 1948 the nationalisation of the rail companies brought about the British Transport Police. 226 forces existed in England and Wales. At the beginning of the First World War there still existed 188 and due to forces being amalgamated at the end of the Second World War balanced the figure at 131.

These 131 forces made up the London Metropolitan Police, the city or borough police and the county police. Each of the three different forces had different organisational structures. The commissioners of the Metropolitan Police were accountable to the Home Secretary.

From the beginning there had always been an opposition to the police. The public were hostile towards them and battled with them over local culture and customs. There was feelings of oppression and victimisation. The police had already identified a 'criminal class' who lived in the slum areas and needed to be 'watched' to protect the wealthy districts. So for most part of the nineteenth century the working class was identified by the police as in most need of being 'watched'. There grew a great need for the police to legitimise their work and the need for a police force.

The legitimisation of the police was to provide a visible body of authority to reduce the public fear of crime enabling the community to feel safe and protected. The police force was intended to be a non-political force and would represent the community. The police force would be a neutral force on all accounts and the use of minimal force would be employed. Various means were used to achieve these aims and uphold the legitimacy of the police. From the establishment of the police to present day the police force has continually defended its legitimacy, as much as its legitimacy has been questioned. There was increasing concern regarding the accountability, effectiveness and legitimacy of the police by the mid to late 1950's due to a number of small corruption and accountability scandals where the media portrayed a corrupt force. The increasing criticism of this lead to the creation of The Royal Commission on the Police 1960. The aim of this commission was the focus on police pay, accountability and the possibility of a national police force. Recommendations made in a final report (1962) formed the basis of The Police Act (1964). This act defined the responsibilities of the three main bodies responsible for the police, these were, the police authority, chief constables and The Home Office. The introduction of Unit Beat Policing (1967) reduced the number of police officers on foot and put them into cars once again raised questions of legitimacy and accountability through visibility and the uncovering of corruption in the 1970's lead to the police becoming increasingly politicised through political allegiances and industrial disputes. In 1981 Lord Scarman's inquiry into the Brixton disorders and policing the miners strike made recommendations which influenced The Police and Criminal Evidence Act 1984 which, with a number of other recommendations, stated that, police powers should be balanced with the protection of the individual, increasing resources and local community consultative committees should be established to encourage communication between the police and the public. This was a recommendation which defended the legitimisation of the police force representing the community. They can only represent the community if there is co-operation, communication and consultation between the police and the community. After all, the main body of police work is within these communities and a great deal of police time is used dealing with working class street crime.

Emanating from the constant questions of accountability and legitimacy raises the question of bias within the police force. The main areas to look at are police discrimination, police discretion and police bias and how bias is originated. Discrimination can be deliberate. A deliberate act out of police officers personal views determining his or her decisions of who is suspected of being a criminal and the discriminatory treatment of the offender. Bias can also originate from unconscious prejudice. A police officer may well hold prejudice ideas through their background, their family upbringing and their social acquaintances. This prejudice has always been present, it is not questioned by the officer in question and can be considered as normal. Bias can also take the form of being unintended consequences out of reasonable attitudes, practices and decisions. Bias operates at every level of the criminal justice system from the first encounter with the police to the penal system. If we take Reiner's perspective that the penal system functions to reinforce the position of the powerful sections of society over the less powerful then this puts the police in the position of being non-rational and socially constructed which would reflect various bias and structural inequalities. The low visibility of police officers while on duty by their higher ranks provides the opportunities for the police officers to exercise personal discretion and bias at a personal and institutional level. Police work is not visible to the general public and it is very difficult to gain access to police information which gives society the impression of a need to protect the way they operate.

Police bias can take a number of forms and it is mainly aimed at the socially disadvantaged and most powerless members of a society this mainly being young blacks and the working class because these are assumed to be of the criminal type. An example of class bias can be seen in the August 2002 introduction of 'on the spot fines' for offenders such as drunkenness or 'rowdy' behaviour. The offence and the crime are decided solely by the police officer in attendance. Shortly after this was introduced by the

Prime Minister's son committed several offences including being drunk and incapable and giving a false name and address to the police. He was not punished as a working class person would have more likely to have been as he received not punishment. If he had received an 'on the spot fine' of, at the time £40, £80 or £100, this would have been a tiny fraction of his parents income. If he had of been from a working class family this fine would have been a large portion of the family's income.

The bia towards ethnic minorities has been a major area of debate for some time. The debate was fuelled further by the introduction of 'stop and search' but not only for young black males but also for the working class. The Police and Criminal Evidence Act 1984 provided all police officers with a general power to stop and search a person in a public place if they have reasonable grounds for suspecting that they would find stolen good or prohibited articles (McLaughlin and Muncie 2002). Stop and search requires reasonable suspicion. The question which arises is, being black, young and male and/or of working class grounds for reasonable suspicion. When an individual is stopped and searched it must be stated why they are being searched and a record of the search would be made available to the suspect. In an attempt to eliminate bias, codes of practice which accompany the act state that a firm basis for the 'reasonable suspicion' must be stated. The Home Office 1991 stated that reasonable suspicion cannot be supported by personal factors such as race, age, sex and dress or that they are known to the police. If these codes of practice were abided to then there would be no bias and the debate would not continue but the debate is still strong and ongoing.

Police bias can also be geographical. Where a person lives can increase the suspicion. An individual from a working class council estate would arouse more suspicion than a middle class individual living on a private newly built housing complex. Indications to this would also be in the way they dress and present themselves. A youth wearing smart, clean designer clothes would be less likely to be suspected by the police. The way a person speaks and acts can also arouse suspicion, if a person is loud and swearing and showing a bad attitude towards the police and others they are more likely to be stopped and searched. Another major factor to being stopped and searched is family background. If a person is assumed to be from a family which is known to them then that person is assumed to be the same as the other family members who are known to the police,therefore more likely to be stopped and searched.

Some of the major problems with stop and

search are, where the search has taken place is the only thing required to be recorded, If the person consents to the search then it does not have to be recorded. Most people would be apprehensive about refusing to be searched or questioned through fears of repercussions. There is no requirement to say why the search has taken place. Some evidence has suggested that police officers have devised procedures and techniques to bypass and avoid safeguards (Bottomley et al 1991) There is very little monitoring of stop and search records and there is a great deal of variation within different forces to the use of stop and search. One of the main ways of identifying bias difficult is because there is no way of knowing if the reason for the stop and search is the reason stated in the record.

The police have the power to stop and search any individual. The decision to do this comes from individual discretion and is based on subjective judgements. There is a great deal of wide discretion and autonomy. The decision to stop and search can come from cultural norms within the individual officer and the police force which supports certain types of stereotyping and prejudice. According to police statistics black people in London are five times more likely to be stopped and searched in comparison to white people.

Another problem within the police force is

what is known as 'cop culture' or 'canteen cop'. This is a structured culture which exists within the police force and is a product of wider structural relations which are based on a white male ideology. Cop culture is seen as a stereotyping of certain types of people and groups. Police culture reflects the power difference within the social structure. If society is seen to be unequal then the police will also be unequal, this suggests that police culture is sociologically generated. The central feature to cop culture is the sense of mission. A police officer feels that the job they do is not just a job but a way of life which has a worthwhile purpose. They see themselves as performing an essential role and safeguard social order. The police have a set of views which have been described by Riener as 'cynical' or 'police pessimism'. They acquire an attitude of constant suspicion which comes from the need to be constantly looking for signs of trouble or danger. There is a bias within this suspicion which comes from a socially constructed bias of types of people. It comes from what society sees as danger signs. This suspiciousness leads to stereotyping certain individuals and groups. Police stereotyping of what is considered as a likely offender leads to a self fulfilling prophecy because these people are disproportionately questioned or arrested it leads to a cycle of deviance amplification (Young 1971) within any society there are groups of people who are seen as disadvantaged or powerless, who are seen as problematic by the dominant powers in society and therefore the task of controlling these people is given to the police force. This has been termed as 'police property'. This police property is difficult to define but can be segregated into five categories which are, the rubbish, challengers, disarmers, do-gooders and politicians. Rubbish, are calls to the police which are considered as unworthy of attention such as domestic disputes, they are seen as wanting a service. although, in recent years attitudes towards domestic violence have changed. The challengers are those who try to penetrate the police secrecy, these include lawyers or even the media. The disarmers are people who are seen to weaken police work like women and children. The do-gooders are anti-police activists and the politicians are remote and do not have a realistic view of police work or street life.

Police culture is seen as an institutional culture, a culture of machismo and sexism. The police force is seen as a macho job, a job for the boys, and offers a sense of excitement and danger and implies a tough character which draws a certain type of person. A new recruit into the police force will tend to take on the culture through mixing with other officers on the beat or patrol or within the 'canteen culture' of the police station, Sexism within the police culture is continually reinforced by the discrimination which takes place in recruitment and promotion of female officers because they do not fit into the macho image of the police and are seen as weak and not capable of doing the job efficiently. Attitudes towards this has improved in recent years but still exists.

The police want to seen as pragmatic. They want to get the job done safely with as little fuss and paperwork as possible, which is easier to do with a collective culture where everyone knows how things are done and the culture is used as a type of guidance. Different cultures exist within different police forces and these cultures are reflected in the structures of the society it is policing. Although the cultures may be different they all appear to have a basic set of cultural norms which exist in all police cultures, that is, bias towards ethnic minorities and the working class.

The bias cultures raise questions of legitimacy and accountability once again. If legitimacy and accountability were upheld as they are supposed to be then there would be no question of bias. If the codes of practice within the police stop and search were applied to all equally regardless of being young, black, unemployed or working class then this would eradicate bias but the continuing establishment of cop culture prevents this. Continued monitoring of all stop and searches could help to prevent bias. The whole nature of police work generates the culture which leads to the discrimination and bias of certain individuals and groups of people.

Primary, Secondary & Tertiary Prevention

Primary Crime Prevention: All modes of crime prevention require community involvement at some level. Its main focus is on the first development stage of crime, that is dealing with the visible problems within the community, the natural environment. This would include broken street lights and windows, abandoned cars and buildings. It is believed that this type of problem leads to crime. It had been described at the medical model like treating the symptoms.

Secondary Crime Prevention: This type of crime prevention focuses on the things that are considered as 'at risk' of offenders and reducing the opportunities for offending. The main aim is to identify potential people, places, situations and opportunities for offending and therefore be able to predict and to prevent further offending. By reducing the opportunities to commit crime this increases the risk of the crime and by minimising the gains of the crime it will deter the criminal from the offence.

Tertiary Crime Prevention: This model focuses on the prevention of further offences after the crime has been committed. It takes steps to make sure the victim is not further victimised. It also aims to reduce the recidivism rate of the offender. The victim would be given advice about home security, being safe when out and about such as, staying in well lit areas, going out at night in groups, rape alarms etc.

In order to have successful crime prevention there needs to be a combination of all types of crime prevention with the police and other agencies working with and alongside members of the community.

Theories of Crime: Rational Choice Theory

Rational Choice theory is based on the fundamental tenets of classical criminology, which holds that people freely choose their behaviour and are motivated by the avoidance of pain and the pursuit of pleasure. Individuals evaluate their choice of actions in accordance with each option's ability to produce advantage, pleasure and happiness. Rational choice provides a micro perspective on why individual offenders decided to commit specific crimes; people choose to engage in crime because it can be rewarding, easy, satisfying and fun. The central premise of this theory is that people are rational beings whose behaviour can be controlled or modified by fear of punishment. In this way, it is believed offenders can be persuaded to desist from offending by intensifying their fear of the punishment. In terms of setting the quantum of punishment, according to this theory, sanctions should be limited to what is necessary to deter people from choosing crime (Siegel and McCormick, 2006)

Rational choice is premised on a utilitarian belief that actions are based on a conscious evaluation of the utility of acting in a certain way. This perspective assumes that crime is a personal choice, the result of individual decision making processes. This means that individuals are responsible for their choices and thus individual offenders are subject to blame for their own criminality. In terms of offending, rational choice posits that offenders weigh the potential benefits and consequences associated with committing an offence and then make a rational choice on the basis of this evaluation. Therefore, before committing a crime, the reasoning criminal weighs the chances of getting caught, the severity of the expected penalty and the value to be gained by committing the act. This means that if offenders perceive the costs to be too high, the act to be too risky, or the payoff to be too small, they will choose not to engage in the act.

The tenets of this theory are based on a number of assumptions about the decision making process and behavioural motivations. It is held that people decided to commit a crime after careful consideration of the costs and benefits of behaving in a certain manner. This involves considering both personal factors, which may include a need for money, revenge or entertainment, and situational factors such as the target or victim's vulnerability and the presence of witnesses, guardians or the police. Rational choice focuses on the opportunity to commit crime and on how criminal choices are structured by the social environment and situational variables.

Research on Rational Choice Theory

There is some research that supports the rational nature of crime. This support, however, is confined primarily to instrumental crimes such as, property and drug offences. There offences are generally crimes of opportunity. In this way, if offenders come across an opportunity to commit an offence, but perceives a high chance of getting caught they will refrain from committing the offence. Property offender will stay away from places that are occupied, have security measures or are in areas with neighbourhood watch schemes or generally look out of one another. Property offender are enticed by unlocked doors and windows and unsupervised property. It also appears that drug dealers tailor their transactions in a similar fashion, as they tend to work in locations where they are able to clearly see anyone approaching and where there is an insignificant presence of watchful guardians.

In terms of common street crime it was found by Clarke and Harris (1992) that car thieves are selective in their choice of targets, selecting different types of vehicles depending on the purpose of the theft. This suggests that the decision with respect to a target and opportunity is rationally motivated. This rationale of decision making is also found to hold true for sex trade workers. Maher (1996) suggests that women rationally choose whom to solicit, whom to engage with and what risks they are willing to take to fulfill an interaction. For substance offenders, the decision to use has been reported as being related to the benefits associated with use. Specifically, according to Petraitis et al. (1995), this means the benefits of consuming illegal substances outweighing the potential costs associated with use. In terms of the distribution of drugs, MacCoun and Reuter (1992) found it to be related to the economics of the trade. Drug dealers often cite the desire for a supplementary income as a prime motivator for getting involved in the drug trade.

With respect to violence, it has been found that perpetrators are selective in their choice of target.

They select people who appear vulnerable and without any means of protecting themselves. Wright and Rosi (1983) found that violent offenders will avoid victims who may be armed and dangerous, preferring to select more defenceless victims who are less likely to resist. More recently, Siegel and McCormick (2006) conclude that although some acts of lethal violence are the result of angry aggression, other seem to show acts of rational planning. Therefore, although violent acts appear to be irrational, they do seem to involve some calculations of the risks and the rewards. In all, these studies indicate that there is an element of rationality in the decision to engage in offending behaviour.

Assuming a rational basis for committing crime overestimates the extent to which people consider the legal consequences of their actions. This theory also focuses on individuals and their choices while ignoring the social constraints and conditions that shape an individual's circumstances, thought processes and life chances. These exert considerable influence on people. Engaging in crime is not simply a rational decision. It is affected by the interaction of a number of factors and influences. Furthermore, increasing the penalty also assumes that offenders were aware of the original sanction and felt it was worth the risk, while the new, more punitive punishment makes it no longer worth the risk in a cost/benefit analysis. This, again, is assuming that offenders are aware of the change in the severity of the sentence and rationally calculate their choice of action. Since this assumption is not supported by the literature, both specific and general deterrence strategies have not yielded the results predicted by the rational choice theorists.

Chapter 12
The Penal System

The History of Prison

In 1166 Henry II built the first jails. There was a number of jails built including Newgate Prison in London. This year also seen the first legal textbook produced and this becomes the precursor to what became Common Law. Common Law is law that is derived from customs and judicial precedent (an act that may be used as an example when dealing with similar instances). He also establishes a court system in England and juries are set up with 12 men to make decisions on land disputes.

King John signed the Magna Carta in 1215 which saw the start of English judicial rights, meaning that no one could be sent to prison without a trial by his peers. Article 39 states "No free man shall be arrested, or imprisoned, or deprived of his property, or outlawed, or exiled, or in any way destroyed, nor shall we go against him or send against him, unless by legal judgement of his peers, or by the law of the land."

During the 1300's people could refuse to be tried by a jury but the consequence would be prison. The conditions in the prisons were very harsh where prisoners slept on the ground and were only given bread to eat and water to drink every other day. Prisoners were also charged for everything, their food, blankets and fuel. There was even a charge for having their manacles removed so for prisoners who did not have any money or any family to pay for any of these things then they would have to go without, even without food.

The 1400's saw the establishment of House of Correction which were to try to control the growing problem of vagrancy. These people were termed the 'idle poor' they were put into prison as a punishment for being lazy. They could only be released with the consent of the magistrates.

By the 1600's the population in prisons grew considerably, seeing the first problem of overcrowding in prisons. At this time juries were becoming reluctant to hang people for minor offences so their solution was to release offender from prison if they agreed to join the Army or the Navy.

By the 1700's prisons in England were still overcrowded and by the end of the century The Industrial Revolution saw a great amount of movement within communities which lead to an increase in minor crime. The conflict with Napoleonic France saw the numbers in prison grow further with the confinement of prisoners or war. This is when the 'Hulks' (derelict ships) came into use as prisons in the

Thames and the southern ports.

Transportation to America was used as a form of punishment, it was considered to be more humane than execution and was a solution to the problem of overcrowding in prisons until it was no longer possible due to the American War of Independence, so transportation to Australia began in 1786 and continued until 1791. Transportation to Australia created the basis of the country's population with the first transportation of 775 prisoners in 1786. Following this, between 1787 and 1791, three more large fleets of prisoners were transported.

In 1777 the High Sheriff of Bedfordshire, John Howard, who had studied prison conditions for 17 years, publishes a jail reform book called 'State of Prisons in England and Wales' which proposes that jailers should not be allowed to charge prisoners and that the prisons should be disease free and healthy. The book, although very influential, was not put into practice widely until the 19th century.

1791 saw the design of the 'Panopticon' by Jeremy Bentham. Jeremy Bentham was a philosopher who based his idea on the notion of 'utilitarianism' which is, the greatest good for the greatest number of people. It focused on new ways of managing prisons and prisoners. The aim was also to make prisons more humane. This brought about change in British law and how criminals were dealt with and saw the beginning of practices with the aim of rehabilitation. He became one of the greatest influences in rehabilitation and reform. The design of the Panopticon was to have a main administrative block with cell blocks interconnected. The Panopticon would be a circular prison with cells around the perimeter. In order to stop the prisoners communicating with each other there was to be wall on each side of the cell with one barred window facing the outside of the building. The window would bring light into the cell enabling the prison guards, who were located in a tower at the centre of the panopticon, to see the prisoners at all times. The walled cells prevented physical attacks between prisoners and to promote moral reform. It is interesting to note that although several prototype panopticons were built, only in America, it never really took off in Europe.

Previous to 1815 jailers charged prisoners of the things they needed like food and blankets but in this year the state began paying jailers and the responsibility of inspecting prisons was given to the magistrates. Prison inspectors did not come about until 1835. It was not until 1877 jailers were appointed on merit and all prison staff received a salary.

Elizabeth Fry, whose image is seen on a £5 note in 2002, sets up the Association for the

Improvement of the Female Prisoners in Newgate after she saw the overcrowding and poor prison conditions. She introduces a prison school for the children of mothers who were imprisoned. A plea is made by her and her brother Joseph Gurney to Sir Robert Peel form more prison reforms.

1878 saw the introduction of the Prison Act which incorporated John Howard's reforms and a movement away from the idea of prisons as places of punishment in order to reform. The ideas of 'decarceration' and 'therapeutic incarceration' were also introduced. Therapeutic incarceration aimed to reduce the 'punishment' of prisons and decarceration was to replace prison sentences with community punishment with supervision. This Act also introduced the Prison Commission which took control of all prisons and saw the closure of the worst prisons, annual report were reviewed by parliament.

Separate confinement was abolished in 1922 due to the suggestion that it created high risks of prisoners going insane due to the long solitary confinements and in 1919 the term 'prison officers' was introduced. Wakefield prison saw the first staff training courses in 1935 due to reforms not being enforced quick enough. The number of female prison officer grew dramatically due to World War II.

The Criminal Justice Act of 1948 outlined a

model for what is now known as the modern prison. Some of the recommendations included the involvement of prison staff in the reform of the prisoners and longer terms of imprisonment in order to rehabilitate and train the prisoners.

The Penal System

We have a criminal justice system which exists to punish offenders for a crime they have committed. The criminal justice system is a range of ideologies, ideologies which include due process, crime control, welfare, power and managerialism. Due process is a legal process which is based on rules and procedures which are intended to be fair, just and impartial. The crime control is intended to control the level of control in society and to punish offenders. Its main value is the punishment of the guilty. Welfare is rehabilitative and concerned with discretion and individual analysis. The power perspective demonstrates power dynamics that exist and justify the existence of the criminal justice system. The managerial aspect states that crime needs to managed, a management of resources and the management of crime to a tolerable level through administration, rationalisation and careful use of resources.

The main aim of the court is to punish people for the crimes they have committed. It has been suggested that the courts operate in a bias manner which contributes to the continuing prison crisis. The courts are responsible for deciding how offenders should be dealt with and operate on three levels, the magistrates' courts, The Crown Court and The Court of Appeal.

The penal system has been in what is termed a 'crisis' for some time. This crisis relates to the number of offenders sent to prison, the definitions of crime, the treatment of offenders and what works. The penal system and the court system are institutions which interact with each other. This came about due to industrialisation and the changing of societies and their needs and changing ideologies and economics. The ideological analysis of the penal system and the courts show how it reflects a society's state at any given time in history. Different ideologies relating to the structure of that society and the ideologies of the ruling power at that time. A number of approaches to punishment have been implemented to relieve the ongoing prison crisis with little positive effect. There has been a utilitarian approach which includes deterrence. The aim being to prevent further crime for the good of society. It includes methods to discourage offending and re-offending by the consequences of the punishment. Reform and rehabilitation aims to re-intergrate the offender into society and rehabilitate them to be socially productive. Rehabilitation approach sees offenders as products of their environment. Incapacitation removes the choice, freedom and ability for an offender to re-offend. This approach usually involves prison. Then there is the retributive approach. The main aim is to punish the act and is incorporated with 'just deserts' meaning that the punishment is deserved, an eye for an eye etc. It sets fixed penalties for certain types of crimes. This retributive approach should take away any bias within the system. Some of the earlier penal codes focused on deterrence, other approaches became more popular in the nineteenth century. the last quarter of the century saw a return to public protection and just deserts. According to Cavadino and Dignan (2002) the system should include all approaches as none of them work individually. They state that society, the penal system and the courts should be looking at new ways of dealing with offenders. Whichever approach is applied bias towards certain types of people and groups exists at all levels of the criminal justice system from the police to the courts.

Each different court, the Magistrates', The Crown Court and The Court of Appeal are staffed by different sets of judicial officials, the powers they have and how they choose to use these powers varies considerably and involves a great deal of discretion.

Responsibility of the courts is shared among three government departments. The courts and judiciary are the responsibility of The Lord Chancellor's Department and The Home Office is responsible for the drafting of legislation within the criminal justice system as well as the police, prisons and probation. The Attorney General is responsible for the Crown Prosecution Service. This shared responsibility causes confusion and tension therefore making it difficult to reform the system. The main problem with the court system is the degree of discretion which is available to all and appears to be exercised with almost total disregard for the impact which a given decision may have on other parts of the system (Cavadino and Dignan 2002)

The Magistrates' courts are the lowest tier in the criminal justice system. It is a system of unpaid, untrained, volunteer, part-time magistrates. The main job of the Magistrates' is to deliver 'summary justice' to people charged with less serious crimes but this does not mean that the punishments they impose are trivial. Magistrates' have the power to send people to prison for up to six months. In 1998 48,000 adults were sent to prison by Magistrates. The Crown Courts have existed since 1972, they replaced quarter sessions and assize courts. More serious crimes are dealt with in the Crown Court with the attendance of a public jury. The judge's role here is to decide on points of law. It is the jury who decides if a defendant is guilty or not. Juries are generally chosen from the upper and middle classes which is a disadvantage to the minority black or working class defendants. The Crown Court also acts as an appeal court against both convictions and sentences by magistrates'. In this case there is no jury. The Court of Appeals deals with any dissatisfaction with the decisions of the lower courts. The decisions they make are based on documents and transcripts and usually include the arguments of barristers. Magistrates' and judges should make decisions based on logical deductions of precedents. In the eighteenth century William Blackstone introduced a theory of law stating that, judges do not make the law but, by rules of president, to declare the law as it is. Judgments should not be made by the judge's personal sentiments or his own judgment. If a judge based his decision on his own judgments then this would be suggesting that the law was wrong. In reality judges make decisions which are not spelt out in presidents, they do tend to be based on personal sentiment and also based on personal and institutional bias. This becomes clear when looking at some of the decisions made by magistrates' and judges and the consequences these decisions have on certain types of individuals and groups. One of the main problems with bias decisions is that magistrates' and judges are predominantly from middle or upper class backgrounds. They usually have been well educated at well established universities and have had a privileged lifestyle. They do not have a realistic view of ordinary working class people therefore base their judgment on their own subjectivities.

In English law suspects are presumed innocent until proven guilty but the practice of remand undermines this. Imprisoning a person before trial assumes that they are guilty to be proven innocent. In some case remand is used as a form of public protection depending on the crime in question. There are other factors which may determine whether a defendant is remanded in custody or released on bail. The Bail Act 1979 was introduced to reduce the number of defendants remanded in custody. It was structured so decisions were recorded and reasons given if bail was refused. It is questionable why the number of defendants detained in remand rose from 5,090 in 1976 to 12,520 in 1999 (Cavadino and Dignan 2002) When the decision is the judge's decision. It is possible that the decision made was based on bias towards race, class, gender or previous record.

A person's class can determine their treatment in court. One class may be prosecuted differently to another, in particular the middle and upper class.

Messerschmidt (1986) looks at the ideology of law. He suggests that the law protects the interests of the middle and upper classes by criminalising certain forms of behaviour, this is a Marxist perspective. An example of this class bias was reported in the Guardian on Monday 27th September 1999. Based on newspaper reports after the first day of the case against the Earl of Hardwicke, it looked as if the aristocrat was bound to go to prison. He and his friend, Stefan Thwaites, had arranged for cocaine to be delivered to a hotel. Hardwicke was actually heard saying, "come on, bring on the charlie. I was a big fat line". He was then videoed snorting cocaine yet he was still freed. If this had been a working class individual no doubt a long prison sentence would have been enforced. In contrast, reported also in the Guardian on Tuesday 23rd February 1999 it was reported that a 55 year old man from Wales used cannabis twice to relieve pain from chronic arthritis. He was sentenced to one year imprisonment. It appears that being of low social class, having a low family income and being unemployed can affect the outcome of a court decision.

Being unemployed can have an impact on sentencing because people who are employed are less likely to be sent to prison and more likely to receive a fine, they have the ability to pay. If they were imprisoned they would probably lose their job. An unemployed person is more likely to be perceived as criminal and therefore more likely to receive a sentence rather than a fine because it is assumed that the defendant will not or cannot pay the fine. There has not been many studies which compare sentencing between working and middle class defendants but some suggest that middle class offenders have already suffered through the disgrace of being convicted, bearing in mind that most judges and magistrates are from the same class. The middle class can also afford better lawyers which gives them an advantage. There is also a difference between working class crime and white collar crime. Companies can lose millions through fraud but the sentencing can be fairly lenient compared to the long prison sentences a bank robber who stole thousands would receive. For example, a three million pound fraud in the 1960's received a sentence which was only a fraction of the sentence received by the two million pound Great Train Robbers.

Race can also be a major factor in determining sentence. Racial discrimination can be conscious or unconscious, direct or indirect which results in black people being sentenced more often and more harshly than white people. It is assumed that black people are disproportionately involved in crime. One of the best known studies of race and sentencing was carried out by Roger Hood in 1992. He examined the sentencing of black people at five Crown Courts in the West Midlands in 1989. He discovered that 57 per cent of black males were sentenced to custody compared with 48 per cent of white males. Taking all other variables into account he found that black males were 5 per cent more likely to be sentenced to prison than white males. It has also been suggested that pre-sentence reports disadvantage black people because, according to de la Motta (1984) in Nottingham black people were three times more likely as those on white people to make no recommendation to sentencing. Probation officers make fewer recommendations for community orders for black people because they lack the confidence to carry them out successfully.

It has been assumed that women are treated more leniently than men in the criminal justice system. This is termed the 'chivalry' hypothesis which believes that because most judges are male the female offender is treated in the same way a mother, wife or daughter would be treated. Other evidence shows this not to be true. The harsh treatment women have received is due to the non-conformity to the traditional role of women. Many women are termed mad rather than bad because their behaviour is in contradiction to the placid, responsible nature which is expected from a woman. Therefore many women are referred to psychiatrists or psychiatric intervention along with a prison sentence. For women this position can be worse if they are mothers, not only for them but also for the children involved. Both main English political parties, when in power, have a policy of separating working class mothers from their children. A judge's bias toward women was shown in a new report in the Times 8th January 2000, it was decided, for no obvious reason, that new mothers should be deprived of her newborn child after being imprisoned for a minor shoplifting offence and the baby taken into care. This only supports the obvious harsh treatment of young mothers. Farrington and Morris carried out a study of magistrates' sentencing in cambridge and found that women who were divorced or separated or had a deviant family background were also more likely to receive harsher sentences. It depends on whether the woman fits the typical feminine role or not, whether she is of working class, middle class or upper class, whether she is a mother or not or whether she is employed or unemployed. All the bias which exists within the criminal justice system, whether it is because of race, gender, class or employment status, it all contributes to the rising prison crisis.

In 1981 Walker distinguishes between 'paper

justice' and 'real justice'. Paper justice would involve men and women given the same penalties for like offences but the real justice would take into consideration the suffering of a child or children if a woman is imprisoned. Although the aim of the criminal justice system is to be fair and equal other factors do need to be taken into consideration. Some measures can be taken to try to eradicate bias within the courts. Sentences should be based in the individual alone regardless of class, race or gender. All personal situations should be considered as well as the effect of imprisonment would have on the individual, their family, social status and employment. The first contact with official authorities when an offence has taken place is the police. Pre-conceived institutional and cultural bias must exist at this level and then spreads throughout the system. The improved monitoring of all arrests and through each stage of the criminal justice system could help with the problem of bias. Everyone who is involved in sentencing should receive racial awareness training as well as the introduction of ethnic monitoring. The Race Relations (Amendment) Act 2000 extended the legal duty not to discriminate on the grounds of race to the police. It also stated that all public bodies are to be put under legal duty to positively promote good race relations and equality of opportunities (The Guardian, 21st

February 2001).

There is no doubt that bias does exist in the criminal justice system but the offender is well aware of this bias. Although they feel powerless to prevent or challenge the bias their expectations of treatment in court are with the magistrates' and judges bias in mind. Offenders are aware of their class, race, gender and position in society and expect to be treated accordingly. Mothers who are imprisoned do not see the imprisonment as the main punishment in itself they feel that being separated from their children is a harsher punishment. It appears as if they are being punished twice, firstly by the imprisonment itself and secondly by the separation from their children. Society appears to accept the bias and lives in accordance to it. It is a self fulfilling prophecy.

The Work of Michael Foucault

Michael Foucault's main concern was with knowledge, power, the body and discipline. What Foucault called the 'human sciences'. Foucault believes that power is created through knowledge and this knowledge is created through discourse. During the pre-enlightenment years god was the source of all knowledge. People turned to religion to develop their knowledge and thereafter their societies through what Durkheim called the 'collective conscience', a group of shared ideas and moral values which derived from religion and shared among society. Durkheim describes these pre-enlightenment years as 'mechanical societies, societies which are based on obligations, customs and sentiment which has collective rules and social practices that are mainly religious in nature and a strong common conscience spread throughout all aspects of life, which existed before industrialisation. These were small close knit communities where everyone knew everyone else and the labour was shared among the community. The collective conscience and social solidarity was enforced by sacred laws based on religion. God was the absolute truth. Before the enlightenment punishment took on a different form of public executions. At this time god and religion were central and was the main source of all knowledge. To commit a criminal act would be considered to be an act against god. To show this disapproval executions were carried out in public as a show of power and control. This horrific act was a message to its audience of what would happen if an individual acted against god. A wide range of acts could be considered to be against god. After the enlightenment and the development of humanisation, rationalisation and human sciences the prison emerged. According to Foucault this change took place around 1750 and 1820 (Garland 1990). The process of punishment was centralised by government agencies. It was no longer acceptable to execute and torture so another method of control needed to take its place. The movement drifted away from physical punishment upon the body to punishment and control upon the body in Foucault's terms, the body meaning the way in which we conduct ourselves and in the way we behave. Within Foucault's work this is also described as 'discipline upon the body' or 'soul'. In the same way as suggested by Garland (1991) to imprison someone only restricts the physical body it does not change the way a person thinks and conducts themselves. In this sense it was a change from physical discipline to psychological discipline.

From a Marxist perspective this change was due to an increase in the need for labour through industrialisation. More workers were needed to supply the increase of the demand for goods.

Unlike Durkheim, Foucault believed that there was no absolute truth and all knowledge was constructed. He believed that we gain our knowledge through discourse and language and as both discourse and language are constructed therefore knowledge is also constructed. This construction of knowledge came with the enlightenment, the rationalisation of man, the realisation that people were different and the so called 'death of god', the movement away from religion. For those who make effective use of discourse to gain knowledge can also make practical and effective use of the power gained through it. For example, a doctor would effectively use his knowledge of the human body to diagnose illness and a teacher would use their knowledge to teach children which would, in Foucault's view, be passing on the knowledge of the teacher to the pupil and therefore enabling them to gain knowledge and according to Foucault gain power. So in Foucault's view we all possess knowledge and power, contradicting the Marxist view that power is held by one particular class to be used to oppress another class. We are all constantly passing on knowledge and recreating power and oppression. Because it is an ever changing construction, knowledge is constantly changing which means that people's ideas of other people and their behaviour are also constantly changing. The more knowledge we possess the more power we possess and unlike Marxism, we do not oppress one class over another but the more oppressed we become ourselves through developing idea of what is considered normal and abnormal. For Durkheim, this movement away from god came about due to industrialisation and the change from mechanical societies to 'organic societies'. Industrialisation brought about larger populations spread over larger areas and an increased complexity of division of labour, meaning when individuals are dependent on others to perform economic and productive functions which they cannot carry out themselves, which leads to occupational specialisation. This was a system of social relations where individuals were linked by contracts rather than by sentiment (Morris 1995) which changed people's ideas about each other.

Foucault based his work on categorisation. These categorisations were based on ideas of what was considered normal and abnormal. The constantly changing constructed knowledge constantly changed ideas of what was considered normal and abnormal and this knowledge, power and ideas of normality could be used to control behaviour. In Marxist terms the lack of knowledge and power between certain groups of people such as the doctor and his patient, the company owners and the workers, could be suggested as a way to oppress and avoid the working class gaining knowledge and subsequently power.

Durkheim claimed that these group categories preceded the formation of intellectual categories. He believed that among the ideas that individuals have, religion must have been the first fundamental system of ideas to explain and classify the external world *Morris 1995) and all the ideas are derived from religion. This could be considered true because there does exist a form of collective conscience in the form of society's agreement that murder is wrong. The idea that murder is wrong comes from the bible and other religions. Therefore it would be possible for a so called 'base collective conscience' to exist in the same way Marxism claims a base and superstructure exists. But, unlike Marxism, the superstructure does not reflect the base because of gained knowledge and power, the rationalisation of man and the changing ideas of what is considered normal and abnormal.

For those who possess the knowledge, possess the power, and this power can be used to place knowledge upon the body. Foucault saw the human body as the ultimate material which is seized and shaped by all political, economic and penal institutions which are systems of production, domination and socialisation fundamentally depend upon the successful subjugation of bodies (Garland 1991). This knowledge can be used to 'normalise' people through the process of what Foucault calls normalisation. This normalisation process is based on the different categories of what is considered normal and abnormal and can be enforced through disciplinary procedure. An example of how power and knowledge placed upon the body can be used to normalise through disciplinary procedure would be to examine the military system. The army prides itself on discipline, regulation and conformity and enforces this through harsh regimes, strict rules and regulation and constant observation.

Foucault discusses 'technologies of power' which are techniques of observation and regulation similar to those used in the military. Knowledge over the body can be used to create more power and the knowledge can be gained through observation through the use of the 'panopticon'. Visibility and inspection was the central feature of Bentham's panopticon prison design in the eighteenth century. The panopticon was a circular shaped building with a tower at the centre. The tower was pierced with wide windows that open onto the inner side of the ring, the outer part of the building is divided into cells, each of which extends the whole width of the building, they have two windows, one on the inside, corresponding to the windows of the tower, the other on the outside allowing light to cross the cell from one end to the other. All that is needed is to place a supervisor in the tower and the individuals are constantly visible, (McLaughlin and Muncie 2001). This enforced discipline at all times. The positioning of the cells and the use of light made this possible. Although the panopticon designed by Bentham was never built, San Francisco's newest prison is that of a panoptic design and has been praised by the inmates because of the way it undermines the culture of rape to be found in other establishments, (Pecora 2002). Foucault argued that other institutions other than prisons began to use this same form of knowledge and power. This form of power, visibility, inspection and surveillance was used to exercise control in factories, with the main office usually higher than the working floor so the management could overlook the workers, in schools, with the increasing use of closed circuit television, high school gates, and in most modern secondary schools the use of swipe cards to gain entry and exit to, not just the school but in individual parts of the school and many of our workplaces, places both private and public. All resembling the panopticon structure and the panopticon was a mechanism of power (Foucault 1977). The main idea behind the panopticon was that the disciplinary power, the visibility, the inspection and the observation affected people's behaviour (Wilson 2001). This is evident not only throughout today's modern prisons but also throughout modern secondary schools and hospitals with the increasing use of surveillance methods including closed circuit television, security doors and passes, well lit corridors and monitoring systems, which according to Foucault have the same disciplinary functions.

The change to rationalisation and observation also brought about a new way of collecting data. At the end of the eighteenth century and the beginning of the nineteenth century a huge interest developed in the ways in which the new data could be put to use. Some of these were new technologies for classifying and gathering figure (Hacking 1990) collecting and processing new information or, in Foucault's terms, collecting and processing new knowledge, which could provide the basis upon which the normal could be defined from the abnormal (Foucault 1991).

Gary Marx (1988) discusses how we all have to take part in this surveillance process by the use of banking, medical care, insurance, jobs, credit and loans and, most of all, a national insurance number. As a result of this many records and data are kept which gives insight to our economy, supporting a Marxist view, and our social lives become components of our social selves (Poster 1991)

Foucault himself never directly addressed issues relating to computerisation, but Mork Poster (1991) talks about the presence of a 'superpanopticon' where information and communication technologies make it possible for huge amounts of data to be regularly gathered and processed at a fast rate. These information and communication technologies are the perfect tools of modern societies to accelerate and amplify the conduct of surveillance, (Innes 2003). When large amounts of data about a wide range of social activities can be gathered this can then be used to monitor how people are behaving and therefore more effective interventions upon the body can be used to control and normalise.

According to Davis Lyon (1994) these developments in surveillance cause changes in social order, social interaction and social relations. He argues that surveillance can be used as a 'surrogate mechanism' for generating some sense of trust between people. This can be seen in the sense of self regulation induced by surveillance. One can be more trusting if both are under constant surveillance or do not know if they are being observed or not. All these mechanisms of power were and are used to 'normalise' the individual through observation and modern law until there is no longer a need to observe because the individual forms a sense of self regulation. They become so used to being observed even when those mechanisms are not in place the individual still abides by the normalisation. It has been suggested this is why many people leaving the armed forces have difficulties in adjusting to civilian life because it is not as obviously observed and regulated as army life where there is a much higher degree of discipline in the form of hierarchy. The Panopticon as a 'technology of power' is used to explain Foucault's notion of 'hierarchical observation'. Observation from a higher status. The higher status which holds the knowledge, power and the ideas of what is normal, which could be considered as, not a collective conscience as Durkheim suggests but a 'false consciousness' created to oppress and control one class over another in a Marxist perspective. Foucault does suggest the penalty legitimates law's role in promoting and protecting the interests of the ruling class. In Foucault's terms even the hierarchy are still subject to the same kind of observation and self regulation as everyone else. More so for people who are constantly in the media. They are constantly being judged on how they behave and are far more likely to be criticised because of our idea of what is normal and abnormal, what is acceptable and what is not acceptable behaviour.

Foucault's focus on power and surveillance has been criticised by Garland for being too reductivist and ignores the guarantees provided by modern law and does not take into account the formation of new knowledge about people and society such as, feminism, civil rights and advances in medicine. Garland does not say that power is not important but Foucault fails to take into account the culture, mentality and sensibility of different groups of people and societies. In the similar way Durkheim assumes everyone thinks the same way in forming a collective conscience, Garland argues that Foucault does not take into account individual thoughts and feelings, or forms of resistance, resistance that can be used to the benefit of societies or individual groups as well as oppress them. Foucault also does not take into account the multi cultural society where many different groups of people have their own beliefs, religions and ideas of what is normal and what is abnormal. What may be considered as normal for one group of people or one individual may be considered as abnormal to the other. He also assumes that there will be no political resistance or objection the the ideas of what is normal and abnormal.

Chapter 13
The Criminal Justice System

The Law and Society

Natural law is the doctrine that just laws are immanent in nature, they can be claimed as discovered and are not created by such things as a Bill of Rights. It can also emerge from a natural process of resolving conflicts which are embodied by what is known as common law. These two aspects are actually very different but can also oppose or compliment each other. They do share a common trait of relying on immanence as opposed to design in finding just laws. The concept of natural law was important in the development of Anglo-American common law. Parliament often made reference to the Fundamental Laws of England which embodied natural law since time immemorial and sets limits on the power of the monarchy. The concept of natural law was expressed in the English Bill of Rights and the United States Declaration of Independence and by the nineteenth century anarchist and legal theorist Lysander Spooner (1808) (Shively 1971). Due to the influence of Thomas Aquinas (1224 - 1274) the Roman Catholic Church understands natural law to be immanent in nature. Theories of law which are based on natural law are, libertarianism and anarcho capitalism where legal positivism rejects natural law and is based on scientific fact, that which can be proven. Natural law views crime as the violation of individual rights. Since rights are considered as natural, rather than man made, what constitutes as a crime is also natural, in contrast to laws which are man made. Adam Smith (1723 - 1790) illustrates this view by stating that, a smuggler would be an excellent citizen, *'had not the laws of his country made that a crime which nature never meant to be so.'* (Smith 1723 - 1790). Natural law theory distinguishes between criminality and illegality, the former being derived from human nature, and the latter being derived from the interests of those in power. This view leads to a seeming paradox, that an act can be illegal that is not a crime, while a criminal act could be perfectly legal.

'Individual rights' is a legal term which refers to what an individual is allowed to do and what can be done to an individual. Individual rights are considered to be central to a 'due process model' of criminal justice. In Western discourse, individual rights are commonly assumed to be inversely related to social control. In contrast, much of recent political discourse on individual rights in China, particularly with respect to due process and rule of law, has focused on how protection of individual rights actually makes social control by the government more effective (China has the lowest crime rate and the fewest number of police). The Universal Declaration of Human Rights 1948 and subsequent declarations, established individual rights, in theory, as the basis of international norms. Individual rights can be divided into negative rights, what the government cannot do to you, and positive rights, what you are entitled to from society. The distinction between negative and positive rights can illustrate the difference between political ideologies. For example, many adherents to libertarian and conservative ideologies believe that the primary role of the government is to protect negative rights, and with restrictions of government control the prosperity that is envisioned positive rights will follow. The issue in ideology is that it can be understood as a source of manipulation. Law as ideology directs its subjects in ways that are not transparent to the subjects themselves, in this view, law cloaks power. The idea of law, in contrast, involves a set of institutions that regulate or restrain power with reference to norms of justice. The presence of the ideology in law must compromise law's integrity. Not only is the view of law as ideology is at odds with a lot of mainstream thinking about law, it seems difficult to reconcile with the central philosophical positions on the nature of law, e.g. a positive conception of law as a set of formal rules, or a natural law conception where law is identified with moral principles (Fletcher 1996).

At one time societies handled their differences in private. Some modern societies still do, like the civil law systems of France and Germany. The decisions of what was considered right and wrong was left in the hands of the people. It was things like folkways, mores, customs and norms that were sufficient for most problems. In contrast, everything about criminal law today is in the hands of the legislators, crimes are 'owned' by the state. According to the government this is because of a duty or obligation to protect certain basic, underlying 'societal interests' that cannot be taken care of by citizens themselves. This paternalistic stance is a rather rudimentary form of the idea of Social Contract, a relatively weak philosophical position that does not benefit minorities very well (majority rule: minority right). This is in direct opposition to the idea of Natural Law, which hold that there are certain universal elements to morality and individual conscience that does not necessarily require the coercive power of the state nor government intervention. Natural Law, unfortunately, does not provide much specific guidance for rule making. Constitutions are largely written in terms of Natural Law which acts as a check on Social Contract judge-made law which by its paternalistic nature is designed for the betterment of society, Positive law.

It has been said that all crime is an injury against society and there does not always have to be a victim. Society, as a whole, via its legislatures, has presumably made a collective judgment that certain behaviours are harmful to certain 'societal interests'. Criminal law is distinguished from all other kinds of law because it carries with it the moral condemnation of all society. The essence of Criminal Law is its common punishment (Hart 1958). Criminal Law defines crime and its elements but it also provides the impetus for voluntary, positive, moral action, as Samaha (1999) puts it, *'a last resort as a method of social control'*. It seems best to think of Criminal Law as, a set of both proscriptive (prohibited) and prescriptive (preferred) rules for conduct. Some crimes are moral or ethical commitments known as the *law behind the law'* (Gardner and Anderson 1996). They are supposed to compel people to a higher standard of conduct which is prescribed by the Criminal Law, such as omissions.

Breaking the law may involve a moral lapse, accident or mistake. Crime ordinarily involves something deeper which is unjustifiable and inexcusable. Sometimes the distinction is made by saying that the Criminal Law is amoral (a set of impersonal, rational rules) and that crime always involves morality. Another way of saying this is that a person accused of a crime is being tried for being a certain kind of person. So called Status Offences, like vagrancy and curfew violation. According to Hall (1949) any crime has seven elements and a crime is any:

* Legally proscribed (the concept of Legality)
* Human conduct (the concept of the Actus Reus, (the act))
* Causative (the concept of Causation)
* Of the given harm (the concept of Social Harm)
* Which coincides with (the concept of Concurrence)
* A blameworthy frame of mind (the concept of Mens Rea (the thinking))
* For which punishment is provided (the concept of punishment)

The most important aspects are the Actus Reus and the Mens Rea. The Actus Reus is a phrase which means evil or bad deed and is derived from an old Latin phrase, and in many ways, is what separates Criminology from Theology because those who work with criminals all the time cannot be concerned with, or inclined to punish bad thoughts. The government is not concerned with evil unless it manifests behaviour.

Religion is concerned with evil as manifested in thought. An act does not make a person guilty unless the mind is guilty. The concept of Mens Rea is a phrase meaning evil or bad mind. The best way to understand Mens Rea is to know that it is always invisible. Intent cannot be proven like a motive can but, you cannot really blame someone for their motive if it is understandable, they can only be blamed for their intent. It is impossible to get inside the mind of every offender. A confession is the nearest thing to direct evidence of Mens Rea.

There is a whole set of laws which exist for what are called inchoate crimes (incomplete crimes) and from a legal point of view 'communication' is a form of action. There are three main inchoate offences, incitement, conspiracy and attempt. An inchoate offence is one that is 'committed by doing an act with the purpose of affecting some other offence' (Allen 2003). It is committed when the defendant takes certain steps towards the commission of a crime. With incitement the defendant must have tried to persuade another to commit a crime. With conspiracy at least two defendants must have agreed to commit a crime and, finally, with attempt, the defendant must have tried to commit an offence and have got relatively close to achieving the objective. With inchoate crimes mental state is irrelevant because the criminal statutes have usually described the behaviour so well that the principle of Vicarious Liability applies. Anyone who participates in the planning, design or cover up of a crime is subjected to the same penalties as a person who actually carries it out. This is very controversial area of law and some statutes require a combination of communication and conduct but once combinations are applied evidence of bad thoughts may be admissible. The closest term we have for when wicked thoughts are assumed to apply to the act is 'malice'. This is an example of natural law being applied but in a positivistic law system it appears to be only of convenience. When applying natural law the problem which arises is, which is more important, guilty actions or guilty thought or must it be a combination of both.

The Actus Reus of incitement is the act of persuading, encouraging or threatening another to commit a crime. In the case of *Most* (1881) 7 QBD 244, the defendant published in a London newspaper an article urging readers around the world to follow the example of those in Russia and murder their Heads of State. This was held to be incitement to murder contrary to s. 4 of the Offences Against the Person Act 1861. It is clear, in this case, that natural law has been applied. The action can be proven and the 'evil thought' has been assumed. It may have been possible that the defendant may not have intended anyone to take the article seriously, the crime was assumed to be, under Natural Law, as morally wrong therefore convicted. The Mens Rea of incitement states that the inciter must intend that as a result of his persuasion, the incitee will bring about the crime. In this case it did not. Generally the incitee must know the facts that make the conduct incited criminal. Which they would have, murder is considered as a universal wrong, hence, Natural Law. A defendant can only be guilty of incitement to handle stolen goods if the incitee knew or believed the goods in question to be stolen. However, the inciter might still be guilty of attempted incitement and if an innocent incitee committed the crime the inciter could be liable as a principal offender acting through an innocent agent. There can be liability for incitement to commit the impossible only if the commission of the crime was possible at the time of incitement. A n offender can still be charged even if the offence is impossible for example, if an offender attempted to steal from a bag that contained nothing under Natural Law it is still morally wrong to steal therefore they would be guilty. One advantage of the offence of incitement is that there can be an arrest before the crime is committed. It can also deter people from committing the offence as it carries the same sentence as actually committing the offence. The moral element of this is that harm was intended complying with Natural Law. But at the same time there has not actually been a crime committed therefore it is punishing people for evil thoughts not facts. According to Natural Law this is immoral thoughts therefore should be punished.

In the case of conspiracy the Actus Reus states that there must be an agreement between at least two people. They both must reach a state where they agree to carry out the commission of the offence so far as it lies within their power to do so. Once agreement is reached it must be communicated (an action) between them both. Section 2 of the Criminal Law Act 1977 places certain restrictions upon who can become parties to a conspiracy. Section 2(1) provides that a person cannot be charged with conspiracy if he or she is the intended victim of the crime. This causes problems in the case of fake death for insurance purposes as a conspiracy must take place and under Natural Law it is still considered morally wrong. Section 2(2) provides that a person cannot be charged with conspiracy if the other party or parties to the conspiracy of: (a) that person's spouse, (b) a person under the age of ten, or (c) the intended victim of the conspiracy. In the case of point (a) under Natural Law the spouse would be just as guilty. They have still conspired to commit an offence, they should be both charged equally. In the case of point (b) it is questionable to consider a child under ten as being morally responsible. One of the strongest examples of Natural Law is the offence of conspiracy to Corrupt Public Morals or Outrage Public Decency. These offences are wide and have no real definition. In the case of *Shaw v DPP* [1962] 2 A11 220, Shaw published a directory of prostitutes. Shaw could not be charged with the offence of corrupting public morals because there was no way of telling if he actually did and at the time there was no charge he could only be charged with conspiring to corrupt public morals. Under Natural Law the moral aspect of the offence should be taken into consideration. In this case the House of Lords held that a conspiracy to corrupt public morals is an offence. In the case of *Knuller v DPP* [1972] 2 A11 ER 898, a homosexual organised a contact magazine for over twenty one's although no offence was actually committed it was held by a majority in the House of Lords that there is a common law offence of outraging public decency and, consequently, it is an offence to conspire to outrage public decency.

Natural Law and the offence of attempt can be more complicated when the basis of Natural Law is morals. Section 1(1) of the Criminal Attempts Act 1981 provides that:

'If, with intent to commit an offence to which this section applies, a person does an act which is more than merely preparatory to the commission of the offence, he is guilty of attempting to commit the offence.

Under s1 (4) of the Criminal Attempts Act 1981, the Criminal Attempts Act 1981 only applies to indictable offences (unless parliament specifically provides in another statute) and s1 (4) abolishes liability for: attempting to aid, abet, counsel or procure the commission of any offence, attempted conspiracy, and attempted to assist an offender contrary to s4 (1) of the Criminal Law Act 1967. The Actus Reus of attempt states, the prosecution must prove that the defendant committed an act which was *'more than merely preparatory acts come to an end and the defendant embarks upon the crime proper.'* When that is will depend upon the facts in any particular case. For example, in the case of *Rv Gullefer* (1990) 91 Cr App R 356, Gullefer put a bet on a dog in a race because his dog was losing he ran onto the track to void the race so he could get his money back, it did not work and the race continued therefore he was found not guilty. He would only have been charged if the race was stopped and he had got his money back. Under Natural Law he should have been found guilty because he had the intent and he also carried out all the actions required to carry out the offence it was just luck on the racers half that he did not manage to stop the race. He still acted immorally. The Mens Rea of attempt states that section 1(1) refers to the defendant acting *'with intent to commit an offence'* Therefore, only intention to commit the offence in question will suffice as the mens rea for attempt. In the case of *R v Pearman* (1984) 80 Cr App R 259, it was held that the word 'intent' in section 1 has the same meaning as in the common law of attempts. The court applied *R v Mohan* [1976] QB 1, where the Court of Appeal held that there must be proved

'a decision to bring about, in so far as it lies within the accused's power, the commission of the offence which it is alleged the accused attempted to commit, no matter whether the desired that consequence of his act or not'.

Once again a person can be committed of an offence when an actual offence has not been committed. The basis of this lies in Natural Law. All the actions leading up to the offence have been carried out and in order to do this the offence must have been thought about therefore the Actus Reus and the Mens Rea have been completed. In the case of murder if a defendant acquired a loaded gun and intended to kill someone and went on to carry out the offence in full and then missed the intended victim then, under Natural Law, they should be found guilty of murder. All the moral implications of the offence have been carried out but under the present law system the offender would be guilty of attempted murder even though they carried out all the required actions and had the guilty mind it does not seem moral that they should be charged with attempt just because they missed their intended victim.

Although our present law system appears to base itself on Positive Law, on scientific facts, Natural Law, the morals of human behaviour still plays a large and influential part, particularly in the case of inchoate crimes. Because the crime has not been complete the main emphasis is on the guilty mind, the moral aspect of the offence. Problems arise when trying to determine at what point the offence constitutes an attempt and an actual crime. This is why inchoate crimes carry the same sentence as the actual offence, once again an offender is being punished for evil thoughts and it is their Actus Reus which proves their Mens Rea. Overall our law system is based on both Positive and Natural Law but it appears that the system uses whichever fits best to which ever crime in order to get the best outcome. We are then left with another question of, for who is the best outcome for, the offender, the public or the authorities.

Magistrates' and Crown Court

Here we will look at the role and workings of both the Magistrates' Court and the Crown Court, we will also look at the role of each member of both courts and look at the differences and similarities between the two. We will also look at the different types of cases and some of the problems within the court system.

Magistrates' Courts are administered through local committees' within a national framework set by the Lord Chancellor. There are two types of Magistrates' within the court, 'lay magistrates' and 'district judges'. Lay magistrates' have no formal legal qualifications but do receive some training, they receive no payment for their services and give their time voluntarily. There are around 30,000 lay magistrates'. They sit in panels of usually two or three but no more than seven and together they hear cases. 97% of all criminal court cases are tried by lay magistrates'

District Judges (previously called a Stipendiary Magistrate) who are legally qualified and are usually trained as a solicitor or barrister. The District Judge is also appointed by the Lord Chancellor and he does receive a salary. There are about 90 District Judges.

There judges sit on their own to hear cases.

The Magistrates' Court Clerk is legally trained and advises the Lay Magistrates' on the law and their powers, e.g as to imprison or to fine a defendant, also to advise them on court procedure.

The Court Usher is the only member of the Magistrates' Court to wear a uniform which is a black gown. They are responsible for the smooth running of the court. They also liaise with the people involved in the case being heard. It is also the ushers job to announce each case.

Facing the magistrates' in court is the Prosecution Solicitor and the Defence Solicitor. The Prosecution Solicitor is a member of the Crown Prosecution Service, this is an independent body which is usually instructed by the police and prosecutes on behalf of the Crown. The Defence Solicitor will come into court with their client and will stand and speak on their behalf. The Defence Solicitor will also put forward any mitigating circumstances, these being anything that might persuade the judge to be lenient. They may also be a member of the Probation Service in court. The Probation Officer is sometimes called upon to give written reports about the defendant or to supervise various sentences such as community service.

All summary (less serious) offences, such as,

criminal damage less than £5000, drink driving or driving without insurance, start at the Magistrates' Court. There will be an initial hearing where the accused first appears in court and it is established which type of case it is, depending on the crime, and committal proceedings take place to establish if their is a case to be heard. This is a way of cutting out unnecessary trials saving time and money. Committal Proceedings are where the defendant is sent by the Magistrates' Court to be tried at Crown Court. This can happen when the offence is triable either way and the defendant has chosen for the case to be heard at the Crown Court or the magistrates' think the offence is too serious to be tried by them. Either way cases are cases with higher significance such as theft, burglary or A.B.H where the defendant is asked which court they would like their case to be tried in. In 1999 and 2000 the Government tried to remove the defendant's right to choose to be tried in the Magistrates' Court or the Crown Court. On both occasions the House of Lords voted against the change. In the Crown Court the case will be tried by a jury.

The magistrates' can also decide whether to grant arrest warrants, if the offence is punishable by imprisonment, search warrants or whether the defendant should be granted bail. If the defendant is granted bail while waiting for the next stage of their trial under the 'Bail Act 1976' states that there is a presumption that the defendant should be granted bail, but they can be refused by a magistrate if they are good reasons for believing that the defendant would not surrender or would commit further offences or would interfere with witnesses. When bail is granted conditions may be imposed by the magistrates' such as, they must reside at a Bail Hostel and/or report daily/weekly to the police. In making a sentence the magistrates' or District Judge will take into consideration the seriousness of the crime, information supplied by the solicitor, probation officer, medical report and previous convictions.

Magistrates' will also hear Youth Courts, these are not open to the public and they must have at least one woman on the bench. This court is much more informal. They also have some civil jurisdiction which includes, licensing pubs, enforcing demands for council tax, hearing family cases and proceedings under the 'Children's Act 1989'.

The Crown Court tries more serious crimes such as, murder, assault and G.B.H. They also hear appeals from the Magistrates' Court. It sits in more than 90 permanent centres throughout England and Wales. Each centre being designated as 1st, 2nd or 3rd tier depending on the seriousness of the offence. First tier deals with both criminal and High Court civil cases. Second tier deals with only criminal cases and the third tier deals with criminal cases and are served by circuit judges and recorders only. Trials in the Crown Court are heard by a jury of twelve people's elected at random from the electoral register. They are directed on matters of the law by the judge, who may be one of 84 High Court Judges. There are currently 78 main Crown Court Centres divided into six regions known as circuits. Within the Crown Court the Judges deal with the law of a case and the jury deals with the facts of the case. The facts must be beyond reasonable doubt. Barristers speak on behalf of the defendant instead of the solicitors in Magistrates' Courts, the solicitor has no rights of audience, only the barrister can speak. Barristers are experts in their field, they have undertaken more education and are very specific in one subject e.g murder cases or family cases. You can only see a barrister through a solicitor, although some solicitors can act as a barrister but only after extensive education.

Once a case has been transferred to Crown Court a plea and directions hearing will be held to establish if the plea is guilty or not guilty. If the defendant pleads guilty the judge will decide the sentence, if the plea is not guilty the trial takes place.

There are advantages and disadvantages to

both the Magistrates' Court and the Crown Court but most importantly by tradition and experience Crown Court juries seem to be more prepared to enter verdicts of not guilty than are magistrates'. The usual reason is that Magistrates' hear hundreds of cases and come to see the defendants in a jaundiced way, where as juries come with fresh minds and probably have a better awareness of the lifestyles of the defendants, but no one can really know for sure. Some unofficial statistics suggest that fifty percent more of those who go to trial in the Crown Court are found not guilty than in Magistrates' Courts. according to 'Mojuk: Newsletter' 'Inside Out No58' wrongful criminal convictions are an everyday feature of the Criminal Justice System. It goes on to say that successful appeals against criminal convictions showed that in the decade 1989 to 1999 The Court of Appeal (Criminal Division) abated over 8,470 criminal convictions, a yearly average of 770. In addition to this there are around 3,500 quashed criminal convictions per year at the Crown Court for convictions obtained at the Magistrates' Court.

Crown Court Judges have greater powers of sentencing than Magistrates'. The most a Magistrate can sentence is six months imprisonment or twelve months for two offences or fines up to £5,000. A six months sentence in the Magistrates' Court could carry three years in the Crown Court. This is an overwhelming advantage for the defendant. There is no longer a waiting time before the matter is dealt with in the Crown Court. According to Home Office statistics there is a national average 68 days for proceedings in Magistrates' Court for indictable cases between 1999 and 2001. In South Yorkshire it is 100 days between the same years but this figure depends on the number of offences cleared up by the police as a result of a charge or summons rather than a caution or other means. Magistrates' may say at the end of a trial if they feel their sentencing powers are insufficient and send the case to Crown Court. A decision to stay in the Magistrates' Court does not promise a sentence in the Magistrates' Court. Another great advantage of the Magistrates' Court is that they are much cheaper to the system and possibly the defendant. If a defendant was to choose a Crown Court for a minor offence they may find they have a lot more costs to pay.

As the main aims of the Criminal Justice System are to,

* Reduce crime and the fear of crime as well as social and economic costs.
* To reduce crime and disorder.
* Reduce the impact of crime and

disorder on lives.

    * To dispense justice fairly and promote confidence in the law.

    * To ensure just process and effective outcomes.

    * To be dealt with at speed.

    * Meet the needs of the victims, witnesses and jurors.

    * Respect the rights of the defendant and to treat them fairly.

According to government statistics, cautions, court proceedings and sentencing in England and Wales, 2000, published in November 2001, there were 1,911,600 completed proceedings at Magistrates' Courts in 2000 that is 1% more than 1999 and 95,300 defendants had proceedings completed at the Crown Court 2% fewer than in 1999. The custody rate indictable offences was 14% at Magistrates' Court and 64% at Crown Court.

In conclusion the statistics show that slightly more proceedings were completed in Magistrates' Court than in Crown Court and the 2% decrease in Crown Court shows that more defendants are wishing to have their trials heard in the Magistrates' Court. The powers of sentencing have an effect on these figures as most defendants are aware of the more severe sentencing in the Crown Court. Overall the

Criminal Justice System continues to make changes and developments to improve the service. Cases are now heard quicker and dealt with appropriately although many may agree that sentencing powers would benefit from an increase. Looking at the aims of the Criminal Justice System there are points that many may be in disagreement over, for example, are the needs of the victims met to a high enough standard? and the defendant appears to have more rights than the victim. Statistically the system seems to be fair and just but as with many statistics they do not portray the true life scenario.

Crown Prosecution Service

The Crown Prosecution Service (CPS) was created in 1985 under the Prosecution of Offences Act and began operating in 1986. It is responsible for prosecuting people in England and Wales who have been charged with a criminal offence following investigations by the police.

It is headed by the Director of Public Prosecutions and is divided into 13 geographic areas across England and Wales, with each area being led by a Chief Crown Prosecutor. The CPS employs over 8,000 people in total.

The role of the CPS?

The main functions of the CPS are:

* to give advice to the police regarding potential cases for prosecution;
* to review cases submitted to them by the police;
* to determine any charges, if appropriate (except for in minor cases); and
* to prepare and present cases at both the Magistrates' and the Crown Courts.

The CPS is made up of prosecutors, who are barristers and solicitors with the role of prosecuting criminal cases at court; paralegals, who assist in the preparation of cases for court; and administrators. There are also two specialist casework groups – the Central Fraud Group and Serious Crime Group – that are responsible for prosecutions on all cases investigated by the UK Border Agency, the Serious and Organised Crime Agency and HMRC, along with terrorism, fraud and serious crime. The CPS deals exclusively with criminal prosecutions.

The Decision to prosecute

In making case decisions, Crown Prosecutors follow the principles contained within the Code for Crown Prosecutors. The decision on whether or not to prosecute a suspect will be made by applying two tests, as outlined in the Code:

    * The evidential test: Crown Prosecutors must first consider whether there is enough reliable evidence (gathered by the police) to provide a 'realistic prospect of conviction' against each defendant on each charge. This is an objective test, meaning that, if it is satisfied, a jury or bench of magistrates will be more likely than not to convict the defendant of the alleged charge. In deciding whether a particular case satisfies this test, Crown Prosecutors must also take the defence case into account. If there is no realistic prospect of conviction based on the evidence available, then the case will fail the evidential test and must not go ahead, irrespective of how serious it may be.

    * The public interest test: if the case satisfies the evidential test, then prosecutors will need to consider whether prosecution in that particular case is in the public interest. In most cases, a prosecution will take place unless there are significant public interest reasons against prosecution, which outweigh those in favour of it. The more serious the offence or criminal record, the more likely it is that a prosecution will be needed in the public interest. Both tests need to be satisfied for a case to proceed for prosecution.

With regard to determining appropriate charges in particular cases, prosecutors will make decisions with reference to Charging Standards for offences, which is agreed between the CPS and the police.

The Use of Juries

The use of juries in criminal trials continues to raise conflicting opinions amongst lawyers, politicians and the general public. The right to be trial by jury can be traced back to the Magna Carta (The Great Charter of Liberties, 1215) and are used in both Criminal and Civil Courts where the judge decide the law and the jury decide the facts of a case. (The Bushell's case 1670 6 St.Tr. 999) established the independence of the jury from the judge so jurors could not be bullied into a conviction by the judge. In criminal cases if the defendant is found guilty the judge decides an appropriate sentence. In civil cases the jury decides on how much damages are awarded.

To qualify for jury service a person must be aged between eighteen and seventy, registered on the electoral roll and have lived in the United Kingdom for at least five years since the age of thirteen. Computers produce a random list from the electoral register and summonses are sent out. Vetting can take place using the police and Special Branch records to check that the potential juror does not hold controversial views, although there are guidelines laid down by the Attorney-General, it is impossible to know if they are being followed since the process in not controlled by legislation. Certain people are ineligible for jury service, these are, people suffering from mental disorders, the judiciary and others concerned with the administration of justice and the clergy. People with certain criminal convictions and those currently on bail in criminal proceedings and are disqualified from becoming a juror under the Juries Disqualification Act 1984. Certain people may be 'excused as of right' these are, anyone aged sixtyfive to seventy, anyone who did jury service in the last two years, members of parliament, the medical profession, the armed forces and practicing members of a religious society. Previously it was common place for a judge to dismiss a juror who had disabilities including deafness, as it was assumed they were incapable of performing their duty. Therefore The Criminal Justice and Public Order Act 1994 introduced a new section 9B into the Juries Act 1974 stating that a person with a disability may be brought before the judge if there is any doubt that they can serve, but lays down a presumption that they will serve unless the judge thinks that that person will not act effectively. although this does not help people who are deaf and in need of a sign language interpreter as interpreters are not allowed into the jury room. There can also be a 'discretionary excusal' which means a person can be excused from service if the judge believes they have a good reason, this could mean holidays booked or a lack of childcare. This seems to rule out a large number of people from attending jury service and they may appear to be left with the people who have 'nothing else to do'. People who are in insignificant low paid jobs which suggests a lower education and who may have difficulties understanding the case. This has been a major issue for the Civil Courts concerning complex fraud cases where the jury may acquit rather than convict an innocent person through lack of understanding of the case. This could be an explanation for the high acquittal rate in jury trials. It has been suggested by Morton (Law Society Gazette 99/48 12th December 2002) that these complex cases should be heard by a judge alone. therefore too many discretionary excusals leads to an unrepresentative jury. Sir Robin auld produced a government commissioned report published 8th October 2001 which recommended a crackdown on this problem. A Home Office study 2000 found that two out of three people called for jury service avoided it through being exempt, disqualified or excused. A way of improving the jury system could be to copy that of New York where judges do jury service where there would be little concern about the understanding of the case. Auld also made a number of recommendations regarding the problem of perverse acquittals, where the jury acquit in the face of all evidence as in the case of R v Ponting (1985 Crim LR 318) where the judge made it clear that the defendant was guilty of an offence under the Official Secrets Act but the jury returned a not guilty verdict. Auld recommends that prosecutors should be able to challenge these perverse acquittals.

Another attempt to reform the Criminal Justice System was the proposal to abolish the right to a jury trial in triable either way cases. In July 1998 the Government issued a paper outlining a number of options for reform. They opted to abolish the election for trial and leave it up to the magistrates' to decide and in November 1999 published a Criminal Justice (Mode of Trial) Bill which was rejected by the House of Lords in January 2000. The Government went on to introduce a second Bill in February 2000 and this too was rejected. It has been suggested that this would reduce costs and free jurors to concentrate on the more serious crimes but it has been argued that this would take away the defendant's right to a fair trial. It has also been argued that the use of juries make the Legal System more open because it involves members of the public yet juries deliberate in private and no one can enquire into what happened in the jury room or between jurors. They do not have to give any reasons as to why or how they reached their decision, therefore there is no way of knowing if the jury really understood the case or came to their decision based on the facts or for the right reasons as in the case of R v Young (1992) Court of Appeal, as reported in The Times, 30th December 1992, known as the 'Ouija' Board case where a number of the jurors' while in the hotel, used a ouija board to contact the dead victim and claimed that they had received certain information from him bearing upon the case but the court could not enquire into what had been said between jurors during their deliberations as specified in section 8(1) Contempt of Court Act 1981. It was pointed out that the ouija board session had took place in the hotel room not the courtroom, affidavits were taken from the jurors and it turned out that they had been drinking and a retrial was ordered, amounting to a great deal of wasted costs. It has been suggested that the Lord Chancellor could make it a rule that drinking while serving on a jury should be strictly prohibited.

It has also been noted that jurors may be bias against certain groups or individuals, as in the case of R v Ford (1989) QB 868 CA involving an Anti-National Front demonstration, the judge ordered that the jury should be drawn from an area with a large

Asian population (English Legal System. Elliot. C, Quinn. F. 2002) this approach was rejected as wrong. The Court of Appeal held that race could not be taken into account when selecting jurors. Within liable cases jurors tend to be prejudiced against newspapers and award huge damages as in the case of Jeffrey Archer who was awarded £500,000 in 1987. These cases are very expensive and juries increase the cost as the cases tend to last longer. The jury does not have to give any reasons for the amount of damages awarded.

Media coverage especially in high profile cases can also influence jurors. The idea of secrecy of the jury room should protect them from outside pressure and influence when deciding a verdic,t but unfortunately this is not always the case, and it is difficult to see how they could have no contact with any media whatsoever while outside the jury room and not to be influenced by it in some way. The disadvantage of jury 'nobbling' must be taken into consideration, as jurors can be intimidated into reaching a certain verdict. A reform was introduced in the Criminal Procedure and Investigation Act 1996 Section 54 of the act states that where a person has been acquitted of an offence and someone is subsequently convicted of interfering with or intimidating jurors or witnesses in the case then the High Court can quash the acquittal and the person can be retried. This, will in no doubt, reduce the risk of jury nobbling.

In November 2002 the Queen gave a speech outlining a number of Bills to reform the Criminal Justice System. One of those is to allow judge and jury to hear all the facts of a case including any relevant previous convictions of a defendant. James Morton (freelance journalist, The Law Gazette, 12th December 2002) states, it is not clear how much of a defendant's previous convictions would be allowed and would this include arrests? And according to Liberty (Liberty's response to Queen's speech 13th November 2002) this may lead to more convictions but far too many of them would be wrongful convictions as previous convictions do not prove that someone committed the offence in question just because they may appear likely to have. Another Bill within the Queen's speech is to abolish 'Double Jeopardy' once acquitted of a crime that person cannot be retried for the same offence. a defendant acquitted could freely walk outside the court and admit to the crime he has just been acquitted from and nothing could be done about it. The Bill will allow retrials for those acquitted of a serious offence where new and compelling evidence emerges. The questions need to be asked, which in itself may cause problems are, what will be considered as compelling evidence?

And what crimes will be considered serious? Liberty's response to the Queen's speech, it may help to convict a few more serious criminals but will lead to repeat prosecutions for many innocent people, even when they are acquitted their ordeal will not be over and the police and prosecutors will know they can have another go and would not have to tackle the real problems of incompetent investigations.

It appears that there are more disadvantages to juries than advantages and all the evidence suggests that there are still many arguments and issues to be resolved surrounding the use of juries both in Criminal Courts and Civil Courts. One of the main issues being the selection of jurors and the amount of excusals occurring with many aspects of the Criminal Justice System. It will take a lot of work and reform to make the system fair and just for everyone. The main point being The Criminal Justice System cannot please all of the people involved both within the courts and the public all of the time.

Chapter 14
Violence in Society

Dark Figure of Crime

The 'dark figure of crime' is a term that is used by sociologists and other who study crime to describe the number of crimes committed that are not reported and therefore concerned authorities are not aware of. This puts into question the efficiency and the effectiveness of official crime statistics and data. When we consider all the crimes committed at any given place and time there is a number of these that are never reported to the police. For some, they may be reported to the police but they are never recorded. The Dark Figure of crime has been described as 'occurrences that by some criteria are called crime yet that are not registered in the statistics of whatever agency was the source of the data being used' by Albert Biderman. Sociologists define the difference between committed crimes and the reported and recorded crimes as the dark figure of crime. Because of this dark figure of crime it comes into question of the true amount of crime within society.

There has been many theories to the roots of crime with some suggesting that it is due to the lack of equality and the cause in urban areas is due to the environment . It is believed by criminologist that the roots of crime are within the neighbourhood (Social Disorganisation Theory). In their 1993 book 'Neighbourhood and Crime' Robert, Bursik and Harold argue that the theory does not take into account the larger political, economic and social forces within the urban setting that surrounds the neighbourhoods. They also argue that it is difficult to understand the crime in these urban areas without considering the ability of the neighbourhood taking in other community residents, schools, churches and other community institutions who are not part of the neighbourhood to practice control over the prevention of crimes. It is established that where a child grows up and the environment they are brought up in has a great influence on the kinds of behaviours displayed by that child as they move into adolescence and adulthood. It is also well established that some areas have a higher crime rate than others but may not be attributed to the fact that many criminals live in that area, but by the fact that the people living in that area support some acts that might grow into more serious crimes when these acts are adapted. Institutionalists claim that an act is not recorded by the police because it does not meet the required criteria defined in order for the act to be considered as criminal therefore the official data does represent the real crimes committed. As the relevant authorities define and classify the crime, the 'crime' will not fall into these definitions and classifications. Therefore according to institutionalists the dark figure of crime does not exist.

There are three things that must be provided in order for a crime to be recorded. Firstly, the knowledge that a crime has been committed. Meaning that the individual committing the crime must be aware that they are committing a crime or the individual committing the crime must have been seen by another while committing the crime (Coleman and Moynihan 1996). Secondly the relevant authorities must be informed that a crime has taken place, either by the individual who observed the crime being committed or by the individual that committed the crime, taking into consideration that it would be very unlikely that the offender will report the crime themselves.Thirdly, the crime that has been committed must be accepted as a crime,an act against the law, by the authorities or police it has been reported to. If any of these three factors do come about then the crime will go unrecognised. However it must be noted that if others have seen the offence being committed or have heard about it they would have the expectation of the police acting upon that offender. When this does not happen the public question their reliability. Complex social protocols have been found to be upon the police official figures of crime. This complex social protocol is built through negotiations with offenders, social relations and the police judgements and decisions as to what to define as a crime and the appropriate action to take.Recording crimes takes place in a three stage process. Firstly, the reporting of a crime by an individual, which is usually the victim or a crime being committed has been observed by the police. Secondly is the recording of the crime. The decision is made by the police after a crime has been reported to record to report or not. Then the number of crimes to record must be determined and the types of offences in the reported crime. The guidelines of the classification of crimes is the responsibility of The Home Office. When several offences may have been committed or where an offence has been committed by a number of people, this classification is important. The third stage is the detection of a crime, after a crime has been reported and recorded then the necessary investigations are conducted that connect the offence to a particular victim, following the guidelines provided by the Home Office within the police department the crime is then detected. Once the victim has been identified the offender is charged with an offence or offences in a court of law or they may be cautioned after the court has considered the report of the detectives (Moore 1996)

Most crime statistics that are available from authorities are considered as unreliable which raises questions on the reliability of the police mainly due to the various limitations they face. The main problem being that many offences are not reported to the police and there are a number of reasons as to why these offences are not reported. One reason being that some crimes that are observed by members of the public are considered by them as not serious enough the warrant the reporting. Another reason is that some crimes committed like rape and sexual assault the victim may find it too embarrassing to report it. Another reason, which is a common reason, is that the victim is not aware that a crime has taken place such as, in the case of fraud. There are also cases where the victim may be unaware that they are being victimised such as, offences against children, elderly or an individual with learning difficulties. Some of the other reason as to why people do not report crime are the fear of victimisation such as, neighbour disputes, victims may decide to take the law into their own hands this can also come about where there is a lack of trust in the police possibly through experience or word of mouth.

Most crimes committed are subject to police judgement and this can also be a problem, some may consider some crimes more important than other crimes therefore putting more into that crime rather than the other. The loss of files is also another problem with in the reporting system. A report may be filed in the wrong department or be lost during transition from one department to another. The reporting of crimes can also be affected by the crime such as, car insurance claims or the loss of property whereas other increases in reporting certain types of crime can be due to campaigns like a drink driving campaign at christmas. The police may also have an influence on the reporting of crime when there is a movement from the informal or community policing to zero tolerance policing (Pasha 1998). Most law enforcement bodies have the power of making a judgement on the offence and can influence the number of crimes that are recorded depending on how they record their own activities (Baltimore 2009). An individual can report their case to the police but it might still not be recorded until it has been proven in such a way that it fits to be incorporated in the crime data. When the police have other serious cases to deal with cases such as that involving the mentally ill may be overlooked. Reporting and recording crime can change due to many factors including the change in legislation and the number of police, employment in the police force is on the increase and with the employment of more community support officers. In addition to this there can be the creation of new classes of offences like compulsory seat belts and the decriminalisation of others. There is also the changes in technology to take into consideration such as the advanced use of CCTV and alarms systems. Mosher (2002) states that the development in criminology has created an awareness within the general public regarding the rate of crime in society and as a result of this they will be encouraged to report crimes to the police.

It has been claimed that the dark figure of crime has fallen because there has been significant attempts made by the authorities involved to wipe out the fears and the limitations that affect the witnesses of crime and the fear of reporting them but it still under question as to the extent of unreported crime.

Trait Theory

Eysenck and Rochman developed the idea of trait theory. The aim of this theory is to establish as to why people behave differently in different situations. Eysenck applied a scientific approach to this question with making use of questionnaires 'Eysenck's Personality Inventory' (EPI) to produce 'psychometric inventories' which are measurements of personality traits. He used this information to attempt to predict how different people would react in a specific situation. Kant believed that traits could be put into categories and each person could be put into one category but no one could be part of any other category. Whereas Eysenck believed that a person could be measured along two continuums. 'extraversion - Introversion' and 'neuroticism - stability'. He suggests that depending on a person's score would allow for the prediction of how they would react to a given situation. It is established by most theorists of trait theory that traits are genetically inherited and biologically determined. Through his studies Eysenck established the two personality features extraversion and neuroticism. He stated these as 'behavioural expressions of differences in biologically based temperament' (Butt 2007). These traits would be stable and change over time or situation was unlikely and levels show by each individual was due to differences in autonomic and cortical arousal.

Personal construct theory (PCT). This was developed by Kelly in 1955 and has a different approach to individual differences. This theory is based in phenomenology (the science of phenomena as distinct from that of the nature of being), It looks mainly at how each person views the same thing differently. Personal construct theory is aimed at the understanding of experiences lived, the making of personal meanings and the different views of the world each person has. Developing a set of personal constructions based on individual experiences is how people make sense of their world. The focus is on recognising that people have different views of the world around them. One of the main differences between Eysenck and Kelly is that Eysenck believes that traits are fixed and Kelly believes that traits can be flexible. But this flexibility is not something that comes about easily as great investments have already been made in constructing an individual's world therefore making it difficult to change these constructions. It is also helpful to note that most of the personal construction that happens does so without the individual knowing it is happening.

Trait theory is a theory that can be understood widely because of the similar way in which people assess others while involved in their everyday lives. Although this theory has came under much criticism the 'Eysenck's Personality Inventory' has been seen as a useful tool of measurement when comparing large samples of individuals on objective measures of personality. They can be used for identifying general traits for different organisations.

According to Eysenck social processes take place outside the individual and are important when influencing and shaping a personality. He believes that the differences between people are mainly driven by inherited biological traits and the influences from the environment and the social aspects shape that personality. The individual personality can range from outgoing and sociable, extrovert, to shy, reserved and withdrawn, introvert, and given the right circumstances some individuals can display a psychotic dimension. Clardige (1986) states that the strength of Eysenck's work is the links he draws between his dimensional theory of personality and abnormal psychology which allows him to make hypotheses about the interaction of three dimensions, neuroticism, extraversion and psychoticism. As an example, someone who was neurotic but are also introverted would be more likely to respond with exaggeration to slightly fear inducing situations. They would also avoid new situations quickly (Boeree 2006). To sum up Eysenck suggests that a trait is the aspects of an individual's personality which makes the individual fairly predictable and constant in their feelings, thoughts and actions over time and across different situations (McCrae 2001)

Eysenck also used genetic studies to along the physiological line to develop his theory of personality further. As he states that the difference between individuals are mainly due to what a person inherits genetically but he also states that these inherited personality traits are not fixed nor may last forever. Although they play a huge part they are not the only factor in shaping a personality although the change in them may be very little the biological foundation of them is there throughout an individual's lifetime.

One of the problems with these ideas of personality trait being inherited biologically is that not all people from violent families go on to become violent themselves. There has been studies on the influence of levels of testosterone on behaviour and Eysenck states that aggression and sexual behaviour may change the levels of testosterone released into the body while being influenced by the levels itself. It has been a long standing question within psychology of whether our external environment or our inner attributes, such as our inherited personality traits, play the most important part in determining and shaping an individual's behaviour (Haynes and Uchigakiuchi 1993). B. F. Skinner believes that conditioning the environmental processes can be far more influential but many other theorists believe that it is a combination of both biological, environmental and social properties that shape a person's personality with the inherited traits being the foundation.

Social Learning Theory

According to the Encyclopedia of Psychology

(2001) social learning theory is based on the psychology concept that the learning processes within our environment establish human behaviour. In order to develop desirable behaviour rewards and/or punishments are used to reinforce that behaviour and determine it. According to trait theories personality is a set of characteristics that are based on the individual's attitude, desires and certain behaviours that form a constant and stable part of our personality. J Rotter believes that cognition plays a large part in social learning and a person's behaviour is determined on what they expect. Therefore, a person will behave in a certain way based on the outcome of that behaviour expected and the value they place on it. Rotter's theory is based on two variables, internals and externals (Mearns 2000). It is based on the premise that individuals different beliefs on their ability to control whether or not their different behaviours throughout life are reinforced. Internals have the belief that they have control over their behaviour whereas externals have the belief that external factors which they have no control over determine their behaviour. But these are not fixed variables so a person can show a combination of both external and internal. Its main concern is with the individual's interaction with the environment. Albert Bandura believed that behaviour, cognition and the environment have a mutual reacting relationship. He suggested that an individual's interpretation and understanding of a given situation for example, if someone is being hostile then that individual will show hostile behaviour and in turn affecting the environment causing others to show hostile behaviours and thoughts. Bandura also noted that people can learn a certain type of behaviour through observation and the consequence of that observed behaviour. As a result of this they will take up the behaviours that give a positive reward and deter from the behaviours that do not receive favourable rewards. He termed the 'observational learning'. It must be noted that although people work and socialise in the same places they perceive that environment in different ways. These expectations play a part in determining individual behaviour for example, being on time for college and getting good grade is determined by the expectation to get into the university of choice. Other factors in determining our behaviour are our personal values, goals and ideas, self regulation and life goals.

Another theorist who believes that the individual environment plays a major part in shaping and forming their personality and their behaviour is Jones (2005). He suggests that family, peers and the neighborhood all have an effect on the social learning that shapes an individual's personality and behaviour. Therefore by looking at the kind of environment which a person lives and has been brought up in would enable us to understand their behaviour. Therefore, a person that has been brought up in a criminal and/or violent environment will have learned that that behaviour brings them a reward by the behaviors observed and it may be said that this would be an indication of poverty which drives them to this behaviour. This reinforces the suggestion that people who are brought up in this type of environment have a high chance of turning to this type of criminal behaviour (Jones 2005). It is likely that a child who is brought up in an aggressive environment will show these behaviours as observed by their family, friends, peers and siblings.

There is no doubt that social learning plays a large role in shaping and developing the personality and once certain behaviours are established in childhood, through the conditions within their environment, it can be very difficult to change that behaviour in adulthood. It leaves the question of what can be done about violent and aggressive criminals if this behaviour is well established.

Chapter 15
Youth Crime

Differential Association

There have be many attempts at explaining youth crime but there is no one explanation. Here we will look at the main theories used in attempts to explain the problem of youth crime in society, they are, differential association theory, labelling theory and rational choice theory all which look at the facts that are related to the criminal behaviour and the type of crimes they commit.

Differential association is a theory which was developed by Edwin Sutherland in 1974 as an attempt to explain why youths engage in criminal behaviour. The main focus of the theory is that criminal behaviour is a learned behaviour which is acquired through social contact with other individuals (Hopkins Burke 2009). This theory explains how an individual can spend a great amount of time with others who engage in criminal behaviour and come from criminal backgrounds and whose attitudes towards breaking the law consider it acceptable and therefore learn the criminal behaviour. According to Sutherland (1974) there are nine different factors which can be used to explain why an individual would engage in the criminal behaviour.

* The behaviour is learned.
* Criminality is learned behaviour through interaction with others in the process of communication.
* Individuals commit crime because they are influenced by the behaviour of intimate people.
* Learning criminal behaviour involves specific techniques, drives, motives and rationalisation.
* Culture.
* Individuals associate themselves with people that engage in criminal behaviour and believe it is acceptable.
* Differential associations may vary in frequency, duration, priority and intensity.
* The process of learning criminal behaviour by association with criminal and anti-criminal patterns.
* Criminal behaviour is an expression of needs and values.

The behaviour is learned.

According to Hopkins Burke (2009) the criminal behaviour is learned and are influenced by the people they associate with. Because most people grow up in some form of family these are the people they spend most of their time with, because of this they develop their social values and 'norms' from them. Sutherland also stated that criminal behaviour is learned, it is not something we are born with and it can only be established with associating with others who engage in criminal activity. They are acquired through the process of learning.

Criminality is learned behaviour through interaction with others, in the process of communication.

This focuses on the development of the child. Children are taught the roles of the people around them and become accustomed to the norms of society at a young age and learn the roles by observing male and female characteristics relating to specific genders. The individual can learn criminal behaviour simply by communicating with the person who is involved with and committing deviant and or criminal behaviour.

Individuals commit crime because they are influenced by the behaviour of intimate people.

This suggests that the youth is influenced by family members and close friends. It has been suggested by Hopkins Burke (2009) that television and media communication are less influential than family and close friends.

Learning criminal behaviour involves specific techniques, drives, motives and rationalisation.

This suggest that just being around family members and close friend who engage in criminal behaviour does not mean that they will also engage in that behaviour. It suggests that it will give them the resources into criminal rational. They will gain the individual knowledge of how to commit certain crimes but they also can make the choice to engage in that crime or not because they know from socialisation and society 'norms' that the act is wrong (Hopkins Burke 2009).

Culture

In many countries there is now a diversity of people all with their own ideas of what is considered acceptable and unacceptable behaviour and specific direction of motives and drives is learned from the different definitions of legal and social codes.

Individuals associate themselves with people that engage in criminal behaviour and believe it is acceptable.

This states that an individual becomes delinquent by association with people that consider the outcomes of breaking the law more favorable than the outcomes of abiding by the law.

Differential associations may vary in frequency,

duration, priority and intensity.

Differential association is not fixed and at different times in a childs life they may be subjected to different levels of intensity, priority and duration.

The process of learning criminal behaviour by association with criminal and anti-criminal patterns.

The process of learning criminal behaviour by association with criminal and non-criminal patterns involves all the mechanisms that are involved in any other learning (Newman 2007).

Criminal behaviour is an expression of needs and values.

It is claimed that this cannot be used to explain why youths commit crime because two people have the same needs where one chooses to meet those needs by legitimate means whereas the other chooses to meet those needs by illegitimate means.

Labelling Theory

Lembert in 1951 was the first to establish this theory and the view of 'deviant', later in 1963, it was further developed by Becker. The basic claims of this theory are that conformity and deviance does not come from the person's actions, it comes from the way in which others respond to the person's actions. It has been stated that labelling theory highlights social responses to crime and deviance by Marcionis and Plummer (2005) Deviance has been defined by online dictionaries as, "the fact or state of departing from usual or accepted standards, especially in social or sexual behaviour". Since it emerged labelling theory has become the main theory in the explanation of deviance. The backbone of the theory is developed by the assumption that not only is it based on the violation of norms within any society which is considered deviant behaviour but also on the behaviour which is defined as deviant within that society. In this instance the deviance is not seen as the act that the person engages in but it is based on the responses of others. Certain acts may not be against the law but are still considered as deviant and therefore the individual will be labelled as so. Becker 1963 states that social groups create deviance because they make the rules which creates the deviance, then those rules are applied to certain individuals or groups labelling them as deviant. He went on to state that, deviance is not the act that the person commits but the consequences of the application of others by rules and sanctions to an offender (Becker 1963). Therefore the deviant individual is the one the label has been applied to.

In 1951 Lemert distinguishes two types of deviance, primary deviance and secondary deviance.

Primary Deviance

Diminutive reactions from others that have little or no effect on an individual's self concept.

Secondary Deviance

People pushing the deviant individual out of the social circle which can cause the person to seek the company of people who condone deviant behaviour.

Lemert also argued that it is possible that instead of the view 'crime leads to control' it would be more productive to view crime as 'something that control agencies structured'. It is Lembert's idea of secondary deviance that leads Goffman 1963 to define the 'deviant career'. He stated that 'people who acquire a label or a stigma, which is a powerful negative label, it changes an individual's self concept and social identity'.

The statement 'stigmatising young people may actually lead them to a deviant career' came from Hopkins Burke (2008). This was inline with Lembert's belief that retrospective labelling distorts a person's life in a prejudicial way guided by stigma. He believes this is an unfair thing to do. It was also claimed by Howard Becker in 1963 that labelling individuals as outsiders creates deviance by certain social groups. The main concentration of labelling theory's approach to deviance is the social reaction to the defined deviant act as well as the interaction process that leads up to the labelling of an individual.

labeling theory can be seen as a socially constructed way of defining crime and deviance and that the police, media, the law etc all play a part in labelling individuals and groups of people as so. This labelling theory may also signify that that the cause of crime may be linked to the inequalities of class, race and gender. It has also been suggested that labelling an individual as deviant can lead to 'self fulfilling prophecy'. This is when an individual or a group are labelled deviant and are treated by the their social environment accordingly, therefore they begin to accept and believe the label and begin to act and behave according to the label given. The self concept is derived from the responses of others.

Strain Theory

Strain theory believes that social structures within a society can influence individuals to commit crimes. It was developed by Merton in 1938 and suggests that there are two types of important elements of social structure, these are, cultural goals and the function of the goals and interests. According to Merton there are five responses to strain that can explain the occurrence of crime and deviance. These are:

* Conformity
* Retreatism
* Ritualism
* Innovation
* Rebellion

Conformity

This makes the suggestion that individuals could alleviate the strain of trying to achieve the 'american dream', (to achieve all the life goals society expects us to achieve) by changing their goals and by withdrawing allegiance to the institutionalised means.

Retreatism

These type of individuals are the ones who reject the cultural goals of society as well as its institutionalised means of achieving the goals. This type of individual is usually considered by society as not part of the society (Hopkins Burke 2008). According to Merton this is the most uncommon path for someone to take.

Ritualism

This type of individual is not very successful at

achieving their goals. They tend to emphasise on the means which obscures their judgements on the attractiveness.

Innovation

This type of individual will use alternative means of achieving their goals if something prevents them from achieving that goal through the legitimate means.

Rebellion

This type is the type who rejects the goals and legitimate ways of obtaining the desired goals. They will want to change and challenge the existing social system and the institutionalised means and its goals. As stated by Hopkins and Burke 2008, they reject socially approved means and the goals of their society.

Strain theory suggests that it can cause negative feelings within an individual from the surrounding environment. The negative feelings can be defeat, despair, fear and anger. Agnew (1992) claimed that the anger tends to be the strongest emotion felt by the individual. He states that when an individual becomes angry they tend to blame others for their negative relationships and circumstances (Agnew 1992). According to Agnew the more strain an individual is subjected to the more likely they are to engage in criminal acts and delinquent behaviour. He states that the individual becomes more aggressive as the anger mounts because they cannot cope with the negative strain (Agnew 1992)

Youth Crime: Summary

The main theories used to explain youth crime do give good explanations. Differential association is used to explain youth crime and deviance. The theory believes that behaviour is learned so therefore deviant and criminal behaviour must be learned with the key variable being, the age of the learner, the amount of good and bad social contacts they have in their lives and how much contact they have with the person or group they learn the criminal or deviant behaviour from.

Labelling theory explains criminal and deviant behaviour as a social process where the deviant individuals are defined by others in society. This theory suggests that an individual only becomes deviant when they have been labelled as deviant by others. Therefore, labelling theory and strain theory explain youth crime and deviance as the outcomes of social strains within the way society is structured.

In summary, an individual or a group of people in any society can be labelled as deviant by others because that society has defined the social 'norms'. For example, an individual who has a lot of tattoos and piercings may be labelled as deviant or a criminal because the general socially constructed view of people with tattoos and piercings is the criminal type. This view may have been socially constructed through news, television, film etc. Another example would be groups of people who follow a certain way of dressing which does not fall into the social 'norms' such as the 'goth' or the 'mods' and 'rockers' in the 1960's or the emergence of the 'punk' and the 'skinhead'.

Although labelling theory shows a good explanation of youth crime it falls short with the statement, 'a burglar does not become a burglar because someone has labelled them so'. It could be due to a combination of many reasons. It could be said that if an individual is consistently labelled as a criminal or deviant they will eventually start to behave that way, the self fulfilling prophecy. Becker (1963) claims that once an individual is labelled and accepts the deviant behaviour, all their other qualities become irrelevant and the label becomes the master status.

Differential association and strain theory can be used to tackle youth crime because the differential association accepts that criminal and deviant behaviour is evident within all social classes and that the criminal or deviant behaviour can be learned through social interaction with groups that are influential to the individual. A problem with differential association is that it is very difficult, if not impossible, to measure the frequency, intensity and duration that an individual has with criminal groups or persons, according to Glueck (1956). We must also remember the possibility of the learned behaviour coming from media sources because they are so readily available to most young people.

Chapter 16
Environmental Criminology

Crime and The Social Environment

Emile Durkheim wrote at a time of great change in the nineteenth century, a great social and economic change. He believed that a certain amount of crime was necessary to develop social change therefore crime was functional. He also made a number of observations about the nature of crime in the social environment. Firstly he thought it was difficult to imagine a society without some form of deviance and crime, therefore, making crime functional so a yardstick would be provided to measure against conformity and moral standards. This in turn makes crime a necessary for any society because it makes the collective conscience clear and promotes the coming together in condemnation of certain types of behaviour within the society. It helped to identify the boundaries of what was considered as acceptable behaviours. Durkheim's view of punishment was a means of reinforcing the collective conscience and not about deterrence, retribution or rehabilitation. This was not his only view of crime and he saw crime as a way of challenging the norms in order to develop progress and healthy social change. This idea can be seen throughout time when individuals or social movement have brought about some kind of change in society resulting in certain types of behaviour no longer being considered as deviant or criminal. Durkheim also stated that although crime, like pain, is not desirable it is a normal part of a society and can be useful to bring about change and solve problems. He also thought that too much crime or to little crime would be a sign that there was something seriously wrong with that society. He claimed that too much crime would lead to the disintegration of the order and values of a society and very little crime would suggest that the social control was too strong and would lead to repression and stagnation.

The great changes that came about during the time of Durkheim was the movement from 'mechanical societies' to' organic societies' through industrialisation. In the mechanical societies there was little 'division of labour'. These communities were based on strong morals and values, close knit communities and conformity. Whereas organic societies contained a high level of division of labour through the rapid industrialisation. There was a great need for workers with specialisation which brought about individualism and a demand for more goods. This division of labour brought about what Durkheim termed as 'anomie' which caused a breakdown in the collective conscience, the set of morals and values held by the smaller communities. A common morality was what regulated these societies which at this time served as a very effective form of social control. As industrialisation spread it caused the breakup of the smaller communities because the new factories that were built to supply the demand were build in the towns. People had to move to find work. It was Durkheim's belief that in time these new communities would settle down and new moral values and beliefs would take shape to fit in with the new communities. The transition from the old to the new communities left people with no sense of moral code or a consensus. A lack of moral standards and no regulation. This is the transitional state of affairs that Durkheim referred to as 'anomie'. He used this to describe a state where there is no 'norm' and no one was clear about what the social rules were, what was considered as acceptable and not acceptable. This great change also, according to Durkheim, encouraged greater aspirations and expectations among the society therefore people were wanting more things and wanting them quicker. As a result of this people saw attempts at some form of control as aimed at preventing them from getting what they want and in turn leading to people committing crimes to obtain the things they want or driving them to suicide being unable to get what they want.

Durkheim claimed that humans are naturally in pursuit of pleasure, satisfaction and happiness. This is difficult in a community where different individuals are pursuing different pleasures, satisfactions and happiness. Anomie results in different cultures with different norms and values conflicting. Durkheim described this as 'everyone being at war with everyone else'. Durkheim's concept of anomie was not picked up again until the 1930's by an American sociologist called Robert Merton. He used and developed the concept of anomie to theorise on crime in the 1930's. The term anomie was used by Merton in a very different social context to that of Durkheim. Durkheim wrote at a time in Europe when it was still under the influence of aristocracy and privileges were for few people. Whereas Robert Merton wrote in the time of the 'American Dream'. Robert Merton, like Durkheim, wrote in a time of great economical and social change. There was a huge rise in the population of America due to migration after the great depression. This was also the time of the 'American Dream'. It was believed that anyone could go from a log cabin to the White House and this opportunity was open to all. It was believed that this could be obtained by hard work and commitment, through legitimate means. For Durkheim, anomie was a temporary state and given time it would develop new regulations. For Merton, anomie was always present and was brought about by the lack of legitimate opportunities to obtain the american dream with the goal of material success.

Anomie arises when the cultural goals cannot be met by certain individuals or groups. They may be committed to the cultural material goals but lack the ability and opportunities to do so, they could be disadvantaged by race or class. For Merton anomie is the strain of the social structure to attain the goal of material success and the future of the social structure to provide the legitimate means to do so. Unlike Durkheim, Merton thought it was not natural for people to pursue material gain and this was culturally induced. Merton described five different reactions to the strain of anomie. These are:

Conformity: This is when the material goals are accepted and the legitimate institutional means are used to do so. Conformity does not involve any deviance and most people do conform.

Innovation: This does involve deviance. This is when the material goals are accepted but the legitimate means to do so are not. Possibly because they do not feel they are adequate or they are not capable of achieving them. Therefore, illegitimate means are used instead. Merton claimed that this was common among working classes because they have less ability and opportunities to conform.

Ritualism: This involves the goals being rejected or lost sight of. These individuals start in pursuit of material goals and use the legitimate means but then become 'stuck in a rut' and lose sight of the goals. The job becomes a ritual. Some are content with what they have through fear of failure or losing what they already have.

Retreatist: This individual rejects both the material goals and the legitimate means to do so. They drop out of society. They are in it but not part of it. This may be of choice to some through spiritualism or communes, but for some they might find themselves homeless or addicted to drugs and/or alcohol. Crimes committed would probably be for self-preservation, such as stealing food.

Rebellion: This is when both the goals and the legitimate means are rejected with a clear idea of what should replace them. This form of rebellion can be deviant with terrorism and bombing but it has also been with peaceful demonstrations and rebellions. Durkheim described one of the functions of crime was to push the boundaries of normality as with Gandhi and Martin Luther King.

Merton used these 'adaptations' to describe people's reactions and stated that people may experience a number of different reactions throughout their lifetime. For example, the ritualistic worker may at some point steal from their boss, which would be innovation, or someone goes on a drinking binge which would be retreatist. Merton also wrote about 'strain theory' which became escalated in the huge growth of mass advertising and media. What was once considered as luxuries is now considered as necessities such as, washing machines and mobile phones. At the time Merton wrote his theories it only applied to America but in today's modern world it can be applied to every city. We are all expected to achieve certain standards and obtain a certain standard of living which is expected to be able to fully take part in society. Leisure activities are expensive and children are under pressure to have the latest designer clothes and products. The rise in tuition fees makes it more difficult for certain members of society to obtain the education they need to get a good well paid job and the higher status.

Broken Windows Theory

George Kelling and James Wilson were social scientists who were the first to introduce the Broken windows Theory in 1982. The idea is that a relatively small crime can take place but this event lead to the gradual build up of similar or the same crime. The main example comes for the title of the theory. Consider any building with windows, if a window is smashed and not repaired there is a tendency for vandals to smash other windows until all the windows are smashed. Eventually the building might be broken into and acquire squatters and be prone to internal vandalism. It is the same premise if someone put an old piece of furniture or a bag of rubbish out on the street, soon after more rubbish is put there, it pile up and then lead s to other crimes being committed near by. It is like it spreads, starting off small and gradually growing larger and spreading further to incorporate other crimes.

Before Kelling and Wilson introduced this theory a psychologist from Stanford called Philip Zimbardo (well known for the Stanford prison experiment) tested the broken window theory with an experiment in 1969. He arranged for a car with the bonnet up and no registration plate to be parked in a Bronx neighbourhood and another car in the same condition to be placed in Palo Alto in California. Within minutes of the car being left in the Bronx it was attacked. Zimbardo noted that the first people to approach the car was a family of three, a mother and father with a young son. They removed the battery and the radiator from the car. Everything of value had been stripped from the car within twentyfour hours of it being left there. After that the car was being used as a play area for the children with the windows being smashed, the upholstery ripped etc. The car that was left in Palo Alto (a much more affluent area) was left there for more than a week untouched so Zimbardo went up to the car and smashed it with a sledgehammer, soon after other people joined in with the vandalism. He noted that the vandals were mainly adult and were well dressed and respectable whites. He concluded that theft and abandoned property are more common in the Bronx so vandalism happens quicker as the community generally seems to show no interest or concern. He stated that similar events can occur in any community when the communal barriers are lowered by actions that suggest a lack of interest or concern.

Developing further on the broken windows theory George Kelling and Catherine Coles in 1996 applied this theory to general crime and suggested that problems in the community need to be fixed while they are small. For example, fixing a broken window within a week and the likeliness of further vandalism will be reduced. Taking these small measures can lead to less people fleeing certain neighbourhoods and problems escalating. Oscar Newman claims that is is not enough to just fix the small problems he suggests that people need to have an investment in the community in order to care about it. Which leads us back to the notion of defensible space.

Crime Prevention Through Environmental Design

Crime prevention through environmental design (CPTED) is aimed at designing community environments using a number of scientific design methods that are engineered with the purpose of creating safer communities and making it difficult for criminal behaviour. Its main premise it aimed at control. This approach was originally developed by Ray Jeffrey in 177 in his book, Crime Prevention Through Environmental Design: Beverly Hills', who incorporated the works of Oscar Newman and Tim Crowe and added the elements of psychology, biology, ergonomics (the study of people's efficiency in their working environment) and human anatomy.

There is much attention on crime control and prevention throughout the criminal justice system and crime prevention through environmental design has shown to be very successful. This method of crime control intends to manipulate the environment in order to influence the offender's choice of criminal behaviour. It is not only to prevent or deter crime but also to reduce the fear of crime in the communities and increase a better quality of life for those living in these areas. This approach requires a number of things to make it successful, firstly being organisations of groups of citizens who will be active in implementing the changes. Secondly, a strong police force and finally, the most important issue, taking action to remove as many of the causes of crime as possible and eliminating the environment and circumstances to which crime thrives. In 'City Planning and Discouraging Crime' 1968, Angel suggests that the crime prevention through environmental design approach that crime settings can be influenced by:

* Increasing or decreasing accessibility.
* Delineating territories.
* Enhanced surveillance by the police.
* Enhanced surveillance by the public.
* The elimination or creations of boundaries.

Summed up by Cornish and Clarke in the 1986 book ' The Reasoning Criminal: Rational Choice Perspectives on Offending', crime prevention through environmental design can be seen as an approach to problem solving that takes into account the environmental conditions and the opportunities they offer for criminal behaviour occurrence.

The approach looks at many areas of everyday life and the areas where this activity takes place. It looks at the environmental area where the criminal behaviour takes place and implements action to prevent this. Research had shown that crimes are specific and situational, Atlas (2008) states that 'crime distribution correlates to land use and transport network and offenders are usually optimistic and commits crimes in an area they know well, as well as that opportunities for crime arise out of daily activities and crime places that are often without observation or observers. The main strategies used to achieve crime prevention through environmental design are:

* Natural surveillance.
* Informal surveillance.
* Lighting.
* Landscape design.
* Alarms, warning systems and physical security.
* Access control to certain areas.
* Target hardening.

Crime prevention through environmental design conduct research and found that an offender's decision to commit a crime or not depended more on the risks perceived of being caught or not and not so much on the effort it would take to carry out the crime or even the rewards of the crime committed. From this research came 'defensible space' which was designed in order to improve the quality of life for people within the communities by reducing the fear of crime by reducing crime.

Natural Surveillance: Offenders are deterred from offending if their is a high likelihood of them being observed committing the crime and subsequently reported. A good example of natural surveillance is neighbourhood watch schemes.

Informal Surveillance: This is aimed at reducing visual obstacles in the community creating less secluded places. Creating these open areas not only deter the offender but make these areas more useable because people can be easily seen.

Lighting: Good lighting is an effective way of discouraging crime. It provides good natural surveillance and also reduces the fear of crime. The level of light is also important, it needs not to be too strong as to cause disturbance at night or to create high light areas and dark shadowed areas, but strong enough to make a people feel safe.

Landscape Design: This is an area of crime prevention through environmental design that is considered the most significant. This is a way of determining different area of the community with the use of flower bed, certain pattern is paving, hedges, fencing, shrubbery etc. The placement of this landscaping is also important to creating obstacles to prevent offending by extending or limiting shrubbery to certain heights as to avoid seclusion and enabling natural surveillance. Another important factor to landscaping is the creation of appreciation of the area. If an area looks nice then people are more likely to feel a sense of pride in the area they live and a wish to maintain it.

Alarms, warning systems and physical security: Any form of alarms and warning system are likely to deter an offender. Extra locks on external doors and windows are also a deterrent as well as securing the surrounding areas with iron fences, buzzers on apartments, glass panels and self locking doors. The most effective physical security is the use of CCTV. This needs to be well placed in areas which are most likely to be targeted by offenders but at the same time not to feel intrusive to the privacy of the residents. Most people do not a problem with CCTV as it instills a sense of safety. All of these deterrents are know as 'target hardening.

Defensible Space Theory

In 1976 Oscar Newman published, with the National Institute of Law Enforcement and Criminal Justice (US), 'Design Guidelines for Creating Defensible Space'. He went on to define this as, 'a residential environment whose physical characteristics - building, layout and site plan - function to allow inhabitants themselves to become key agents in ensuring their security'. He claimed that in order to help residents feel a sense of ownership and responsibility for their own areas, good design was needed. This would then lead to the residents wanting to defend this space. He believed that the more control and influence they had over their own areas diminished the ability for the offender to operate within it.

This idea of defensible space was adopted by the British Police in 1988 with the 'Secured by Design' initiative. The idea of defensible space relies a great deal on the willingness of the residents to participate as well as the ability to and the idea of self policing is forefront. Time has shown that this initiative has been very successful. Oscar Newman identified the four main factors of defensible space which was later developed further by Ray Jeffrey, these are:

* **Territoriality** - This is intended to emphasise the notion that a 'man's home is his castle'.
* **Natural surveillance** - The ability of the residents to be able to see what is going on in their own neighbourhood.
* **Image** - This is the physical attributes of a development that makes it defensible.
* **Milieu** - (surroundings) This is about

making the most of a development's location to places that will help to prevent crime.

Bearing this in mind, there is the question of, is defensible space just expanding our own personal space? When we first think of personal space we tend to think of what is close to us, say as far as you can stretch out your arms, as many people find it uncomfortable when on a very busy train or in a packed lift. These examples are when we are out in public places and usually do not include our friends or family members. Once we are in our own home then the home becomes the defensible space, Even though the average teenage my show signs of defensible space in their bedrooms. We could look at this as an extension of our personal space. Then this extension spreads out further to include our gardens, garages, sheds etc. Therefore, when people are involved in their communities and have a sense of pride, ownership and some control in the community they become to view this as further extension of their own personal space. This further outreached personal space will be set by what is known as 'symbolic boundaries' these are pathways, fences, gates etc. These areas are comprised of private areas, our own dwellings and gardens or private grounds. Semi-private areas such as, private car parks for residents of apartments. Then there is the public areas such as, parks, shopping area etc.

The main drawback of defensible space is that this can lead to what is know as 'gated communities' some of these do exist. This is when a whole community is surrounded by walls and/or gates and access is restricted to the residents of that community only. There is also the idea that this could lead to segregation of certains types of people, it may be only the richer members of society that could afford to live in these gated communities.

Opportunity Theory

This theory believes that the offender will choose the targets that offer the biggest reward for the littlest amount of risk and effort and that the offender makes a rational choice to do so. We can look at crimes as all needing the opportunity to commit but we must acknowledge that all opportunities to commit are taken upon. According to opportunity theory there must be two factors in place for the commission of the crime, these are, the presence of at least one motivated offender who is willing to take the rational decision to commit the crime and the right conditions within the environment which creates the opportunity to commit the crime. If an offender is motivated to commit a crime they first must have the opportunity to do so therefore in order to reduce crime the opportunities to commit the crimes must be taken away. Manipulating the environment by applying theories such as Defensible space would reduce the opportunity for crime.

Routine Activity Theory

Routine activity theory is a theory which attempts to explain the supply of criminal opportunity. According to Cohen and Felson (1979) there needs to be three elements in place for an offence to take place. These are:

* A motivated/likely offender.
* A suitable target.
* The absence of a capable guardian.

This theory suggests it is the daily activities that create the relevant time and space for the three elements to come together for the crime to occur. It is suggested that the lifestyles of the potential victims can create the opportunities for crime to take place. This probably applies more to modern day lifestyles. Firstly, we have the motivated offender. Today it is far more common for both the parents of the family to be working, whereas years ago the mother mainly stayed at home taking care of the home and the children. With both parents working and the children with childminders or at school from early morning until evening the house is empty giving a suitable target, an area where most families are working or away from home, and the absence of a capable guardian. Therefore creating the opportunity for crime.

Chapter 17
Victims of Crime

Victimology

The term 'victimology' is defined in different ways by different people therefore only a broad definition of the term can be given and considering Victimology is a relatively new concept in Criminology. The focus of victimology is on the victim of crime equally as it is on the crime itself. It focuses on the victim's experience of crime and the events that lead up to, and the taking place of the crime. Victimology also looks at social reaction to victimisation and the different organisations available to victims. It is in essence 'a system of knowledge' of victims (Dussich 2006). The Crown Prosecution Service (2001) define a victim as 'a person who has complained of the commision of an offence against themselves or their property'. According to Kearon and Godfrey (2007) victims of crime have been central to the justice processes. Crimes were recorded before the end of the 19th century because of the activity of the victims of crime. During Anglo-saxon times victims made their complaints directly to the courts and this usually resulted in financial compensation paid to the victim by the offender. (Kearon and Godfrey 2007). It is difficult to pinpoint the origins of victimology but it is considered by many that the origins lie with Mendelsohn and Von Hendig. According to Von Hendig victims have 'crime provocative' functions, meaning they have a proneness to crime (Hendig 1967). On the other hand, Mendelsohn describes victims in terms of their responsibility for their own victimisation. (Marsh 2004). Goodey (2005) stated that there are three categories of victimology that have their basis within criminology,

> 1. The positivist position which looks at the scientific nature of victimology. It defines victimisation according to the criminal law and is linked with the idea of blaming the victim (Goodey 2005).
> 2. The radical position. This concentrates more on human rights with the focus on the rights of the victim. It includes all aspects of victimisation, even the aspects which are outside the law as well as looking at the role of the state alongside the law in producing victimisation (Walklate 2007).
> 3. The critical position. This combines positions A and B. It looks at the individual victims experiences and how society and the state influence them (Goodey 2005). It also is concerned with

the invisible victims as well as the visible victims of crime. It states that policy should take both into consideration. The main focus of this critical position are the rights, citizenship and the state being the main 'policy oriented concepts' which are linked to other versions of victimology (Walklate 2007)

The development of victimology as a field of study

According to Dignan (2005) what lead to the development of victimology was the significance of the visibility of the victims and that visibility is the focus on the victims of crime rather than the offenders. He goes on to suggest that the penal reformers in the 1950's considered crime as not just a violation of legal obligations but as a violation of the rights of the individual victim. These penal reformers had a huge impact on policy making and the development of victimology. It has also been the view that the mass media had an impact on the visibility of victims of crime by focusing strongly on the victim and the families of victims. The media coverage focused upon the impact of the crime upon the victim (Dignan 2005). The late 1960's saw a growing recognition of particular vulnerable groups of people, in particular, abused women and child abuse. Then with the growth of feminism came the focus on women and children as 'victims of interpersonal crime' (Goodey 2005). This then lead to concerns regarding the 'handling of victims' (Dignan 2005).

One of the main and more prominent increases in the visibility of victims of crime came about with the growth of victimisation surveys which in turn led further to the growth of victimology. These surveys provided invaluable information regarding the nature and extent of criminal victimisation (Dignan 2005). These surveys came about in the late 1960's and their initial intentions was to discover more about the 'dark figure of crime'. Included in the crime surveys were information about the financial loss, injuries and the emotional impact the crime had on the victim. The 'British Crime Survey' was later known as 'The Crime Survey for England and Wales' and the information it collected was part of the official crime data (Green 2007). Previous to this research data focused on delinquency but the newer crime surveys focused on victimisation which also led to the further development of victimology. It had been claimed by many that these victimisation surveys had a direct impact on criminological theory, policy and societies view of crime (Maguire and Pointing 1988). During the 1070's the courts in Britain began to put more focus on the victim and began to offer the victim retribution (Maguire 1988). There was a shift from the focus being on the rights of the victim to focus on the services for victims. This became known as the 'victims movement' and was largely run by the 'National Association of Victim Support Schemes. The aim of these services was to improve the links between local communities (Maguire 1988). It is suggested the the emergence of victim support schemes was due to the rising crime rates at that time. With this also came the rejection of the rehabilitative criminal justice model (Goodey 2005). In England and Wales the criminal justice system replaced the rehabilitation model with the restorative justice model. This new restorative model made victim the central focus in the justice process. This model is underpinned by the notion that justice can be gained through problem solving and restoring the damage caused to the victims. To demonstrate, we must note that the compensation order of 1872 and the community service order of 1988 were put into place to provide a making of amends for the damage caused to the victim and/or the community by the offender (Dignan 2005).

As with other models victimology is not without its problems. Firstly there is the definition of victim and the focus of victimology being on the visible victim but falls short when considering the less visible crimes and the less visible victims as well as the problem of the issues around under-reporting and the dark figure of crime, which indicates a problem with methods used to gather data. Along with this are the problems with the Crime Survey for England and Wales. Green (2007a) states problems with the survey by claiming that these surveys do not tell anything about the victims and the impact the crime has had on them. He also suggests that the survey does not attempt to explain trends in offences or to interpret what they find, it does not take into consideration the conditions of which victimisations are based. As well as this the surveys cannot tell why some people are more vulnerable to victimisation than others. It cannot say what factors contribute to victimisation of certain individuals and different groups of people (Green 2007). To add to this, the survey does not include under sixteen years old who are considered as vulnerable and are prone to victimisation. It has been suggested that the Crime Survey for England and Wales should be more focused on the impact of crimes upon the victim and less about the description of the crimes.

Types of Victim and Risk

Victimology is the scientific study of victimization, including the relationships between victims and offenders, the interactions between victims and the criminal justice system, the police and courts and the connections between victims and other social groups and institutions, such as the media, businesses, and social movements.

Victimology examination is a major component of a crime scene investigation.

Victimology within the Crime Scene Investigation

"In the rush to examine a criminal's behavior, it is not difficult to become distracted by the dangling carrot of that criminal's potential characteristics and forget about the value of understanding his victims" –Brent Turvey

Victimology is important in the overall investigative process because it not only tells us who the victims were, their health and personal history, social habits and personality, but also provides ideas as to why they were chosen as victims. In many situations the offender will hold back from choosing a victim until one that meets his needs comes along, possibly allowing him to fulfill some fantasy or desire he has. Because of this, the way the victim is chosen is important and gives an insight into how the offender thinks, which subsequently affects how the perpetrator acts. If we are able to determine how the offender is acting now, we may be better able to determine his future behavior, possibly leading to a successful arrest.

Closely related to victimology are the concepts of method of approach, method of attack and risk assessment. If we know details of the victims' personalities (i.e. they may be naturally cautious), then we may be able to determine, in conjunction with an analysis of the crime scene, how they were initially approached by the offender. The same will apply for the way they were attacked and overpowered. If this information is not distinguishable through the crime scene, then an analysis of the victims' overall risk, that is, the chances of them becoming a victim, may be of some help. If we examine this along with the risks the offender was willing to take to acquire a certain victim, then we will have an overall picture of who the victim was and what drove the offender to choose this particular person as a victim.

Ideally, with a good victimology analysis, and information both on the state of the victim post-crime, and their history and background, the crime scene profiler should be able to start to formulate some answers around questions like –

* Why was this particular person

targeted?

    * How was the person or persons targeted, or was the person a victim of opportunity?

    * What are the chances of the person becoming a victim at random (and therefore opportunistic)?

    * What risk did the offender take to commit the crime?

    * How was the victim approached, restrained and/or attacked?

    * What was the victim's likely reaction to the attack?

    * What was the offender's likely method of approach, method of attack, m.o., signature behaviour, and likely offender risk assessment.

Victim and Offender Risk Assessment

Risk assessment involves determining the risk of a particular person becoming a victim of crime. Occasionally we will hear reports about violent crime stating that the perpetrator had gone to great lengths to acquire the victim. In other cases, we may hear that the perpetrator has acquired a victim of opportunity. Perhaps in this last instance, something that the victim had done, or was involved in, had elevated their risk of becoming a victim of that crime. This is not to suggest that the individual was somehow responsible for being a victim, just that certain factors about lifestyle or situation had increased the chances of victimization. This may include such things as prostitution, excessive drunkenness, drug use, or traveling alone late at night in an area known for criminal activity. A risk assessment may also include an examination of the risk an offender was willing to take in acquiring a victim. This is known as offender risk assessment.

Victim risk is broken into three basic levels: low risk, medium risk, and high risk. They all refer to the degree of chance of someone coming to harm by virtue of their personal, professional and social life.

High Risk Victims: Victims in this group have a lifestyle that makes them a higher risk for being a victim of a violent crime. The most obvious high risk victims are prostitutes. Prostitutes place themselves at risk every single time they go to work. Prostitutes are high risk because they will get into a stranger's car, go to secluded areas with strangers, and for the most part attempt to conceal their actions for legal reasons. Offenders often rely on all these factors and specifically target prostitutes because it lowers their chances of becoming a suspect in the crime. Therefore, in this example, the prostitute is a high risk victim creating a lower risk to the offender.

Moderate Risk Victims: Victims that fall into this category are lower risk victims, but for some reason were in a situation that placed them in a greater level of risk, (in the wrong place at the wrong time) A person that is stranded on a dark, secluded road due to a flat tire and accepts a ride from a stranger and is then victimized would be a good example of this type of victim level risk.

Low Risk Victims: The lifestyle of these individuals would normally not place them in any degree of risk for becoming a victim of a violent crime. These individuals stay out of trouble, do not have peers that are criminal, are aware of their surroundings and attempt to take precautions to not become a victim. They lock the doors, do not use drugs, and do not go into areas that are dark and secluded.

Victim risk is further broken down into several subcategories (mainly taken from *Turvey*)

The victim lifestyle risk refers to the overall risk present by virtue of an individual's personality and their personal, professional and social environment. Lifestyle risk is basically affected by who that person is, and how the person relates to certain risks in the environment. There are certain factors which will increase a person's lifestyle risk, and these include the following:

* Aggressiveness
* Anger
* Emotional outbursts
* Hyperactivity
* Impulsivity
* Anxiety
* Passivity
* Low self esteem
* Emotional withdrawal

The victim incident risk refers to the risk present when an offender initially attacks a victim by virtue of a victims state of mind, or hazards in the environment. Say for instance, that a person has just left work after being fired from his job. He has just invested a lot of money in property and is preoccupied with paying off his financial commitments. When walking to his car in the evening, he fails to notice the person waiting around the entrance to the car park. The fact that he is preoccupied by his newly acquired financial state increases his incident risk because he is failing to notice unusual or potentially dangerous factors in his surroundings.

The offender risk is very important as it tells you what risks the offender was willing to take in order to get this particular victim, at that particular time, and in that particular location.

* modus operandi risk. The MO risk refers to the nature and extent of the skill, planning, and precautionary acts taken by the offender before, during and after the crime. As the MO refers to those things the offender had to do to successfully complete the crime, the MO risk refers to those things that the offender does to reduce his own risk of being disturbed, thwarted or apprehended.

* The MO risk is broken into low risk (referring to those offenders who show a high amount of skill, planning and precautionary acts) and high risk (referring to those offenders who show a low amount of skill, planning and precautionary acts). The MO risk is low because the offender plans many aspects of the crime, thereby reducing their risk for committing the crime. The opposite applies to high MO risk offenders.

Offenders may also be exposed to incident risk, which refers to the possibility of them suffering harm or loss. Offender incident risk is subjective in that it is the risk perceived by the profiler for that offender. The following example will provide an idea as to how an offenders perceptions of a situation will misinform them as to the offender incident risk:

Victim Proneness / Victim Blaming

Research into ways in which victims "contribute" to their own victimisation is considered by victims and victim advocates as both unacceptable and causes more harm to the victim. Victim proneness is also known as victim blaming. One theory suggests that the context and location for the crime bring the victim and the offender together. For example, if the woman had not been walking home alone from the party late at night and walked down a street when the offender was close by then the offence would not of happened.

There has been a number of theories to explain victim proneness, a few of these are:

Situated Transaction Model. (Luckenbill 1977)

This is based on an interpersonal level and suggests it is character based. Fists is the insult, for example, regarding the other person's mother. Then there is the clarification of the insult, 'what did you say about my mother'. Then the repeat of the insult, the retaliation. Next is the counter retaliation and finally the clenching of fists or the production of a weapon. The presence of others escalate the situation.

Threefold Model. (Benjamin and Master)

This view suggests there are three general categories of conditions that support the crime.

1. Precipitating factors. Time and space, being in the wrong place at the wrong time.
2. Attracting factors. Opinions and choices as well as lifestyle meaning the daily routine activities and the events we go to on a regular basis which can be predictable.
3. Predisposing factors. This refers to the sociodemographic characteristics that make up the victim 'type'. Being young, male, poor, a minority, being single or unemployed.

It is important that some of the above should be understood when in a courtroom situation. It is possible that some of the jurors may make allowances or contributions on the victims proneness rather than that of the offender.

Victim Recovery Phases

If a victim is going through a lengthy court case, the judicial support system should be aware of the stages of recovery that a victim might go through after a crime. These stages may well have a bearing on the victims testimony and behaviour before court. Support and therapy sessions must also be taken into account through any criminal proceedings. *The Crime Victim's Book* recognises 3 stages of victim recovery.

1. The impact stage, where the crime has just occurred and the victim may feel 'numb'.

2. The recoil stage, when what has happened finally "hits" the victim, causing them either to go into denial and detach themselves from the event, refusing to accept what really happened or to continually relive the trauma and going over the details.

3. The reorganisation stage is where things seem to get better but the victim is still having flashbacks, especially in the case of those who have repressed the memories. This may be the time the victim finally gets help and goes into therapy.

Others suggest stages similar to that of grieving or mourning, particularly for violent or sexual crimes. The following is for rape crimes (*Source: Laura Berman*), but relevant to others without sexual content.

1. **Denial:** After experiencing sexual assault, there's such total confusion and disbelief that a person often goes 'numb' the mind-body

system has to shut down. It is also common for a survivor to deny that what happened was rape or to downplay it by possibly believing "it wasn't so bad." A common form of denial is where the victim accepts that an assault occurred but avoids recognizing that it was of a sexual nature.

2. Anger: The second stage of grieving a sexual assault is anger. A victim's anger is directed not only at the perpetrator but also at themselves. Since we live in a society that tends to blame the victim, especially a rape victim who knew their attacker, the victim might become angry at themselves for dressing a certain way, putting themselves in a certain situation, or even having drank alcohol. This anger is misplaced and there is nothing a victim can do that can make them 'deserve' to get raped.

3. Bargaining: Bargaining is the third stage of grieving following a rape. The victim's objective is to minimize the emotional trauma. Often, the bargaining is of a spiritual nature: The victim will make a deal with a higher power, asking for the pain to go away in return for certain prescribed behavior.

4. Depression: The fourth stage of grieving over rape is often depression. The reality of the sexual assault sinks in and they have feelings of hopelessness and shame.

5. Acceptance: At this final stage the

victim has some sense of acceptance. At this time the victim is able to begin to get back to a sense of normality to their life. For many victims, letting go is often difficult because they have put so much into simply surviving that they might feel like being a survivor is the only thing that defines them. But at this stage, the victims have incorporated what happened into their lives. It is not the definition of who they are, it is just a part of who they are. They'll likely think about what happened a lot less and feel more like a stronger version of their "old selves."

Survivor Guilt and Stages

Victims of Violence Canada have a good resources page on attempted homicide survivors, and the processes they go through. This, again, should be taken into account through areas like crime scene investigations, interviews and court proceedings if a violent offender is being prosecuted.

The page discusses the loss experience for attempted homicide survivors (which includes a grieving process), and also points out that some survivors may be witnesses, and there is a risk of them feeling as though they have been victimised again during the court trials – both from media intrusiveness, and the court environment itself. These factors should always be taken into consideration, when taking victims of violent crimes into these environments.

Victimhood Culture

The study of victimology may also include the "culture of victimhood," wherein the victim of a crime revels in his or her status. Some interesting references from this particular culture sit with those crimes done under the Munchausen by Proxy syndrome, where the offender portrays themselves as a hero and victim at the same time, by making a family member or another person ill. See more on this in the P for Profit / Comfort Killers post.

Supporting Victims

The study of victimology includes assessment of the criminal justice systems role in crimes with victims, advocacy of victims rights, and understanding the motives and behaviours behind victims going through these systems.

In 1994 an international symposium on victims was held. The AIC (Australian Institute of Criminology) has published selected papers from this *8th symposium on Victims as PDF extracts* on one webpage. These PDF's include papers on politics, sex, gender issues in victims, victim surveys and methodologies, and several papers subjected around the criminal justice and support systems for victims including topics such as victim compensation, victim impact or impairment statements, types of victims (ie. females) through the courts, and finally – several on victim prevention methods.

The World Society of Victimology

The purpose of the WSV is to advance victimological research and practices around the world; to encourage interdisciplinary and comparative work and research in this field, and to advance cooperation between international, national, regional and local agencies and other groups who are concerned with the problems of victims.

Victims as Witnesses

Witnesses are called to give evidence in court to an offence they have been a victim to but a number of flaws have been identified in witness identification and it can lead to wrongful convictions. Witnesses play a huge part in the Criminal Justice process and it is difficult to imagine a criminal case in court without any witnesses but we must look at how reliable these witness are. Here we will look at the following problems.

* Mistaken identification
* Witness perspective
* Environment and vision

* The decline of memory
* The weapon-focus effect

Mistaken Identification

In England and the United States the greatest cause of wrongful convictions is mistaken identification. Since the introduction of DNA testing, according to valentinemoore.co.uk the U.S Innocents Project has lead to 183 prisoners being found innocent and that mistaken eye witness identification was the main factor in three-quarters of these wrongful convictons. There are many factors which can make an eye witness account and identification unreliable.

Witness Perspective

A witness is asked a set of general questions to describe a suspect such as, height, build and age. They will also be asked to describe their surroundings and course of events. These witness guidelines are set out and regulated in the Police and Criminal Evidence Act 1984 Code D. It should be taken into account that the witness's own height, build and age can distort the perception of a suspect. For example, a young woman of 22, 5 feet 4 inches tall and of slim build, when asked to describe the suspect, she describes him as tall, around 6 feet to 6 feet 2 inches, early to mid forties and of slightly larger build . When, in fact, the suspect was of average height, 5 feet 9 inches. He is in his late thirties and of average build. These witness mistakes occur because of at the age of 22 the suspect may look older in the same way you might hear an elderly person saying, that boy does not look old enough to drive a car. At 5 feet 4 inches and slim build, the witness would be looking upwards at the suspect giving him the appearance of being taller and larger than he actually is.

Environment and Vision

It is a studied factor that environmental conditions can limit a witness's vision. Dr Paul Michel explains in his online publication 'The Eyewitness Expert' how vision can be limited by such things as, eye disease, distance, movement and low lighting as well as the many other factors which can make a witness unreliable. He also suggests that eyewitness observations should be evaluated by an expert to determine the credibility of the witness's account. This suggestion could lead to witnesses in court being more reliable and the possibility of a wrongful conviction less likely.

When the police document a crime they do not document on the visual aspects of the crime. They concentrate on the physical aspects of the crime only. Evidence is collected when the lights are turned on and photography is used to document the crime scene but no visual information was collected as standard procedure this too could also help to reduce the number of wrongful convictions due to unreliable witnesses. Pre trial witness interviews are conducted in the court procedure to establish the reliability of a witness but these interviews are on a voluntary basis on the part of the witness and are based on the statement given they do not include any vision factors.

The Decline of Memory

Live or photo line-ups are a common practice in identifying suspects. The guidelines for this procedure are stated in the 'Visual Identification of Suspect: Procedures and Practice' It recommends that the fillers of these line-ups and photo identifications by known innocents, non-suspects. The purpose of this is to test the witness's memory and the reliability of that witness's memory. If they select someone other than the suspect then they are shown to be an unreliable witness.

In a research paper by Wendy Kneller, Amina Memon and Sarah Stevenage in 2000 at the University of Southampton, titled, 'Simultaneous and Sequential Line-ups: Decision Processes of Accurate and Inaccurate Eyewitnesses' They proved that simultaneous line-ups increase the possibility of a witness picking out the person who simply looks most like the perpetrator according to their memory. In a number of tests the witness has picked out a suspect even when the suspect was not in the line-up. There is also the possibility that the witness may feel under pressure to 'pick' someone therefore picking the one that looks most like the suspect.

The rate at which an eyewitness's memory declines can have an effect on the identification of a suspect. Research by, S.M. Kassin, P.C. Ellsworth and V.L. Smith of the Department of Psychology, Williams College, USA, 'On the "general acceptance" of eyewitness testimony research. A new study of the expert' shows that memory declines quickly, dropping considerably after only twenty minutes. It is not slow and consistent over time, which is more commonly believed. Memory then continues to fade into the second day where it begins to level off at a dramatically reduced level of accuracy. Therefore, the longer the time gap from the event to the witness giving an account will be affected dramatically by memory decline.

The Weapon Focus Effect

It has been shown in many studies that the presence of a weapon can affect the accuracy of a witness account dramatically. This referred to as the 'weapon focus effect'. The basis of this theory is to show how, when a weapon is present at an event, the focus of the witness is on the weapon and not on the suspect or the surrounding environment. The presence of the weapon attracts the witnesses attention and the longer the weapon is in sight the less likely it is that they will be able to give any accurate information, if any information at all on the suspect or the surrounding factors. This weapon focus effect combined with the decline in memory can make it very difficult for a witness to identify a suspect.

References

Sexual Offences Act 2003

Criminal Justice Act 2003

Human Rights Act 1998 (European Convention of Human Rights)

Sanders. A and Young. R. (2000) Criminal Justice, Butterworths.

Ashworth. A (2003) Principles of Criminal Law, Oxford: Oxford University Press.

Floud. J and Young. W (1981) Dangerousness and Criminal Justice, Cambridge: Studies in Criminology XLVII.

(http://www.scie.org.uk/publications/guides/guide03/law/leg.asp)

Cavadino. M and Dignan. J (2002) The Penal System An Introduction. London: Sage Publications.

McLaughlin. E and Muncie. J (2002) Controlling Crime. London. Sage Publications.

Morgan. R and Newburn. T (1997) The Future of Policing. Oxford: Oxford University Press.

Reiner. R (1996) The Politics of The Police. Oxford: Oxford University Press.

Wright. A (2002) Policing An Introduction to Concepts and Practice. Devon: Willan Publishing.

http://hunteremkay.com/2012/04/v-for-victimology/

Brent E. Turvey, 'Criminal Profiling, An Introduction to Behavioral Analysis', 3rd Edition, Academic Press,

2008.

Deviant Crimes: Victimology

AIC (Australia Institute of Criminology): 8th symposium on Victims as PDF extracts (1994) http://faculty.ncwc.edu/mstevens/ 300/300lecturenote01.htm

Dr Laura Berman – Rape Grieving Stages

Victims of Violence, Canada : Homicide Survivors

The World Society of Victimology

Morton Bard & Dana Sangrey The Crime Victim's Book

http://hunteremkay.com/wp-admin/post.php? post=1570&action=edit&message=10

(Source for 2,3 & 4: faculty.ncwc.edu)

Biderman, A, and Reiss, A. 1967, 'On Exploring The Dark Figure of Crime', Washington, Bureau of Social Science Research.

Coleman, C. and Moynihan, J. 1996 'Understanding Crime Data: Haunted by The Dark Figure' Buckingham: Open University Press.

Mosher, C. 2002 'The History of Measuring Crime' London: Sage Publications.

Moore, S. 1996. 'Investigating Crime and Deviance' Harpers Collins.

http://www.findlaw.co.uk/law/criminal/ other_crime_and_justice_topics/500493.html

Allen, M. (2003). Text Book on Criminal Law. 7th ed.

Oxford: Oxford University Press.

Fletcher, G. (1996). Basic Concepts of Legal Thought. London: Oxford University Press.

Gardner, T. and Anderson, T. (1996). Criminal Law: Principles and Cases. 6th ed. Minneapolis: West Publishing.

Hall, J. (1949). Cases and Readings on Criminal Law and Procedure. U.S.A: Bobbs-Merrill.

Herring, J. (2004). Criminal Law: Text, Cases, and Materials. Oxford: Oxford University Press.

Samaha, J. (1999). Criminal Law. 6th ed. Belmont, CA: West Wadsworth.

Knuller v DPP [1972] 2 a11 er 898

Most (1881) 7 QBD 244

R V Gullefer (1990) 91 Cr App R 356

R v Mohan [1976] QB 1

R v Pearman (1984) 80 Cr App R 259

Shaw v DPP [1962] ac 220

Burke, Hopkins, R. (2001) Criminological Theory. Devon: Willan Publishing

Foucault, M. (1994) Micheal Foucault 'Power' Essential Works of Foucault 1954 -1984 Volume 3. London: Penguin Books

Garland, D. (1991) Punishment and Modern Society, A Study in Social Theory. Berkshire: Open University Press

Innes, M. (2003) Understanding Social Control,

Deviance, Crime and Social Order. Berkshire: Open University Press

Morrison, K. (1995) Marx, Durkheim, Weber, Formations of Modern Social Thought. London: Sage Publications.

Rabinow, P. (1991) The Foucault Reader, An Introduction to Foucault's Thought. London: Penguin Books

Burke, R. H. 2001. An introduction to criminological theory. Cullompton, Devon, UK: Willan Pub.

Downes, D. M., & Rock, P. E. 1982. Understanding deviance: a guide to the sociology of crime and rule-breaking. Oxford: Clarendon Press.

Duff, A., & Garland, D. 1994. A reader on punishment. Oxford: Oxford University Press.

Hughes, G., McLaughlin, E., & Muncie, J. 2002. Crime prevention and community safety: new directions. London: SAGE.

Innes, M. 2003. Understanding social control: deviance, crime and social order. Maidenhead: Open University Press.

McLaughlin, E., & Muncie, J. 2001. The Sage dictionary of criminology. London: SAGE.

Morrison, K. 1995. Marx, Durkheim, Weber: formations of modern social thought. London: Sage.

Muncie, J. 1999. Youth and crime: a critical introduction. London: Sage.

Parkin, F. 1992. Durkheim. Oxford: Oxford University Press.

Slapper, G., & Kelly, D. 2004. The English legal system. London: Cavendish.

Williams, K. S. 1991. Textbook on criminology. London: Blackstone Press.

This Criminology Beginners Guide can provide you with a wide range of the underpinning theories developed to explain many different types of crime. With straight forward easy to read text, listed historical events and facts for easy referencing and further research. The ideal book for the beginner in Criminology

Printed in Great Britain
by Amazon

32975193R00224